FORMAL SPECIFICATION OF ADVANCED AI ARCHITECTURES

IAIN D. CRAIG B.A., M.A., Ph.D.
University of Warwick

ELLIS HORWOOD
NEW YORK   LONDON   TORONTO   SYDNEY   TOKYO   SINGAPORE

First published in 1991 by
ELLIS HORWOOD LIMITED
Market Cross House, Cooper Street,
Chichester, West Sussex, PO19 1EB, England

A division of
Simon & Schuster International Group
A Paramount Communications Company

Printed and bound in Great Britain
by Hartnolls, Bodmin, Cornwall

British Library Cataloguing in Publication Data

Craig, Iain D.
Formal specification of advanced AI architectures. —
(Ellis Horwood series in artificial intelligence).
1. Problem solving. Applications of artificial intelligence
I. Title
006.3
ISBN 0–13–325200–0 (Library Edn.)
ISBN 0–13–328832–3 (Student Edn.)

Library of Congress Cataloging-in-Publication Data

Craig, I.
Formal specification of advanced AI architectures / Iain D. Craig.
p. cm. — (Ellis Horwood series in artificial intelligence)
Includes bibliographical references and index.
ISBN 0–13–325200–0 (Library Edn.)
ISBN 0–13–328832–3 (Student Edn.)
1. Artificial intelligence — Data processing. 2. Z (Computer program language)
3. Expert systems (Computer science) 4. System design. I. Title. II. Series.
QF336.C73   1990
006.3–dc20   90–44152
                                                                              CIP

To Margaret,
my wife and the best friend I could ever have,
with all my love, now and always.

Table of Contents

CONTENTS

Preface

Preface AI software, like most software, is rarely specified formally. Indeed, for most AI programs, there may hardly be anything that resembles an informal specification because the code keeps changing as the experimenter/programmer's ideas change and deficiencies in the program are found—the deficiencies are often ascribed to a poor understanding of the problem. On the other side of the coin, there are those who insist that everything should be written in first-order or intensional logic, and once this has been done, a program can be written to derive inferences from the logical sentences. Despite the goal of formalizing the reasoning processes claimed to be necessary (and this is a debatable point), they write a program to do the job: to my knowledge, the program has been constructed using conventional techniques.

In advanced software engineering, the fundamental (although still controversial) requirement is that *all* software be given a formal specification and that it be derived using mathematical techniques. This, it is claimed, gives the best possible guarantee of correctness: if there are proofs and the proofs are correct, the program must meet the specification. There is still the possibility that the original specification was incorrect, but the software will still meet that (incorrect) specification.

An argument one hears in AI against formal specification is that the software represents an evolving understanding of the problem. Since understanding is evolving, so must the program. This makes specification useless because the formal activity cannot keep up with the differing perspectives of the experimenter. It is the case, though, that there are software structures which are used in a rather different way: these are the architectures from which one develops the so-called "shells". With a shell, one has a relatively stable piece of software, and all one has to do is to encode knowledge and fill the shell—this is "all" one has to do!

It would seem reasonable to give a shell a formal specification just so that one can rely upon it. Another aspect of the formal specification of AI software is the formal specification of that which is loaded into a shell—an encoding of knowledge—but this has received little or no explicit attention. The knowledge representation community are mostly concerned with the development of knowledge representation *languages* and have no time left over to examine the way in which knowledge can be given a formal encoding. That is, the other aspect of the use of formal techniques is to show that a mapping between some body of knowledge and its encoding is, in some sense, correct. Hayes has argued for many years that this should be undertaken, and has argued that a representation with a semantics *as well as* a syntax should be used (he suggests using classical first-order logic). The issues raised in the mapping problem are probably very interesting, but the concentration, here, is on the formal specification of AI software—this is a more immediately tractable problem.

This book is concerned with the formal specification of two "shells" (actually, with two separate architectures). Whether they actually are shells in the conventional use of the word is irrelevant. The first architecture, and the one that receives the greater emphasis, is the blackboard architecture; the second is my own CASSANDRA architecture. The reasons for selecting these two out of the many architectures that one can find were, initially, due to familiarity and complexity. After working with them for a number of years, I feel sufficiently confident to be able to express my understanding of blackboard systems using a formal language. The CASSANDRA architecture is of my own invention, so I feel that I should know it relatively well. Both of the architectures are complex: they are much more complex than production systems and have properties that are not easily discovered. The complexity is also an issue when trying to tell people about, say, the blackboard architecture: it is a surprisingly difficult activity. If formal techniques can help here, it will be for the good.

The formal specification of software is a long and complex process. In a book of this size, it is not possible to document the entire process. Instead, what I have done is to give a relatively complete account of the top-level specification of the blackboard architecture. A first refinement of a part of this initial specification is presented in an appendix. The treatment of the CASSANDRA architecture is somewhat shorter, and relies upon the blackboard specification for a good many of its constructs: the CASSANDRA architecture is a derivative of the blackboard architecture, so this seems to be one way of presenting a specification that is not overly long. There is no refinement of the second architecture, because the formal specification is intended as a formal *definition*.

This point leads me onto the possible uses of formal specification in AI. I currently see four main uses of formal specification in AI, and in other branches of computer science, for that matter:

- Providing a secure foundation upon which to base an implementation (this is the most conventional of the reasons, and it coincides closely with the software engineering approach).

- Making an interpretation precise. With the blackboard architecture, for example, opinions differ as to what a blackboard system really is. Much of the discussion involves pointing to example implementations and then stating principles. By use of formal specification, it is possible to give a precise account of what one understands by an architecture. The blackboard specification given below is part of an account of *my* interpretation of the architecture: it is partial because I have had to leave out some aspects because of lack of space (these aspects relate mostly to control).

- Giving a definition of a new architecture in as unambiguous a fashion as possible. This is what I have tried to do with the CASSANDRA architecture. The reason for this is that I have a definition of what a CASSANDRA system should look like and I want to state that definition so that there can be no argument. Of course, that definition does not pin down *every* aspect of the architecture—indeed, I want to leave some room for exploration—but I do want the basics to be stated clearly, unambiguously and as clearly as possible.

- Opening up opportunities for the exploration of systems without being tied down to a particular implementation or programming language. A formal specification is an excellent structure within which to explore different aspects and ideas: one can change one's mind relatively easily without all the problems of having to wait while the software is being rebuilt. Indeed, because a formal specification is an abstract structure, it is possible to explore totally wild ideas and not have to drudge through the entire program making tedious changes, or yet throw it out and start again.

The first three points are really the motivation for various parts of this book. The final point is one that I am currently actively exploring and results may be reported in the future. This last aspect of the formal specification concept seems extremely exciting and worth following up.

The current book has been written as a prelude to a full implementation of a blackboard system: this implementation will be based on the specification given in Chapter Four and in the Appendix. The fate of the CASSANDRA architecture is more doubtful. The specification in Chapter Six concentrates on the sequential aspects of the architecture, and relegates parallelism and distributed implementation to the realm of future projects. In both the blackboard and CASSANDRA specifications, interesting discoveries were made: for the most part, they related to parallelism. However, it was decided that the CASSANDRA specification should concentrate on sequential matters, even though I would very much like to develop a parallel and distributed implementation of the architecture. This, at present, is not possible because it is a time-consuming and expensive exercise, and I have not been given an opportunity to undertake it. Given the lack of interest and lack of funding, I think it is now time to lay CASSANDRA to rest and concentrate on other matters.

To end this Preface, there are people whom I would like to thank in connection with this book. Firstly, I would like to thank Sue Horwood for being so understanding when decorating and moving into a new flat took me away from writing, and for being patient during the year of illness which further delayed things. Second, I want to thank John Campbell for being so positive about the project and for being so generous in his editorial remarks. Next, I would like to thank Bill Ferreira for reading and suggesting corrections and improvements to the proofs in the blackboard Chapter and in Appendix A,d for pointing out errors in the text, and for suggesting general improvements to the presentation: all errors are, of course, my own responsibility. Finally, I want to thank my wife Margaret for her constant encouragement and understanding while I was writing and revising the text. Without her, this book would not have been half as much of a pleasure to write. I hope the result is something that is worthy of her.

Iain Craig
Knowle,
July, 1991

1

Introduction

1.1 Introduction

This book is about the formal specification of two Artificial Intelligence architectures: the blackboard (Erman, 1975; Nii, 1986a; Craig, *in press*) and CASSANDRA (Craig, 1988a, 1988b) architectures. The subject matter may appear strange to many readers. It is not often the case that problem-solving *architectures* are subjected to formal specification and analysis: instead, knowledge representations are typically treated formally. The production system architecturei (Newell, 1973; Waterman, 1978; Anderson, 1983) is based upon Post systems (Post, 1943), so one would expect formal issues to be considered, but it is on the properties of production systems and representations that emphasis is placed (i.e., *what* is represented within a production system is that which receives the most formal attention, not the properties of the architecture as a whole). It is usually considered that the basic software in an AI system works properly because problem-solving systems generate the correct (i.e., expected) results—that is, they seem to behave properly with respect to representations.

The book is about the basic software that is always assumed (and sometimes neglected) when building AI systems. The architectures that have been chosen are complex. This complexity is one reason why formal specification has been attempted.

The reasons for formally specifying conventional software are, by now, well-known, and have been eloquently advocated by a number of researchers (Dijkstra, 1976) over the years. One particularly good reason why software ought to be given a formal specification and developed in a rigorous fashion is that the formal development method preserves validity—that is, a property that is true in the original specification will remain true in the implementation (the code). If software is developed in terms of proofs at different levels of abstraction, this preservation of validity entails that the code will behave exactly in accordance with the specification. If there are deviations, they will be documented in the proofs that constitute the code's derivation (for example, a specification may be written in terms of infinite objects which cannot be implemented on a physical machine, for obvious reasons). The concept of preservation of validity will be encountered again when the Z specification language is discussed below.

Formal specification of software has been used for software of a "conventional", that is non-AI, kind. Why should the techniques be applied to AI systems which are usually highly complex and sometimes ill-defined? There are, in fact, a number of reasons for doing this. Before giving them, it is necessary to note one thing: if an AI system is ill-defined, it cannot be constructed—in other words, a precondition of the existence of software is that the problem it is supposed to solve must be defined with sufficient clarity for the code to be written. Perhaps it would be better to say that AI software changes rapidly (i.e., is frequently modified): this property—of, essentially, being a prototype—can still benefit from formal treatment, as will be pointed out below.

The problem-solving systems considered in this book have the property that they are relatively stable. These systems are used to construct applications which actually solve the problems; on their own, they are really only *frameworks* or interpreters. (The terms "blackboard system" and "blackboard interpreter" will be used below to denote this interpretive component. The terms are used interchangably, and it is hoped that no confusion with the application software will arise.) In these cases, it is the application that changes with time, and only very rarely does the interpreter need modification. This stability suggests that a formal specification is possible.

The architectures considered in this book are used in the construction of systems that solve problems in complex domains—the resulting systems are, themselves, highly complex and are frequently constructed on an *ad hoc* basis. The ability of the architectures in complex domains makes them prime candidates for application to real-time problems such as speech understanding, scene analysis, sonar processing and air traffic control. With the application to real-time problems come two issues:

- reliability. Real-time systems cannot fail with only a short period of operating time between failures (i.e., have a relatively short mean time between failure). In some domains, lives depend upon the correct functioning of software systems, so reliability issues impact upon safety, as well as upon convenience.

- responsiveness. Fast response times are inherent in these applications. In laboratory experiments, slow systems can be tolerated (at least for while), but the application of AI systems "in the field" requires that response times be adequate to cope with real data rates, not simulated ones.

In this book, reliability is the main justification for the formal approach: if we want AI systems to assist in solving safety-critical problems, they must be as reliable as possible. A formal specification of the basic software goes some way to achieving this goal: a much more difficult task is to show that the knowledge encoded in a problem-solving system is correct or even adequate for the task—unfortunately, we must ignore this issue completely.

The reason given in justification above may appear very pragmatic to some. There are two other reasons for the current exercise that are somewhat more theoretically motivated.

The first of these "more theoretical" reasons is concerned with the establishment of standards. The blackboard architecture has been the subject of considerable activity by a number of different research groups. This has led to a number of different interpretations of the basic architectural prescriptions. Although these interpretations vary in what may appear to be relatively minor details, they are all couched in rather different sets of terminology: formal specification can show *precisely* what one means by a particular construct, in fact, far more precisely than a purely verbal statement. In addition, the differences themselves can be considered very much more clearly, and can be compared in detail once they have been stated in a clear fashion: again, formal specification can help.

Given the fact that the blackboard architecture has been used in so many applications, a formal standard, naturally, turns out to be extremely difficult to achieve: making clear *exactly* how one interprets the basic prescriptions appears still to be very useful. The interpretation given below is the author's (though it has much in common with that of Hayes-Roth (Hayes-Roth, 1983)): for the initiated, it should be pointed out that the specification given here is neutral with respect to the role of opportunism—the reasons for this are given by Craig (1988a) and Craig (*in press*) (indeed, we do not consider the scheduler in any detail, below). In addition to presenting the author's interpretation, other constructs are specified so that different interpretations can be considered (although this is left as an extended exercise for the reader).

With the CASSANDRA architecture (Craig, 1988a, 1988b), matters are very different indeed. This second architecture was defined by the author for use in high-integrity domains where real-time performance may be required (the original implementation dealt with air traffic control), and is intended as a *distributed* architecture. The CASSANDRA architecture has the advantage of having been relatively little used, so the definition given by Craig (1988) still stands unaltered. The reason for including this architecture in a formal specification study is that it is possible, in this case, to define a *standard* against which all future implementations can be measured. In addition, this formal statement may turn out to be an advantage in future developments and may help this architecture in avoiding the problems that have (quite naturally) arisen around the blackboard architecture.

Finally, there is the point that a formal specification of a problem-solving architecture, as with that of any system, allows us to prove properties about the architecture in general, and, thus, gain knowledge about it without needing to engage in an implementation. This fact is clearly of considerable importance in may situations. Furthermore, it allows us to make explicit those properties of the architecture which would otherwise have remained implicit (and remain either part of the folklore or cause problems for the unwary).

Most of the reasons given so far have been intended primarily for the AI community. It is equally important to justify the use of such relatively little-known systems as the basis for a book on specifications. The novelty of the subjects makes them attractive for formal treatment, and there is their relative complexity. As can be seen in the number of pages devoted to the specification of the blackboard system, a large and complex formal specification is the result of this exercise. Large specifications are comparatively rare in the literature, so it should prove illuminating to present a relatively complete one, and to show that it *can* be done. As with a large program or system, a large specification poses management problems, and a clear presentation is required for the specification exercise to be successful: the organisation given below can also be viewed as an attempt to articulate a moderately large specification in such a fashion.

The scope of the specification given below is that of an almost complete (with the exception of user-interfaces and one or two details—local variables, for example). An entire blackboard system is specified; the CASSANDRA specification is equally complete, but "borrows" constructs from the blackboard system—this is because these constructs are required in the original definition (Craig, 1988, Chapter 4). As has already been stated, many properties of both architectures are given proofs. The blackboard specification is intended to be the basis of an implementation—in the Appendix, it is shown how to proceed towards implementation. An implementation using this specification is being undertaken by the author: the implementation is fully rigorous in the sense of Jones (Jones, 1980, 1986) It is, in some ways, to be regretted that there is insufficient space here to give the details of the implementation process, together with the necessary proofs.

1.2 Problem-solving Architectures

Having briefly investigated the reasons for formally specifying problem-solving architectures, it is necessary, if only for completeness, to state what one of these is.

Above, the term "problem-solving architecture" was related to the concept of an interpreter. This relationship is close in some ways, but it is not accurate in others (for example, a problem-solving architecture need not provide a syntax, whereas interpreters in the conventional sense of the term require one).

A problem-solving architecture defines the ways in which knowledge can be applied to solve a problem. It specifies basic constructs and the ways in which they are organised in a system, and it also defines structures that form the basis for the control of the application of that knowledge.

The production system architecture will be familiar to many readers. Because of its relative simplicity, an account can be given here by way of an example.

The production system architecture is composed of the following constructs:

- A representation for knowledge in terms of *production rules*. A production rule has two components: a *condition-part* and an *action-part*. The condition-part (sometimes called the *condition* or *situation-fluent*) states those conditions under which a production rule is appropriate to the current solution state and under which it can make a contribution to the solution process by executing its action-part. The execution of an action-part generates one or more inference steps that alter the solution state. Condition-parts are usually composed of one or more *condition-elements* which can be thought of as predicates. A production rule can be thought of as an *if ... then* rule similar to the single-arm conditional in programming languages.

- A *working memory*. This is a database of items that represent the current state of the solution process. The condition-parts of production rules are *matched* against the elements in working memory to determine whether actions can be executed. When the actions in a rule are executed, elements are inserted into working memory or are deleted from it: in other words, the operations performed by a rule's action-part alter the solution state which is represented by the contents of working memory.

- A *production rule* memory (or *production memory*). This holds the production rules in a system. Production memory is effectively searched when matching the condition-parts of rules. Production memory represents the long-term store in a production system; working memory represents the short-term store in which intermediate results are deposited until a solution is reached. Unlike working memory, production memory is relatively stable in the sense that production rules are not updated or modified as often (if at all) as working memory (such modification to production memory is found only in learning systems, and of course when constructing the production system or modifying it to erase some bug or to cater for a new behaviour).

- A match-deliberate-execute cycle. This is the fundamental control structure in the architecture. This part of the architecture states that the condition parts of the production rules in a system must be matched against the current state of the working memory. Those rules whose condition-parts match the current state are further considered by some explicit selection process until one or more is finally selected to have its action-part executed and thus cause alterations to the state of working memory (i.e., to generate one or more inferential steps).

We need now to reflect on what this example architectural statement actually does. Firstly, it defines a knowledge representation, at least in outline: it states that all the problem-solving knowledge is represented in the form of production rules—they resemble the **if** ... **then** statements found in programming languages. This interpretation is given by the statement that the execution of a rule's action can occur only if its condition-part matches the contents of working memory. It also states that working memory is composed of items that can be matched against conditions (or their components) and that they are created and modified by actions. The architecture does not state exactly what the form of a working memory element is—something similar to a predicate or relation is a common interpretation since, the function of a condition element is often interpreted are being to return a truth-value.

The architecture defines two memories or databases—one for production rules, and one for working memory. It states that working memory contains relatively short-lived intermediate results which are generated during the course of problem-solving activity (the application of production rules). Working memory contents determine which production rules can be applied to alter the state, since it is required that conditions are matched by working memory contents.

Finally, the architecture provides the basics of the control mechanism for production systems: this is the match-deliberate-execute cycle. This cycle continues, once the system has been started, until a solution is found. The cycle requires that all applicable production rules be found during the match phase. Next, these rules are subjected to further analysis (called the *conflict resolution* process) during the deliberation phase: the deliberation process selects some rules (typically one) whose action-part is to be executed in the act phase in order to update working memory. The updated working memory is then used during the next match phase. It should be noted that nothing is stated about the details of the match phase (this depends upon how working memory items are structured), nor about the details of the deliberation phase (those properties of matched rules to be used in the selection phase are not discussed at all), nor does it say what constitutes the execution of actions (are they procedures or are they interpreted in some way?)

The architecture states the *what*, not the *how*. It also provides the basis for the construction of a production system: it states that problem-solving knowledge should be organised as a collection of **if** ... **then** rules—in other words, it suggests a decomposition and structuring method for a body of knowledge, so it provides the basis of a methodology.

In order to move to an implementation, the concepts introduced by the architecture have to be interpreted in computational terms. The architecture can be considered as a very high-level specification dealing with the major aspects of a problem-solving system: knowledge representation, organisation and control. As can be seen, the production rule architecture deals with these aspects. In other words, a problem-solving architecture defines a framework within which to construct systems.

The are a number of different problem-solving architectures described in the literature. The blackboard architecture is one of these, and is a development of the production rule architecture. The blackboard architecture introduces many additional components. The CAS-SANDRA architecture is based on the blackboard architecture and adapts it to the needs of high-reliability, distributed environments.

1.3   The Reasons for Choosing Z

In recent years, many different specification languages have been proposed: VDM (Jones, 1980, 1986) and Z (Spivey, 1988, 1989) are relatively popular. Both of these languages have been developed for the specification of sequential programs and systems; other languages such as CSP (Hoare, 1985) and CCS (Milner, 1980, 1989) have been proposed for concurrent systems. The CASSANDRA architecture specifies that a distributed system be composed of a set of sequential modules; the blackboard architecture is usually interpreted in a sequential sense, although parallelism within these sequential structures may be introduced. At the level of specification in this book, the details of distribution and concurrency are largely irrelevant—nondeterminism is considerably more important because it gives implementers considerably more freedom (a point stressed by Jones (1980, 1986), for example).

Given this fact, the major decision to be made when selecting a specification language is whether a *model-* or *property-* oriented specification is preferred. Z (Spivey, 1988, 1989) is a model-oriented language (as is VDM) in the sense that its components represent models of the states and operations of the system being specified. When writing a specification in such a language, one is constructing a model of the program or system that is to be implemented. The concept of validity-preservation seems natural within the context of a model-based specification. One aspect of Z that was immediately appealing is that it lends itself to a highly *modular* form of specification: this modularity comes directly from the *schema* construct (see Chapter 2). At the time the specification language was being decided upon, it was determined that any blackboard system that would be constructed as a result of a formal specification exercise would be implemented in the C++ (Stroustrup, 1986) programming language for portability reasons. Since C++ is extremely modular, it seemed perfectly natural to adopt a specification language which would endow formal specifications with this property. Although the choice of programming language should not influence the specification in any way (just as implementation considerations should not influence it), in this case, the implementation language pointed in a natural fashion to the specification language to be used. Once Z had been chosen, C++ was forgotten and the specification was carried out purely in terms of the concepts that seem most natural in Z.

In addition to the modularity aspect, there were other reasons for selecting Z. These are:

- Formal semantics. Z is a specification language with an explicit semantics (Spivey, 1988, 1989). The existence of a formal semantics means that every construct in Z has a definite interpretation. This, in turn, means that the interpretation of a Z specification is given unambiguously. Furthermore, it ensures that proofs are well-founded. VDM, on the other hand, relies much more on an intuitive concept of meaning: to the author, this seemed less attractive.

- Schema combinators. Z provides means to combine schemata. The schema is the basic unit of a Z specification and defines, for example, a state space. It is often necessary to combine the basic units of a specification, a process that can become rather tedious unless the specification language comes to one's assistance. Z allows users to combine schemata to form larger ones, and provides facilities for manipulating schemata as "first-class" objects. This property makes Z very attractive for the specification of large systems.

- Natural interpretation. To the author, the interpretation of Z objects as objects in a typed, constructive set theory is most appealing, as its view that functions are explicitly to be represented by their graphs, and that predicates define subsets. As will be seen in Chapter 4, the first-order nature of Z can, occasionally pose some problems, but in the majority of cases it does not. A natural interpretation makes a language or a notation very much easier to use and to understand. Since formal specifications are intended to be, at least partially, a means for communicating ideas between people, a natural interpretation would appear to be a bonus.

- Elegance. To the author, Z is a very elegant language. The elegance comes, in part, from the natural, intuitive (and very familiar) interpretation of Z objects, and, in part, from the schema construct. The notation used for Z is economical, and this, too, contributes to its appeal. This aspect of Z was not too important in deciding which specification language to employ, but it is one that had to be considered. In addition to purely technical ease, the aesthetic appeal of a specification language can be employed to make formal specifications attractive.

As a result of these considerations, Z was finally chosen for the specification and for use in this book. It is possible to convert between VDM and Z, for example, provided that the original is in a suitable form. However, the reasons given above should indicate that the author considers Z to be the most appropriate language for the current task.

Some readers may be wondering why a specification language that applies to sequential systems has been used to describe a distributed system. The non-determinism argument given above does not seem to hold much water after a litttle consideration. The reason is that the CASSANDRA architecture, in fact, only specifies the constructs that have to be present within a (logically) single node in a distributed computer network: in other words, as will be seen below, the architecture, essentially, specifies a sequential program that must be instantiated at each node. The network topology is not considered part of the architectural specification. Some might argue (correctly) that there are aspects of the overall network structure that are important for the behaviour of each node (for example, the existence of loops in the communication paths—this property can lead to deadlock): as is stated in Craig (1988), inter-communication between nodes is highly problem-specific and cannot be treated within a general architectural specification. As a result, it is possible to ignore the communications mechanisms and to concentrate on the specification of the structure of the generic problem-solving node (which is exactly the approach taken here). An interesting problem, which is not tackled here, is to turn the sequential programs that reside at each node into parallel programs: this exercise can be eased because of the non-determinism that is used in the Z specification—once again, there is a good reason for selecting to engage in a formal specification using a language like Z.

1.4   The Organisation of this Book

The book is organised as follows. In Chapter 2, a tutorial on the Z specification language is given. This overview presents the majority of the Z constructs that are used in the two specifications that follow. The tutorial chapter is aimed at providing the reader who does not know Z with all the tools needed to understand the system specifications that are the real subject of this book. A sizeable subset of Z is presented, and a number of example proofs (some taken from subsequent sections of the book) are given. It is to be hoped that the reader can use the material in Chapter 2 as a basis for exploring Z specifications on his or her own, and that the coverage is sufficient that the interested reader can engage in program specification using Z.

Chapter 3 begins the specification of the blackboard system by presenting, first, a general description of the blackboard architecture, and then a detailed and informal description of the system which will be formally treated in Chapter 4. The informal specification covers all aspects of the blackboard system so the reader can approach the formal specification with a very much better understanding of the subject matter. The informal specification is presented so that the reader is not forced to acquire alien concepts while trying to understand a large

Z specification. The formal specification of the blackboard system is given in Chapter 4. The formal specification is organised in exactly the same way as the informal one. The formal specification contains explanatory material (it is not, therefore, a large tract of mathematical symbols) in order to help the reader further (this explanatory material also contains justifications and clarifications so that the reader will understand why a particular choice was made).

Chapter 5 is concerned with an informal (English) definition of the CASSANDRA architecture. Its role is exactly analgous to that of Chapter 3. Chapter 6 contains the formal specification of the CASSANDRA architecture: this specification is the *standard* specification of the architecture, and all implementations must conform to it.

Finally, the Appendix deals with the implementation of the blackboard system. It deals with the refinement steps necessary to move from the formal specification given in Chapter 4 to a coded version and describes the proofs that must be undertaken to ensure correctness. Interested readers can use the contents of Chapter 4, together with the Appendix, to construct a blackboard system. The approach described in the Appendix is being used by the author to construct a system, so the suggestion is not merely theoretical.

All relevant proofs are given where they illustrate interesting or important points. In many cases, though, proofs are omitted or merely sketched: this is for reasons of space.

2

The Z Specification Language

2.1 Introduction

In this Chapter, we will present an introduction of the Z specification
language (Spivey, 1988, 1989). This is the language which we will be
using in the rest of the book. The introduction will be sufficient for
the two formal specifications that we give in the sense that it explains
the syntax and semantics of all of the Z constructs that we will use.

We do not pretend that the Chapter can serve as a *general* introduction to Z: the reader should consult (Spivey, 1989). We do not cover the proof techniques that are applicable to Z specifications, although we do present some example proofs—in other words, we will rely on the general mathematical and logical intuitions and knowledge of the reader.

It must be emphasised that we can only cover that part of the Z language which is used in this book, nor do we give a list of the various properties of the operators that we will use (such a list can be found in (Spivey, 1989)). We have not had occasion to use a number of facilities provided by Z: in particular, we do not use λ- or μ-expressions, we do not use finite surjections and injections, and so on. These omissions are for a number of reasons:

1. We simply had no occasion to employ a number of these features— this is the most important reason, for we do not believe in using a feature simply because it is there. In the specifications that we present, the features that we have employed are, we believe, those which are most conducive to a clear presentation of our ideas and intentions. Perhaps because of bias, perhaps because of background, we have tended to concentrate on the first-order logic and set-theoretic constructs in the specifications: for our part, these constructs have a clarity which would not have been equalled if we had introduced other, possibly less familiar, concepts.

2. The specifications that we present are top-level descriptions of the two architectures. In this book, we are not concerned with the implementation of these architectures, and, equally, we are not concerned with the refinement process that leads from our specifications through a series of other, more detailed ones, until a level is reached at which code can be produced (although the Appendix briefly outlines the refinement process). As a consequence, we have only used those features and facilities which we believe are most suited to top-level specifications.

The second point relates to the fact that we make no use of finite functions, and to the fact that we do not use finite sets. We want to pause for a second to explain why we have consistently used infinite objects such as infinite sets and why we have not constrained our functions so that they, too, are finite. This is because we believe that the top-level specification should be as general as possible, and also that it be somewhat detached from the refinement and implementation processes. In other words, we do not feel that because a structure is infinite, we should not use it in specifications. On the contrary, we feel free to use whatever we see fit in order to make our intentions as clear as possible. The specifications that we give in the next few Chapters are guided by a need to refine them into executable code, and this must be stated quite clearly; however, they are not *constrained* by this need. We believe that top-level specifications should be relatively abstract (although we would not be doctrinaire on this) and as clear as possible: in other words, constraints on size may, in some cases, simply obscure matters rather than making them clear. To be sure, on later stages of the specification process (the refinement stages), it will be necessary to worry about finitude just so that an eventual implementation is possible.

In this Chapter, we will explain the concepts of *type* and *schema* as they are interpreted in Z. The schema (plural *schemata*) is the main construct in Z specifications. A specification is composed of a set of type definitions, possibly some axiomatic definitions (to express functions and relations), and a set of schemata. Schemata are used to specify data structures (actually state spaces) and the operations defined over them. The main effort in constructing a Z specification is in the definition of schemata. To make this process easier, Z provides a number of facilities for the combination of schemata: these facilities are reminiscent of the connectives and quantifiers of first-order logics. We will explain the use of schema combinators as well as schemata themselves. As will be seen, all schemata define types and are composed of typed objects, and there are type rules that must be respected when operating on schemata.

Axiomatic definitions occur with some frequency in the specifications that we give below. Axiomatic definitions are typically used to define functions and relations over various types. For example, if we were defining a binary tree type, we might define a predicate which is satisfied if and only if a tree is ordered: that predicate can be expressed using an axiomatic definition. Although the Z language provides a considerable number of functions, it is often necessary (unless one is very lucky) to define additional functions, relations and operators which act on the objects that are defined in the specification: this is a primary role for axiomatic definitions. In addition to this role, axioms can also be used to introduce global variables: in such cases, the axiom supplies the type of the variable and any constraints that are imposed upon the values that it may take. We make very little use of this second form of axiomatic definition below.

2.2   Types in Z

Everything in a Z specification has a *type*. In other words, every object in a Z specification has a type.

The concept of type should be familiar from programming languages if not from mathematics, and we will assume that the reader is comfortable with the concept. Z admits rather more types than do most programming languages. The interpretation of a type in Z is that it is a set of objects, all of which have a common property. This implies that all Z types are relatively small.

For example, in Z, the following are types (amongst others):

- Numbers (which can be natural, written $\mathbb{N}$, integers, written $\int$, or reals);

- Sets. Sets can be defined by comprehensions or by display: a set must contain objects of a uniform type. For example, the set of the first five naturals (excluding zero) is: $\{1, 2, 3, 4, 5\}$. The elements of this set are of type $\mathbb{N}$, and the type of the set is $\mathbb{P} \, \mathbb{N}$. The symbol $\mathbb{P}$ is the (infinite) *power-set* constructor, and is read "set of". The above set can be written as the comprehension:

$$\{x \mid 1 \leq x \leq 5\}$$

and also has the type $\mathbb{P} \, \mathbb{N}$. For any type T, the type of the infinite set of objects of type T is written as $\mathbb{P} \, T$. We will see many examples of types in the two specifications that are given below.

- Sequences. Sequences are interpreted as mappings from the naturals to objects of some other set. The sequence of the first five naturals (excluding zero) is written as $\langle 1, 2, 3, 4, 5 \rangle$, and is of type seq $\mathbb{N}$. This sequence is shorthand for the set:

$$\{\ 1 \mapsto 1, 1 \mapsto 2, 3 \mapsto 3, 4 \mapsto 4, 5 \mapsto 5\ \}$$

  where the symbol $\mapsto$ (called "maplet") represents the association of an element of the domain of a mapping or function with an element of the range of the mapping or function. The type seq $\mathbb{N}$ contains the *empty sequence*, which is written $\langle \rangle$. If we want to exclude the empty sequence from a sequence type, we use the constructor seq_1. A type $\text{seq}_1\ T$ for any type T represents the set of all sequences *except* the empty sequence. If we have a sequence of type seq T, we can obtain the domain of the underlying mapping using the dom operator; similarly, we can obtain the range using the ran operator. These last two operators apply to *all* types that can be expressed as the *graphs* of functions or relations.

- Functions and relations. Z provides a rich collection of basic constructors for function and relation types. For example, the set of functions whose domain is the naturals and whose range is the naturals is written in Z as:

$$\mathbb{N} \to \mathbb{N}$$

  and we can declare a function with this type in the following way:

$$f : \mathbb{N} \to \mathbb{N}$$

  We can apply dom and ran to f to obtain the domain and range sets. A binary relation can be defined by:

$$r : \mathbb{N} \leftrightarrow \mathbb{N}$$

  where the symbol $\leftrightarrow$ is the constructor for binary relation types.

- Schema types. We will have more to say about schemata in the next section.

- Products. Cartesian products are allowed in Z. For example, an object $(1, 2)$ is a product of type $N \times N$. Note that $(1, 2)$ is not the same as $(2, 1)$, and $(1, (2, 3))$ is not the same as $((1, 2), 3)$. The interpretation of products is the usual one. Z defines two operations, *first* and *second* to project a product onto its first and second components, respectively.

In Z it is possible to determine whether two objects are identical or equivalent. This applies to all objects. In particular, it is possible to determine when two functions or relations are equivalent. For this to be the case, they must have the same type. The interpretation of functions and relations in Z is in terms of their graphs. For a function of type $N \rightarrow N$, its graph is the set of all ordered pairs of natural numbers. Two functions of type $N \rightarrow N$ are equivalent if and only if their graphs are equivalent (i.e., contain exactly the same ordered pairs of naturals). This definition of equivalence extends to relations. In Z, the relation:

$$r : N \leftrightarrow N$$

and the function:

$$f : N \rightarrow N$$

are considered to have the same type ($N \times N$), and so their graphs can be the same. This leads immediately to the possibility that they may be equivalent. It also leads to the possibility that the function may be used in place of the relation, and vice versa, because the two objects are of the same type. We do not make much use of this property in the specifications that we give below. Note that this definition of equality is not, in general, effective.

Z provides two constants, *true* and *false*. There is no explicit type for truth-values (booleans). Since Z specifications are based around the concept of a relation, it is not, in general, necessary to define objects that return truth-values. The equivalence between functions and relations means that a function can be "thought of" as a relation, and so a range type of truth-value is not needed. In the two specifications that we present below, we have need of truth-values, but we define our own: this is partly a matter of convenience, and partly because of our views on the appearance of these two constants in first-order languages.

There are a number of ways in which types can be defined in Z. The simplest forms are by type synonym and by enumeration (free-types can also be defined, but we do not use them in the specifications that follow: see Spivey, 1988, 1989). In addition, it is possible to declare *atomic* types.

Since atomic types are by far the easiest to understand, we explain them first. We can define two atomic types as follows:

$$[ATTR, VAL]$$

(We have defined two types because we will use them in the next section.) This definition introduces the identifiers $ATTR$ and VAL as names of types: the enclosure of identifiers by square brackets on a new line serves to introduce the identifiers as names of types. The two types are atomic in the sense that their components cannot be further subdivided. Each of the two types we have defined above is assumed to be a set of values (we can also assume that neither of them is empty).

We can declare an object of type $ATTR$ thus:

$$a : ATTR$$

where a is a variable. The variable a is of type $ATTR$, and can be bound to any value of type $ATTR$.

The symbol $\twoheadrightarrow$ denotes the *partial function* constructor. A partial function is a function which relates domain elements to elements of its range, but it is not the case that all elements of the domain are related to elements of the range. In other words, there may be some elements of the domain for which no corresponding range element exists: if such a function is applied to one of these domain elements, it is *undefined*.

Given the atomic types $ATTR$ and VAL, we can define a new type:

$$ENTRY == ATTR \twoheadrightarrow VAL$$

This is a *synonym type*, and is introduced by the $==$ symbol. This construction introduces the identifier $ENTRY$ as the name of a type which is defined as the set of partial functions from $ATTR$ to VAL. Whenever $ENTRY$ occurs in a specification, it is possible to substitute $ATTR \twoheadrightarrow VAL$ for it. In order for this definition to be legal, both $ATTR$ *and* VAL must have been previously defined in the specification (in other words, they must be *in scope*—Z uses *lexical* scope rules). This kind of definition merely attaches a name to a type: it does not specify any constraints on the type.

The final kind of simple type definition, the one we called an "enumeration" above, is similar to the enumerated types to be found in **Pascal** or **Ada**. We can define a type:

$$ANSWER ::= yes \mid no$$

This type is composed of two values only: the value *yes*, and the value *no*. These are alterantive values. A variable:

$$ans : ANSWER$$

can clearly only have one of these two values at any time. The alternatives in the definition of the type are separated by vertical bars ($\mid$). The symbol $::=$ serves to introduce the type definition. (This syntax is also used to introduce "free types": we do not use them in the specifications given below, so the reader is referred to (Spivey, 1989) for more details.)

2.3 Schemata

In this section, we will be concerned with the concept of a schema in Z. As we have said, a Z specification will be composed, for the most part, of schemata. We have also said that schemata in Z represent types, as well as data structures and operations. We will explain this duality below. We will begin with a discussion of the form and interpretation of the Z schema, and then move on to a discussion of its interpretation.

As we have said, operations and state spaces (data structures and data types) are represented by schemata in Z specifications. The following is a version of a schema that we could define for the blackboard specification (Chapter 4):

$$
\begin{array}{|l}
\hline
\_Entry \underline{\hspace{6cm}} \\
\hline
slots : ATTR \nrightarrow VAL \\
knownslots : \mathbb{P}\ ATTR \\
\hline
knownslots = \mathrm{dom}\ slots \\
\hline
\end{array}
$$

We introduced the types *ATTR* and *VAL* in the previous section, and so they are in scope.

The schema has the name *Entry*. It is important to notice that the spelling is important: in Z, upper and lower case are distinct, so *Entry* is not the same as *ENTRY*. The *Entry* schema has two parts: the part above the line (called the *signature*) and the one below the line (called the *predicate*). The signature is used to declarei variables and to introduce other schemata: it defines the types of the objects that are used in the predicate *and* it defines the type of the schema as a whole.

The predicate is a logical expression which defines situations: specifically, if the predicate is satisfied by some situation, we say that the schema is satisfied by that situation also. A situation is an assignment of values to variables (note that the variables can be global ones, as well as those defined in the signature of the schema). The variables that are declared in the signature are in scope in the schema's predicate. All variables in a signature *must* be typed.

In the case of the *Entry* schema, the signature introduces two variables, *slots* and *knownslots*. The variables are both correctly typed (in the sense that their types are well-formed and in scope). The predicate merely asserts that *knownslots* is the domain of *slots*.

The *Entry* schema serves to define a new type. It can be instantiated, and variables can have type *Entry*. It is therefore legal to write:

ent : *Entry*

in which case, the variable *ent* will be of type *Entry*.

The predicate of the *Entry* schema serves a particular purpose. Since it is a schema that defines a new data type, the predicate is used to express the *invariant property* of that data type. This can be more clearly seen if we consider the following schema:

```
┌─ BCount ─────────────────────
│  val : ℕ
│ ─────────────────────────────
│  val ≤ 10
└──────────────────────────────
```

This schema defines a new (abstract) data type which represents a bounded counter. The predicate of the *BCount* schema states that *val* may never be greater than ten. This expresses an invariant property of the data type: any attempt to assign a value greater than ten to *val* should result in an error (in the case of the specification, it results in a false condition).

When we define a new data type or state space, we clearly need to initialize it. This operation is represented by a schema. We use the convention that the initialization schema for a data type T will have a name composed of the prefix *Init* and the name of the type: thus, the initialization schema for T would be *InitT*. For *Entry*, we have:

```
┌─ InitEntry ───────────────────────────────
│  Entry
│ ─────────────────────
│  knownslots = ∅
└───────────────────────────────────────────
```

By definition of *knownslots*, this expands into:

$$\text{dom } slots = \varnothing$$

and represents the assertion that, upon creation, there are no attributes in the entry. In fact, the initialization schema says something else. The reader may wonder why it is that the range of *slots* is not mentioned: this is because, if the domain of a function is empty, the range, too, must be empty (in fact, it might be a set with large cardinality, but, because there is no way of accessing the values via the function, we cannot obtain those values—this is simply because we do not *know* what the association between the domain and range elements is).

The initialization schema has a signature which refers only, in this case, to the name of the original schema (the one whose initialization conditions we are specifying). In some cases, input variables might appear in the signature, if the initialization is to set the state to some particular (and reachable) value. Here, we only have a reference to *Entry*. The initialization schema expands to:

```
┌────────────────────────────────────────────
│  slots : ATTR ⇸ VAL
│  knownslots : ℙ ATTR
│ ─────────────────────
│  knownslots = dom slots
│  knownslots = ∅
└────────────────────────────────────────────
```

The initialization schema, therefore, declares all the relevant variables and states the initialization condition.

It is one thing to specify something using the schema language and logic, it is quite another to be sure that that specification is implementable. In the case of initialization, we need to show that it is indeed possible to initialize the schema in the way we desire. In other words, we need to prove a theorem. For the *InitEntry* schema, we need to prove that:

$$\vdash \exists\, Entry \bullet InitEntry$$

This is an example of quantification over schemata. The theorem states that there exists a particular entry (value of type *Entry*) such that the predicate of *InitEntry* is satisfied. This expands to:

$$\vdash \exists\, slots : ATTR \nrightarrow VAL;\ knownslots : \mathbb{P}\,ATTR \bullet$$
$$knownslots = \mathrm{dom}\,slots \wedge$$
$$knownslots = \varnothing$$

which is similar to the expansion we gave above, the difference being that all the variables of the signature are now bound by the existential quantifier. We can now use first-order logic and mathematics to prove this assertion.

With schemata that define data types, there are associated two derived schemata. These are the Δ and Ξ forms of the schema. We give the Δ and Ξ forms of the *Entry* schema and then discuss them.

```
┌─ ΔEntry ─────────────────────────────────
│ Entry
│ Entry′
│
└───────────────────────────────────────────
```

(notice that there is no predicate: sometimes, a predicate may be needed in order to relate a part of the state of the unprimed schema to the state of the primed one—there is an example of this in Chapter 4).

The $\Delta Entry$ schema has no predicate: it only has a signature which consists of references to two other schemata, one of which we have not defined. The schema *Entry′* is:

```
┌─ Entry' ─────────────────────────────────────────────────
│  slots' : ATTR ↦ VAL
│  knownslots' : ℙ ATTR
│ ─────────────────────────────────────────────────────────
│  knownslots' = dom slots'
└───────────────────────────────────────────────────────────
```

The difference between this schema and the *Entry* schema is that every variable is primed. In Z, the convention is that primed variables refer to the contents of the variables *after* an operation has been performed. The unprimed version represents the contents of the variable *before* an operation. The Δ version of a schema is a shorthand for the introduction of all the primed forms of the variables that appear in the base schema (a *base* schema is the basic form—in this case, it is the *Entry* schema we defined above) as well as the unprimed (base) form. The Δ form of a schema introduces those variables that are needed to relate the state of a schema before an operation is performed to the state after it has been performed. In other words, Δ forms are used in the definition of operations that change the state of a schema.

```
┌─ ΞEntry ─────────────────────────────────────────────────
│  ΔEntry
│ ─────────────────────────────────────────────────────────
│  slots' = slots
│  knownslots' = knownslots
└───────────────────────────────────────────────────────────
```

The Ξ form, on the other hand, contains a predicate which identifies the after state with the before state. In other words, it is a shorthand for the statement that the state of the schema is invariant under some operation.

We will see these two schemata in use in the examples that follow.

The *Entry* schema can be thought of as defining a record in a database. There are various operations that can be performed. The easiest of the operations to define is that of extracting a value. The values of *ATTR* are intended to represent retrieval keys (they are called *attributes*), and objects of type *VAL* are the values that are stored under keys. Since the variable *slots* is defined as a function, we can apply *slots* to a suitable element of *ATTR* to obtain an element of *VAL*—that element is the value that is stored under the attribute. The operation that we have defined is represented by the following schema:

```
┌─ GetValue ─────────────────────────────
│ ΞEntry
│ a? : ATTR
│ v! : VAL
├────────────────────────────────────────
│ a? ∈ knownslots
│ v! = slots(a?)
└────────────────────────────────────────
```

This schema represents an operation that can be performed over objects of type *Entry*. The operation does not change the state of the entry (the object of type *Entry*), so the *GetValue* schema contains a reference to Ξ *Entry*. The new schema contains two variables, $a?$ and $v!$. The first is an *input* variable: input variables are decorated with a "?" symbol (question mark). The second variable, $v!$, is an *output* variable: output variables are decorated with a "!" (exclamation mark). The interpretation of input and output variables is as one would expect from programming.

The schema relates the input variable to the output variable. The variable $a?$ represents the name of an attribute whose value is to be returned. Before the value can be returned, it must be in the domain of *slots*: i.e., it must be an element of *knownslots* (this is the first line of the predicate). If $a?$ is in *knownslots*, *slots* can be applied to it to yield a value which is bound to $v!$. To make the interpretation of the predicate clearer, we can re-write it thus:

```
┌─ GetValue ─────────────────────────────
│ ΞEntry
│ a? : ATTR
│ v! : VAL
├────────────────────────────────────────
│ a? ∈ knownslots ∧
│ v! = slots(a?)
└────────────────────────────────────────
```

In other words, it is conventional to consider a predicate as a *conjunction*. This applies in particular when the predicate is written as a sequence of expressions, one per line, and without connectives (as was the case in our initial definition of the schema).

Given the interpretation of schema predicates in terms of conjunctions, the interpretation of the *GetValue* predicate is now clear. If $a?$

is not an element of *knownslots*, the entire predicate is false. The predicate is true only when *a?* is in *knownslots*. The case in which the predicate is false represents an error condition or a situation in which the program cannot work correctly.

The role of Ξ *Entry* is to introduce the before and after states of the schema and to identify them. A full expansion of the *GetValue* schema therefore becomes:

$$
\begin{array}{|l}
\hline
\underline{\;GetValue\;} \\
slots : ATTR \nrightarrow VAL \\
slots' : ATTR \nrightarrow VAL \\
knownslots : \mathbb{P}\,ATTR \\
knownslots' : \mathbb{P}\,ATTR \\
a? : ATTR \\
v! : VAL \\
\hline
a? \in knownslots \wedge \\
v! = slots(a?) \wedge \\
slots = slots' \wedge \\
knownslots = knownslots' \\
\hline
\end{array}
$$

(We have written each variable declaration on a separate line, although we could have joined them and separated them using commas, for example:

$$slots, slots' : ATTR \nrightarrow VAL$$

We chose to write the schema in full for the sake of clarity.)

The effect of fully expanding the schema is to show that textual inclusion is just a shorthand for the inclusion of variables in the signature and the conjoining of the predicates.

We can show the effect of the Δ form when we define the next schema:

```
┌─ ModifyAttribute ────────────────────────────────
│ ΔEntry
│ a? : ATTR
│ v? : VAL
├──────────────────────────────────────────────────
│ a? ∈ knownslots
│ slots' = slots ⊕ { a? ↦ v? }
└──────────────────────────────────────────────────
```

This schema represents the operation of overwriting the value that is
stored in an attribute. This schema has two input variables, $a?$ and $v?$.
It also relates the before state to the after state in its predicate. The
predicate states that the after state represented by the overwriting of
the value stored in some attribute (overwriting is represented by the
$\oplus$ operator). This relationship is expressed in terms of an equation in
slots' and *slots*. When an operation modifies the state of a schema, the
relationship between the before and after states is very often expressed
in terms of such an equation (it is, though, always expressed in terms
of some relation containing the before and after variables). The reader
should be careful not to confuse before and after variables with input
and output variables.

We can expand *ModifyAttribute* in full to give:

```
┌─ ModifyAttribute ────────────────────────────────
│ slots, slots' : ATTR ↦ VAL
│ knownslots, knownslots' : ℙ ATTR
│ a? : ATTR
│ v? : VAL
├──────────────────────────────────────────────────
│ a? ∈ knownslots ∧ slots' = slots ⊕ { a? ↦ v? } ∧
│ knownslots = dom slots ∧
│ knownslots' = dom slots'
└──────────────────────────────────────────────────
```

This schema is derived by merging the signature and predicates of the
various schemata. We have included the necessary conjunction symbols
for clarity.

Sometimes it becomes necessary to refer to the components of schemata. There are different ways to do this. The first is reminiscent of
the field reference construct for **Pascal** records. We could refer to the

slots variable in an instance, *ent* of *Entry* as:

$ent.slots$

Although this is perfectly legal, it does present the problem that *slots* might not be bound to what one thinks it is. In other words, this construction is highly context-dependent. We use this construct just once in the specifications that follow: in that case, we are careful to ensure that everything is as it should be.

An alternative is to use *quantification*. We can quantify over schemata using the universal ($\forall$), existential ($\exists$) and unique ($\exists_1$) quantifiers (we have seen an example of quantification above when we considered initialization). We can also form sets and sequences of schemata, as well as using other constructs. Here, we concentrate on quantification. A fuller treatment can be found in (Spivey, 1989). If, for example, we have:

$\exists\,Entry \bullet \ldots$

we are stating that there exists a schema of type *Entry* such that the formula in the scope of the existential quantifier is satisfied (the formula is elided as three dots). The effect of such a quantification is to quantify over the variables in the signature of the schema. The quantification shown above is equivalent to:

$\exists\,slots : ATTR \twoheadrightarrow VAL; \; knownslots : \mathbb{P}\,ATTR \bullet \ldots$

Inside the scope of the quantifier, we may have any expressions we want. The point is that the variables of the schema over which we originally quantified are in scope and can be treated as ordinary bound variables. Given the context-dependency mentioned above, such quantification is usually constrained (and many examples of such constraints can be found in the formal specification chapters below). This is so that the schema is bound correctly, and so that the variables in its signature are also correctly bound.

The reader should be aware that we chose existential quantification above because of its commitment to existence. We could have given an example in terms of universal or in terms of unique quantification:

the basic properties of quantifying over schemata remain the same. We could, for example, have:

$$\forall\, Entry \bullet \operatorname{dom} slots \neq \varnothing$$

which states that every entry has a non-empty domain (this assertion is false).

Quantification in Z is not restricted to quantification over schemata. There are, again, numerous examples of quantification over simple variables in the specifications that we present below and in the specifications contained in (Hayes, 1987).

One of the more convenient features of Z schemata is that they can be combined. We have seen one simple way of performing such a combination above: textual inclusion. Quantification is another way of combining schemata (there are examples of this in the two specifications). In addition, it is possible to combine schemata using conjunction ($\wedge$), disjunction ($\vee$), negation ($\neg$), implication ($\Rightarrow$) and biconditional ($\equiv$). In the specifcations that we present below, combinations of the first three types are most common.

The negation schema is the simplest to explain. Consider the following schema:

$$
\begin{array}{|l}
\hline
\textit{AttribPresent} \underline{\hspace{5cm}} \\
\Xi Entry \\
a? : ATTR \\
\hline
a? \in knownslots \\
\hline
\end{array}
$$

This schema is true in just those situations in which $a?$ is an element of $knownslots$.

We define the negation of this schema

$$\neg\ AttribPresent$$

as:

$$
\begin{array}{|l}
\hline
\Xi Entry \\
a? : ATTR \\
\hline
a? \notin knownslots \\
\hline
\end{array}
$$

The negation of a schema has the same signature as the un-negated schema, but its predicate is the negation of the original schema. Care should be taken in writing the negations of predicates, for errors can easily creep in.

Imagine now that we want an operation that will return the value stored in an attribute, provided that the attribute is an element of *knownslots*, and imagine that we require that *knownslots* must be non-empty. We can define a schema:

$$\begin{array}{|l}
\underline{\ NonEmptyAttrs\ }\rule{3cm}{0pt} \\
\ \Xi Entry \\
\hline
\ knownslots \neq \varnothing \\
\end{array}$$

The effect that we desire is a predicate of the form:

$$knownslots \neq \varnothing \ \wedge$$
$$a? \in \operatorname{dom} slots \ \wedge$$
$$v! = slots(a?)$$

We can obtain this by combining *NonEmptyAttrs* with *GetValue*:

$$NonEmptyAttrs \wedge GetValue$$

This expands to:

$$\begin{array}{|l}
\ \Xi Entry \\
\ a? : ATTR \\
\ v! : VAL \\
\hline
\ knownslots \neq \varnothing \\
\ a? \in knownslots \\
\ v! = slots(a?) \\
\end{array}$$

The schema that results from this is the *conjunction* of the predicates of the two component schemata (we have omitted the conjunction symbols), and it contains the union of their signatures.

We could define the disjunction of the two schemata:

$$NonEmptyAttrs \vee GetValue$$

which gives:

$$
\begin{array}{|l}
\hline
\;\Xi Entry \\
\;a? : ATTR \\
\;v! : VAL \\
\hline
\;(knownslots \neq \varnothing) \vee \\
\;(a? \in knownslots \wedge \\
\;\qquad v! = slots(a?)) \\
\hline
\end{array}
$$

(We have fully bracketed the predicate for clarity, and we have introduced conjunction symbols as necessary.) The resulting schema again
contains the union of the two signatures, but the new predicate is now
the *disjunction* of the two component predicates.

The implication and biconditional combinators operate in ways directly analogous to those in which conjunction and disjunction operate.

The final schema combinator that we discuss is the sequential composition operator (this is used below). This combinator is written ⨾,
and is rather more complex to describe than the others we have considered. The idea behind this combinator can be expressed as follows.
Let S and T be two schemata, then

$$S \mathbin{\fatsemi} T$$

represents the schema that results from first evaluating S and then
evaluating T: in other words, it holds true in those situations in which
first the predicate of S holds, and then, after some change to the state,
in which the predicate of T holds. Quite clearly, there must be a change
to the situation in this case, so S and T can be assumed to be schemata
that represent operations over state spaces. Furthermore, the result of
executing (the operation represented by) S must be a state which is
valid for T to execute. In other words, the state which results from
executing S must be such that it satisfies the before variables of T.

Before two schemata S and T can be composed by ⨾, a number of
conditions must be met. Firstly, the decorated components of S must
match the undecorated components of T: that is, if S has a variable x',
then T must have a variable x. Also, the types of all input or output
variables must be the same. This second requirement entails that if S

has an output variable $os!$ and T has an input variable $it?$, the types of these two variables must be the same because they are the means by which S communicates its results with T. The after state variables (the primed ones) of S must be identified with the before state variables of T (the unprimed ones) in the following way: take all after state variables of S that have the same base name (name with the prime omitted) and replace them with new variables (this is most conveniently done using a subscript composed of one or more + symbols), and replace all those before state variables of T with the corresponding base name with the newly created variables. Thus, if S has the after state variable s', and T has the before state variable s, we create a new variable, say s^+ and uniformly substitute it in S for s' and in T for s. Third, the predicates of S and T are conjoined and the new variables (in this case, s^+) are hidden using existential quantification.

The following example (from (Hayes, 1987), pp. 22-23) shows how the $\mathbin{\mathring{,}}$ operation works. Let S be the schema:

$$
\begin{array}{|l}
\hline
\,S \rule{3.5in}{0pt} \\
\hline
x? : \mathsf{N} \\
y! : \mathsf{N} \\
s : \mathsf{N} \\
s' : \mathsf{N} \\
\hline
s' = s - x? \wedge y! = s \\
\hline
\end{array}
$$

and let T be:

$$
\begin{array}{|l}
\hline
\,T \rule{3.5in}{0pt} \\
\hline
x?, s, s' : \mathsf{N} \\
\hline
s < x? \wedge s' = s \\
\hline
\end{array}
$$

The composite schema $S \mathbin{\mathring{,}} T$ is:

$$
\begin{array}{|l}
\hline
x?, s, s', y! : \mathsf{N} \\
\hline
(\exists\, s^+ : \mathsf{N} \bullet \\
\qquad s^+ = s - x \wedge y! = s \wedge \\
\qquad s^+ \wedge s' = s^+) \\
\hline
\end{array}
$$

The variable $x?$ appears in both S and T, and in both schemata it has type $\mathbb{N}$. The after state variable in S and the before state variable in T are identified and replaced by s^+. Notice that in the predicate of T, we have:

$$s' = s$$

In the composite schema $S \, \fatsemi \, T$, we have

$$s' = s^+$$

the s' refers, here, to the state after the execution of T.

The predicates of S and T are conjoined (the "and" on the third line of the composite schema predicate), and the intermediate state variable s^+ is hidden by existential quantification: since the variable is bound by the quantifier, it is not in scope outside of the schema's predicate and so is hidden. The variable s^+ does represent the intermediate state because the variable has been substituted for *both* the after state of S and the before state of T.

The $\fatsemi$ operation may appear a little forbidding at first, but it is a powerful method of combining schemata. We use this combinator a number of times below, and are careful to explain why we have chosen it. Sequential composition (which is what $\fatsemi$ represents) imposes a strict ordering on the execution of schemata because it forces the identification of after and before states. In general, we believe, a top-level specification should not impose such constraints: we prefer initial specifications to be non-deterministic in their orderings because this affords additional freedom during the refinement process. In the cases in which we have used $\fatsemi$ below, we do so because we have good arguments to support the assertion that the ordering which $\fatsemi$ imposes will be respected during the entire refinement process. In other words, when we have $S \, \fatsemi \, T$ in the top-level specification, we give arguments to support the assertion that during the refinement process, every time we create a refined schema S' of S, a refined schema T' of T, in order to create the refinement of $C \, (= S \, \fatsemi \, T)$, S' and T' will be composed as $S' \, \fatsemi \, T'$ and not in some other way.

2.4   Proofs

We have now seen the major component of a Z specification, the schema, and we have seen that it is a mathematical object. It is evident, then, that proofs can (and indeed should) be performed on the specifications that we produce. The reason for this is that we have a mathematical guarantee of correctness if we prove properties of the specification. There are two classes of proof that need to be performed:

1. Proofs of internal consistency, and

2. Refinement proofs.

Internal consistency involves proving such things as the fact that one schema does not contradict the predicate of another, or that a schema does not leave the system in an impossible state. They can also involve proving properties *of* the system being specified: proofs of this nature can be found in Chapters 4 and 6 of this book. As examples of the latter, we offer the following:

- If we create a new entry on the blackboard (add a new record to a database, in more conventional terms) and then add a new attribute-value pair (add a new field and value), we have performed the same operation as we would have done if we had created an entry which contained the attribute-value pair that we added as an extra step.

- In a blackboard system, if we add a new attribute-value pair to an entry (i.e., if we add a new field and value to a record) and then modify the value that we have just stored, this operation is equivalent to adding an attribute-value pair with a value equal to the modified one.

We give proofs of these propositions in Chapter 4.

The second class of proof is related to the refinement process. Under refinement, we begin with a high-level specification of the system. Then, we successively refine the specification so that, on each iteration of the refinement process, we obtain a specification that is just a little closer to the implementation language. This process partly involves the transformation of the specification so that constructs and operations that are closer to those provided by the implementation language are obtained. The process terminates when a specification is obtained that can be directly translated into the implementation language.

Refinement involves the development of new schemata which represent data structures and types and operations. These new schemata are more "concrete" in the sense that they are closer to the implementation language than the schemata from which they were derived. The refinement process involves proving that the newly derived schemata can serve as an implementation of those from which they were derived, and proving that they leave all original properties invariant. Jones (1980) discusses this approach to the development of programs in some detail.

In this book, we are not concerned with the refinement process. This is because of lack of space. We do, though, give an outline of the process in the Appendix, and we give an example refinement there. In the Appendix, we will discuss the kinds of proof that are necessary during refinement.

In the remainder of this section, we will give an example proof of the first kind. We are going to prove a simple property of one of the operations we defined in the last section. We will prove that:

$$ModifyAttribute \vdash \text{dom} \, slots = \text{dom} \, slots'$$

The *ModifyAttribute* schema is:

$$
\begin{array}{l}
\underline{\quad ModifyAttribute \quad\quad\quad\quad\quad\quad\quad\quad\quad} \\
\Delta Entry \\
a? : ATTR \\
v? : VAL \\
\underline{\quad\quad\quad\quad\quad\quad\quad\quad\quad\quad\quad\quad\quad} \\
a? \in knownslots \\
slots' = slots \oplus \{ \, a? \mapsto v? \, \} \\
\end{array}
$$

The proposition above says that if we assume that the schema has acted upon some entry, the right-hand side will obtain. This amounts to proving that the predicate of *ModifyAttribute* implies the desired property. In other words, we want to prove that:

$$slots' = slots \oplus \{ \, a? \mapsto v? \, \} \vdash \text{dom} \, slots = \text{dom} \, slots'$$

The proof is by properties of $\oplus$ (the domain over-riding operator) and properties of dom and sets.

$$\begin{aligned}
\operatorname{dom} slots' &= \operatorname{dom}(slots \oplus \{\ a? \mapsto v?\ \}) & \\
&= \operatorname{dom} slots \cup \operatorname{dom}\{\ a? \mapsto v?\ \} & \text{[property of dom]} \\
&= \operatorname{dom} slots \cup \{\ a\ \} & \text{[}(*)\text{]} \\
&= \operatorname{dom} slots & \text{[since } a? \in \operatorname{dom} slots\text{]}
\end{aligned}$$

The line marked $*$ is obtained by observing that:

$$\operatorname{dom}\{\ d \mapsto r\ \} = \{\ d\ \}$$

since $\{\ d\ \}$ is the domain of the map $\{\ d \mapsto r\ \}$.

This property turns out to be quite useful because it tells us about other aspects of the specification. In particular, it shows us that there is a problem with asserting that an entry is the "same" after an operation as it was before (this will become clearer in the section on blackboard invariants in Chapter 4). Many of the properties that we actually prove in Chapter 4 (and which we state without proof in Chapter 6) are of this nature. Without such proofs, we contend, many properties of the system that we are specifying (and also many of the consequences of the way in which we model the system in our specifications) remain at best implicit (and at worst un-noticed): one of the justifications of formal specification is that we can make properties explicit, and therefore subject to argument.

There are many mathematical concepts and structures that can be used in specifications. In this book, and in this Chapter in particular, we cannot hope to cover them all. For those readers who are unfamiliar with the additional apparatus needed, we recommend that (Spivey, 1989) be used as a guide to the concepts that we employ below (everything that we use in the specifications Chapters 4 and 6 can be found there, particularly the mathematical "tool-kit" to be found in Chapter 4 of (Spivey, 1989)).

In addition, we endeavour to define all Z-specific operations when we use them for the first time: this applies in particular to the hiding operations that can be performed on schemata. The last type of operation is used in order to render some of the variables in a schema invisible to anything outside of the schema. In general, we expand schemata where necessary so that the reader can see the effect of the transformations that been applied.

We are now in a position to move on to the informal presentation of the blackboard architecture. The informal specification will serve as the basis of the formal treatment that we give in Chapter 4. We recommend that the reader refer back to this Chapter when reading Chapter 4 and Chapter 6 (which contains the formal definition of the CASSANDRA archicture—an informal specification of it is to be found in Chapter 5).

3

The Blackboard Architecture

3.1 Introduction

This chapter is concerned with an informal presentation of the blackboard architecture (Nii, 1986a, 1986b; Craig, *in press*). It is included so that those readers who are not familiar with the architecture can gain enough background information to understand the formal treatment given in the next chapter. The presentation of an informal account may also be of benefit to those who understand the architecture, for it will give a flavour of the interpretation preferred by the author: this interpretation is the basis of the formal specification which follows. As was stated in the Introduction, there are many interpretations of the blackboard architecture and a formal statement in terms of some unambiguous language (in the present case, Z) is necessary to make precise exactly what one means. However, before engaging in such a formal exercise, it is worth clarifying notions: the present chapter can be seen in this, latter, light, as well as serving as an informal reference with which to compare the Z specification.

Rather than present a simple outline of the blackboard architecture, the chapter begins with an outline of the fundamental principles that underpin it. This serves to motivate the following sections—the architecture is intended as a model for group problem-solving in the context of problems that are too difficult or too large for an individual to solve alone. The fundamental principles constitute the *blackboard metaphor*. Once the metaphor has been presented, we move on to more concrete matters and describe the interpretation of the metaphor in terms of structures that are more readily identifiable as computational: this description forms the concrete context within which to describe the details of the blackboard architecture, at least as far as the author's interpretation is concerned. The latter discussion is somewhat more implementational than is common in the literature: this is because the (semi-) operational concepts that are employed will assist in the formal specification exercise that forms the next chapter. The formal specification that is given in the next chapter differs in some respects from the informal one given below; at the end of this chapter, we will indicate these differences and give justifications for them.

The discussion of the architecture presented in this chapter is necessarily brief. For a more detailed account, the reader should consult other material (e.g., Nii (1986a), Craig (*in press*)).

3.2   The Blackboard Metaphor

In this section, we examine the *blackboard metaphor*. The metaphor is about problem-solving in the context of a group of (human) experts who have been set the task of solving a problem which is too difficult for them to solve individually. The problem is assumed to be such that each expert does not possess all the knowledge required to create an adequate solution. The ignorance of one expert is compensated by the knowledge of another. It should be noted that this difference in knowledge is important to the metaphor: it implies that the experts possess different knowledge and capabilities and that they are not merely "copies" of each other—put another way, it implies that the experts come from different fields, all of which are relevant to the problem under attack.

In the case which we do not consider (the case in which the experts have similar skills), it may be assumed that the problem requires more than one problem-solver because of its sheer size: there are interesting problems in this area (for example, the problems tackled by Lesser and Corkhill (Lesser, 1983)), but they are outside the scope of blackboard systems *per se.*

The metaphor can be expressed in the following way (which is similar to that given by Craig (*in press*), Nii (1986a) and Hayes-Roth (1983)):

> Imagine a group of experts who are collaborating to solve a difficult problem. The experts stand around a blackboard, and are able to write and draw on it. When they have a contribution to make to the emerging solution, they write on the blackboard; otherwise they do nothing. In addition to writing and drawing, the experts are allowed to connect items already on the blackboard by drawing arrows. The problem is solved when the experts agree that an adequate solution has emerged: the solution is to be found on the blackboard.

The experts record their contributions to the solution process by writing on a blackboard: when they have a contribution to make, they write or draw something, and when they have nothing to contribute, they do nothing. The blackboard represents a generally accessible record of the solution process. It can contain records of failed attempts to find a solution, as well as one or more promising routes to a solution. This last remark implies that more than one solution may be recorded on the blackboard: in such a case, the experts have to decide which is the better or more preferable of the proposed solutions.

In all cases, it may be assumed that the experts respond to something that is already on the blackboard. A sentence or a figure that has been drawn by one expert may cause another to record something else which will later be connected (via an arrow or some other method) into an adequate solution. This assumption leads to the observation that unless an expert sees something on the blackboard he or she is not permitted to make a contribution—they are not allowed to engage in private discussions during the problem-solving episode (we could assume that they are deaf and dumb, in other words).

It should be noted that nothing has been said about how the experts make their contributions other than the fact that they respond to items written (or drawn) on the blackboard. Nothing has been said about turn-taking, nor is there anything about priority—it is assumed that an expert *will* make a contribution *whenever* he or she is so able. In other words, there are no assumptions about how the problem-solving episode is conducted. When people are solving problems in similar situations, they often defer to others in the group—say, out of politeness or deference—and they will engage in discussions as to the merits of a contribution. Both of these aspects are excluded from the metaphor because it is intended to capture only the *essence* of the process. In addition, nothing is said about where the initial problem statement comes from, although it can be assumed that it is written on the blackboard by some external agency before the problem-solving episode begins.

Finally, it must be noted that, in the above description, we have concentrated on the terms *adequate solution*. There are reasons for this. Firstly, because of the complexity of the problem or because of the amount of available data, it may be impossible to achieve a complete or perfect solution: some approximation to a solution may be all that is possible (or even desirable). Second, because of the fact that competing solutions can be developed in parallel, an evaluation may have to be made before one of them is adopted: the decision criteria may rest on the fact that one of the competing solutions is more adequate than the other. (It should be noted that, in the case of competing solutions, no decision may be possible, and so all of the competitors are put forth as solutions, as was the case with HASP/SIAP (Feigenbaum, 1982).)

These two points are highly relevant to the kinds of problem that blackboard systems are used to solve. Typically, it is the case that multiple sources of expertise, from different domains, are required to solve the problem. Because of search space size, it may be impossible to determine that a complete solution has been achieved, so criteria of adequacy must be adopted. In some cases, the quality of the data on which the blackboard system operates may be so low (for example, due to noise) that a solution can only be putative: this was the case for the HASP/SIAP system (Feigenbaum, 1982), in which the term "solution" was redefined in such a way that the most refined account of the data, nomatter how incomplete, was to be counted as a solution.

One final point is, perhaps, worth making: it concerns a property of the problems that blackboard systems are intended to solve. This property is implicit in the description of the metaphor given above and is about the organisation of the space generated by the problem. In his book, *Sciences of the Artificial*, Simon (1969) gives a definition of a *nearly-decomposable problem*. A problem of this type is such that its component sub-problems do not interact significantly and can thus be tackled in a relatively independent fashion. A problem in which sub-tasks interact is typified by the blocks world case (Sacerdoti, 1977) in which the movement of one block prevents the movement of another: this is a case of a *negative* interaction, and positive interactions have been observed (see, for example, Wilensky, 1983) (an example of a positive interaction is one in which the solution of one sub-problem has the side-effect that it generates a solution for another). A totally decomposable problem is one for which all sub-tasks can be solved totally independently of the others and for which there are no inter-problem interactions of the kinds mentioned above. In a nearly-decomposable problem, there are inter-problem or inter-task interactions, but their effects can be neglected for the majority of the time.

The property of near-decomposability can be seen in the blackboard metaphor when it is considered that experts can react to anything that is placed on the blackboard. If there were serious interactions in the problem, the contribution of one expert could seriously affect that of another. The assumption is that the contribution of an expert is made at the most appropriate time: this may lead to clarification of the relationships between previous contributions and may lead to the development of a new line of reasoning in the future. However, the order in which sub-problems are tackled is not assumed to be important so multiple lines of reasoning, for example, may occur in parallel. For non-decomposable problems, the order in which sub-problems are tackled, of course, can have serious consequences for the success of the attempt at finding a solution. Near-decomposability allows us to assume that sub-problems may be tackled in (approximately) any order, but still retains the property that a solution to a sub-problem *may* have conse-queces for previous solutions or for sub-problems yet to be attempted. As Simon remarks, the assumption of near-decomposability is relatively mild.

3.3   The Architecture

3.3.1   Introduction

In the last section, we introduced the blackboard metaphor and discussed some of its implications. A metaphor is a guiding principle and, on its own, can only guide us towards an implementation. This section is concerned with the general principles on which blackboard systems rest: that is, it contains a definition of an *architecture* which is more readily amenable to interpretation in terms of a computer program. The architectural statement can be considered to be a high-level specification of a generic structure which is then refined (and interpreted) to form the basis on which an actual system is implemented. The metaphor, on the other hand, is really only a set of guiding principles which illustrates one or more points without suggesting an immediate realisation.

In this section, we will examine the metaphor by extracting its components and giving them an interpretation. The next step will be to extend these interpretations so that an implementation becomes possible.

We begin this examination with the blackboard structure and its contents. We then move onto the question of the role and behaviours of the problem-solving experts. Finally, we need to consider the issue of control. It was stated above that the metaphor contains no statements about how to control problem-solving activities. Quite obviously, any computer implementation will require a control structure: this issue must then be addressed when defining the architecture.

3.3.2   The Blackboard

The blackboard serves as a globally accessible database which records the intermediate states in the solution process. The metaphor states that the experts record information on the physical blackboard: this corresponds exactly to the role of the blackboard database in blackboard systems. From this statement, it is immediate that the computational counterparts of the experts must inspect and modify the blackboard database during problem-solving. Whenever an expert decides (for whatever reason) that it can make a contribution to the solution, that contribution is stored in the database. The blackboard database (which we, henceforth, will simply call the *blackboard*) is globally accessible, because *all* the experts in a blackboard need to be able to inspect and update it.

Organisation of the blackboard

In the metaphor, of course, the blackboard is assumed simply to be of the conventional type: that is, a wooden blackboard attached to a wall. Material can be written on any part of the blackboard at any time, and the structure of the emerging solution is that imparted to it by the experts. In the blackboard architecture, on the other hand, it is assumed that the blackboard has internal structure along at least two dimensions. Since the two-dimensional case is the easiest to understand, it will be presented first and the generalised case will only be mentioned briefly.

The blackboard architecture assumes that the development of a solution takes place over some period of time. The first dimension of the blackboard database is very often considered to be that of time: this serves to locate the components of emerging solutions. In signal processing applications (e.g., HEARSAY-II (Erman, 1975), HASP/SIAP (Feigenbaum, 1982), signal data arrival time clearly serves to order the temporal dimension. In planning applications, the time at which a decision is taken serves a similar purpose. The temporal dimension is frequently (e.g., Hayes-Roth 1983) referred to as the *horizontal* dimension, and is often ignored when describing systems (this is probably because most systems have been implemented on serial hardware where time ordering is obvious). The reader should note that time need not be the horizontal dimension: it is merely a fact that it is typically assumed to play this role.

The second dimension of the blackboard is considerably more interesting. Unlike the physical blackboard of the metaphor, the blackboard in the architecture is assumed to be divided into a number of *abstraction levels* (or more simply, *levels*). An abstraction level is a representation of the problem being solved. Two different abstraction levels view the same problem at different levels of abstraction. In the speech domain, two such abstraction levels are the word and phrase levels. Both of these abstractions are based on primary structural units of an utterance, but the word abstraction views an utterance as being composed of a sequence of words with structural relationships obtaining between the components of words (i.e., between phonemes), whereas the phrase abstraction considers it to be a sequence of words with structural relationships obtaining between them (that is, the standard grammatical relationships). The phrase level represents a more abstract view of the sentence than does the word level (it also represents a more general view) because it contains the structures defined by the word level (words) as components. This idea leads to a common structuring principle for abstraction levels: they are often organised by a *part-of* relationship—for the speech example, it is clear that words are part of phrases.

As has been stated by a number of authors (for example, Nii, 1986a, Hayes-Roth, 1986, Craig, *in press*), the identification of the correct abstraction levels for a given problem represents the difference between a successful system and one that does not work. However, the task is not complete when the abstraction levels have been identified: they must, in addition, be ordered into an *abstraction hierarchy*. This hierarchy contains abstraction levels as its elements and must be a *linear* ordering—it can be viewed as a total ordering on the abstraction levels, and therefore contains *unique* least and most abstract levels (in other words, the abstraction levels are organised as a chain). Furthermore, the architecture states that there must be only one abstraction hierarchy for the blackboard: that is, the abstraction hierarchy must itself be unique. In other words, the blackboard database must be organised as a *chain* of abstraction levels (i.e., a total, linear ordering).

For a great many problems, these constraints can easily be satisfied with a little effort. Some problems, however, require a more relaxed organisation for their global database—errand planningi (Hayes-Roth, 1979) and protein structure analysis (Terry, 1983) are two cases in point—and require a partial ordering. This relaxation can be achieved by considering that a system to solve such problems contains not one but many blackboards, each with its own linear hierarchy.

The abstraction hierarchy determines, amongst other things, where data is input and where solutions are collected. In a synthesis problem such as speech recognition, data is input at the lowest level of abstraction and solutions are collected from the highest level of abstraction. In analysis tasks, the opposite is to be expected. In addition, the organisation of abstraction levels determines the general way in which solutions are developed. In synthesis tasks, we normally expect information stored at low levels of abstraction to be processed in an upward fashion: that is, towards increasingly more abstract regions of the blackboard. In analysis tasks, solutions move from an abstract representation towards increasingly more concrete ones.

Interestingly, the architecture, at least in its most commonly accepted form, does not state *how many* abstraction levels need be present. A single abstraction level on its own logically forms a hierarchy, but for practical purposes, it can safely be assumed that the blackboard will be composed of two or more abstraction levels. The debate concerning the minimum number of abstraction levels required before a system can be considered to be a blackboard system is typical of the informal character of the architecture. Since this debate has been going on for some time without any resolution (although all implemented systems have had considerably more than two abstraction levels), we will not make any further comments.

Blackboard contents

Having described the general organisation of the blackboard, it is necessary to say a few words about the structures that are placed on the blackboard (an operation that is commonly referred to as *posting*) and about what they represent.

Since the blackboard is intended to act as a common database for recording the decisions made during problem solving, it should come as no surprise to discover that it contains structures that represent steps in the solution. These structures are posted on the blackboard by the experts and are accessible to all experts. The structures (called *entries*) contain information that represents a step that has taken towards a solution. In terms of a search tree, entries represent the nodes of the tree. In theorem proving, the search tree contains nodes which represent the sub-formulae that have been derived from the axioms and initial formulae by the action of the inference rules. In a blackboard-based theorem prover, each entry on the blackboard would contain a sub-formula and would act to record that sub-formula for future use. The relationship between blackboard entries and working memory contents in the production rule architecture is immediate: working memory elements represent intermediate data that has been derived by the application of production rules (problem-solving knowledge). In a similar way, entries represent intermediate steps that are generated by the actions of the experts, but in the blackboard architecture, as will be seen, entries that are only provisional may, eventually, make a direct contribution to the final solution. In computational terms, the nodes in a search tree represent partial results.

A critical point about entries is that they are each assigned to *one and only one* abstraction level. In other words, an entry cannot be placed simultaneously on two or more abstraction levels. The reason for this is that an entry represents an element in the developing solution: that element represents an object which is to be manipulated by the problem-solving processes embodied in the experts. Since an entry represents an object, that object must belong to a description at some level of abstraction. It is implicit in the definition of abstraction levels that they are disjoint: that is, the representation at one level of abstraction uses a vocabulary which is logically distinct from the vocabulary of any other level. If this were not the case, it would be an easy matter to prove (by contradiction) the existence of only one abstraction level, and the hierarchy would be destroyed. Since abstraction levels represent different views of the problem using different abstractions, an entry at one level of abstraction must necessarily represent an object which can be described in that abstraction level's representational vocabulary. Hence, it is necessary that an entry be located at *exactly* one level of abstraction, for if it spanned abstraction levels, it would, necessarily, represent different structures (and, thus, could be split into many, separate, entries, each one of which would belong to a different abstraction level).

Entries are added to the blackboard by experts. They can be modified so as to reflect the actions of experts at times later than that at which they were added to the blackboard. The addition of an entry to the blackboard can cause one or more experts to alter existing entries or to add new ones. The addition of an entry to the blackboard corresponds exactly to the addition of text or diagrams to the physical blackboard in the metaphor. Just as items on a physical blackboard remain available for inspection until they are erased, so entries remain available for inspection or modification. It is, though, uncommon for entries to be removed from the blackboard—this is for reasons that cannot be considered in this relatively elementary presentation (the interested reader should consult Craig, 1988a, for an account of deletion).

It is usual for entries to be structured as sets of *attribute-value pairs* (structures that are very similar to records in **Pascal** or structures in **Algol-68** or **C**). The reason for this is that entries typically have to contain large amounts of information (amounts much greater than a single literal in a resolution theorem-prover), Some of which is useful to the control structure. The amount of information in an entry is determined by the problem under attack, but since blackboard problems are typically large, it is to be expected that entries are large structures. In addition to the complexity reason, entries are relatively large structures because they aggregate information. In a clausal-based system (such as **Prolog**), information tends to be represented by small structures which are placed in a database with an accepted search overhead. In blackboard systems, there is an economy of scale, and, in order to reduce the overhead imposed by search, entries tend to collect related information: this entails that only a few entries need to be located in order to gather a considerable amount of information from the blackboard. Finally, the structures represented by entries are usually quite complex, and, as we will see, entries have a representational role in terms of the objects assumed by the problem: the structural complexity of the objects being represented is reflected in the complexity of the entries that represent them.

Attribute-value representations describe objects in terms of their *attributes*. One attribute of an apple is its colour; another is its size. Both colour and size are attributes in an attribute-value representation of an apple. The value component of the representation is a filler for values which represent how much of a given attribute is present in the object. In the case of colour, this would be, in the case of apples, a value which specified "red", for example. The size attribute might have a value which specified that the apple was very large.

The value held on any particular attribute can be changed at any time (this is similar to the values stored in records): such changes can be the addition of a new value (if the attribute takes aggregate values such as lists or arrays), the removal of a previous value or else a value can be assigned to the attribute (i.e., any previous values are simply discarded and the new one inserted in their place—this is very much akin to assignment to a variable). Under certain circumstances, it is also necessary to add (and less frequently, delete) attributes. New attributes are added when the object being modelled is observed to have more attributes than was originally thought (attributes can also be added as a result of an inferential process, of course). For example, the sweetness attribute might be added to the attribute-value representation of an apple when its value has become known (by, for example, trying to eat it). The addition of attributes to a set, and the operations performed on values (storing and replacing them) are fundamental to this representation. In blackboard systems, as in production systems, there are no restrictions on what an attribute might represent: indeed, as we will see in the next subsection, entries (which are basically sets of attribute-value pairs) can refer to other entries on the blackboard and this is a very important aspect of the development of solutions in such systems.

Relationships on the blackboard

The solution that a blackboard system develops for a problem is not typically represented by a single entry on the blackboard. This contrasts with the case for resolution-based theorem provers which represent the solution as the empty clause. Instead, a solution generated by a blackboard system is typically represented as a set of entries whose elements are each at a different level of abstraction—that is, it is, typically, composed of an entire network of entries. These entries span one or more abstraction levels. This means that the representations used for solutions in blackboard systems are *distributed* and not centralised as is the case in theorem provers.

The distributed representation clearly requires that entries be related to each other. One emerging principle in blackboard systems is explicit representation: this first emerged in control, but is tending to spread to other aspects. The explicit representation of relationships between entries is also required in blackboard systems, and is implemented using the attribute-value structure of entries. In this representation, some attributes stand for relations that can obtain between entries. Very often, relationships have information associated with them (for example, confidence values), and this, too, is recorded in entries (either by assigning a complex value to an attribute, or by creating a new attribute to record the confidence value).

In the attribute-value representation, if a relation, say *supports*, exists between entries E1 and E2, entry E1 will have a *supports* attribute whose value is E2. Since the values stored in attributes are retrievable, it is possible for any of the experts in the system to extract the name of the entry which E1 supports. A relation like *supports* is useful when dealing with hypotheses: the evidence for the hypothesis can be said to support the statement of the hypothesis. In the above example, the entry E1 represents (some aspect of) the evidence for the hypothesis represented by entry E2. From this example, it can be seen that the value of an attribute that represents a relation is simply the name of another entry on the blackboard (in other words, a reference to that entry). Since many relations have an arity greater than one, it should come as no surprise to learn that relation-representing attributes frequently contain lists or sequences of entry references, in which case the relation is taken to hold between the entry in which the relation attribute resides and the (set of) entry references which are its value. It is possible, as is the case in BB1 and PROTEAN, to have executable code stored in entry attributes—this is somewhat rare, however, because it violates the informal constraint that the blackboard should contain only passive data.

Relationships between entries are as old as blackboard systems themselves. HEARSAY-II (Erman, 1975), which was the first implemented blackboard system, had a rich complement of relation-denoting attributes. Many relation-denoting attributes also had additional information associated with them (see Hayes-Roth, 1985a, for details).

The importance of the explicit representation of relations (sometimes called *links*) is that they allow sets of entries to be associated with each other. This is part of the explicit representation of the solution on the blackboard. It is also part of the distributed representations that are characteristic of blackboard problem-solvers.

The existence of explicit links allows the problem-solving experts in a blackboard system to locate related and potentially relevant information by, essentially, pointer-chasing. When an entry is to be located from a link, it can be retrieved directly by requesting the blackboard database manager to return the entry structure which is referred to by the link. The blackboard manager is a software sub-system which manages the addition and modification of entries: it deals with entries as logical units and not as sets of attribute-value pairs. A request to locate an entry by name (there are other operations which the manager has to perform, as will be seen) causes the manager to search for the corresponding entry and to return it as a complete structure. Once the entry has been located, operations can be performed on its attributes (such operations are the addition of a value, alteration of a value, and so on). Without the provision of links, such an operation would entail searching the entire blackboard database matching entries against their name or against some other key (typically, an attribute—this operation is actually needed, as will become clear below).

In addition to the efficiency point, links collect entries into distinct sets or regions of the blackboard: these regions represent subsets of the entries on the blackboard. In addition, links partition the blackboard in a *dynamic* fashion into structures called *solution islands*. The intuitive interpretation of a solution island depends upon the problem being solved, and upon the stage in problem-solving. However, they can represent a number of distinct structures:

- a solution which is competing with one or more other solutions.

All or any of the solutions may be in the process of being constructed, or they may be completed and undergoing evaluation.

- A cluster of related items that, taken together, represent an important step in finding an overall solution.

- A context within which future problem-solving activities can take place (this interpretation is less formal than the others and is, in fact, the one which motivated the concepts). The idea of the context is that the entries are related in the sense that they represent structures (objects or inferences) that will be used in the future by the system's experts in the derivation of solutions—such solutions may develop into complete, new islands.

- A group of entries which represent objects that constute the object represented at the highest level of abstraction.

Many other interpretations of solution islands are possible: they tend to be application-specific. The interpretations given above are more or less fundamental since the other aspects can be seen as extensions of these basic ideas. The HEARSAY-III system (Balzer, 1980) reified solution islands as *contexts*: these are independent blackboard regions that are treated as logical units by the HEARSAY-III system. A similar idea can be found in the *spaces* in GBB (Corkhill, 1986).

One view of the problem-solving activity in blackboard systems is that it is based on the formation of increasingly larger solution islands. The islands that are initially developed are later linked to form islands of larger scope until complete solutions emerge.

It should be noted that competing (or indeed co-operating) solution islands may share entries. That is, one island may contain entries that are contained in another island. Where the relationship between the islands is one of co-operation, this can be seen as the development of a larger island (and it requires the observation that islands need not be joined at the highest abstraction level only). Where the relationship is one of competition, the shared entries may be receiving different interpretations in the two islands. It is worth emphasising that we have described the island-merging process in terms of entries: it is, of course, possible that the process be viewed in terms of islands themselves—that is, that entire islands can be subsumed to form larger ones, which is a natural process in a working blackboard system that is solving a problem.

3.3.3   Experts

So far, we have had nothing to say about how experts are interpreted in the architecture. We have said that entries are posted on the blackboard by the system's experts, and we have said that experts inspect entries when making problem-solving moves. In this subsection, we will concentrate on the role and structure of experts.

In order to work out what the minimal structure for experts (which are commonly called *Knowledge Sources* or *KSs* in blackboard systems—In the OPM planning system, Hayes-Roth and Hayes-Roth (1979) actually call Knowledge Sources "experts"), it is necessary to recall what the metaphor has to say about their behaviour.

The experts in the metaphor respond to what has been written on the blackboard. This entails that they can respond to items that have just been placed there, *or* they can respond to items that have been present for some time. The second case may occur when, for example, some other expert has made a connection between two or more existing items—this may make a particular item more "visible" to another expert, who can then respond to it. The metaphor requires that the experts write or draw items on the blackboard: in other words, they change the blackboard state by adding or modifying items.

In terms of implementation, these facts suggest that Knowledge Sources are implemented as condition-action structures which are quite similar to production rules (Newell, 1973; Waterman, 1978; Anderson, 1983). The condition part, which we will call the *precondition* or *trigger*, checks the blackboard for the existence of specific entries. The action part is that component which updates the blackboard database. The action of a particular Knowledge Source can be executed to cause blackboard changes *only when* that Knowledge Source's precondition has evaluated to *true*.

The precondition can be divided into two, logically distinct, components. The first responds to changes in the blackboard state—these changes are called *events*. The second is concerned with the state of the blackboard over some more extended period of time. The reason for this division is that a Knowledge Source may be relevant to some change on the blackboard, but may also need access to other state information. The metaphor in its usual interpretation requires Knowledge Sources to respond to blackboard events: that is to the addition and modification of entries. It has been observed above that entries do not exist in isolation of each other and that they are typically connected to form solution islands. Given the essentially distributed nature of the solution, the addition or modification of a particular entry may require other information for its interpretation. Thus, a Knowledge Source may need to be notified of some operation (i.e., an addition or modification) before its precondition becomes true. The truth-value computed by the precondition determines whether a Knowledge Source's action will be executed to cause more blackboard state changes. In other words, a Knowledge Source needs considerably more information at its disposal when evaluating its precondition than simply the the fact that there has been an addition or modification of some particular entry.

In the author's interpretation of the metaphor, the evaluation of Knowledge Source preconditions *must* begin with some blackboard event. When an event occurs, the first part of the precondition (which we will call the *trigger*) is evaluated. If the trigger evaluates to *true*, the second, state-based component (which we will, perhaps a little confusingly, call the *precondition*) is then evaluated. The truth-value of the precondition (in our terms) depends on the values of some predicates which are true of the entry which was implicated in the event which caused the corresponding trigger to be *true, and also on* predicates and relations which range over other entries and links that were on the blackboard before the event occurred. In other words, preconditions are typified by the properties of *sets* of entries; triggers are principally concerned with single entries. This serves to introduce another distinction of value between the two concepts. The reader should note that we do not forbid the possibility that preconditions can be composed of predicates which refer to the entry that was implicated in the event which caused the trigger to become *true* (which we will call the *triggering* event): in other words, preconditions in our interpretation are able to range over the *entire* blackboard.

In order to make the concept of event more precise, it is necessary for us to say more on what can be done by a Knoweldge Source when updating the blackboard. As has already been stated, entries can be created and added to the blackboard, the values stored in their attributes can be modified, or new attributes can be added. These three fundamental operations cause the events which drive the precondition satisfaction (or more precisely, the trigger satisfaction) process: the events are called NEW, ADD and MODIFY, respectively. In the next section, we will discuss the event system in considerably more detail. For the time being, it is enough to know that triggers are predicates over these events. Triggers can also inspect the contents of the entry which has caused the current event: this allows the values of its attributes to be supplied as arguments to the predicates which comprise the trigger. In case the reader is curious, it is necessary to state immediately that triggers (and preconditions) are typically conjunctions or disjunctions—this allows many attributes to be considered when evaluating the truth-value of the trigger (or precondition), and not just the event type (one of NEW, ADD or MODIFY) itself.

A typical trigger will be a conjunction of a (finite) number of predicates. The first of these is usually the event itself: in other words, the trigger as a whole is *true* if the event type it specifies is the current one. The other predicates are concerned with the abstraction level on which the event has occurred (i.e., the abstraction level on which the event-causing entry resides), and with the values of the attributes in the entry. Disjunctions allow more than one event type to be considered by a trigger, and, hence, more than one set of attributes. In some cases, it is necessary for a trigger to evaluate to *true* under all circumstances, so the constant *true* can also legally form an entire trigger.

The case for preconditions is slightly more complex. This is because preconditions are allowed to inspect entries other than the one which caused the triggering event. It is assumed that the identity of the event-causing entry is retained as part of the local state of each Knowledge Source (i.e., is bound to a variable which is local to every Knowledge Source) so that it can be inspected by the precondition (and possibly by the action). The fact that preconditions are able to inspect other entries means that they must be found, and a primitive function called FIND is provided to do this. (Application functions, predicates and types will uniformly be printed in sans serif; event types will be printed in small Roman capitals, and pseudo-code will be printed in Times bold.) FIND takes a predicate as its argument and returns all those entries which satisfy the predicate. The FIND function returns a set of entries, and set operations (for example, difference, intersection and union) are of considerable importance to preconditions. The idea behind preconditions is that the predicates that they contain are satisfied by *any* entries that are on the blackboard. This entails that any entries in a set which satisfies some generator predicate can be considered by preconditions. As with the case of triggers, the predicates are typically concerned with the values that are stored in the attributes of the entries that the FIND operation returns, as well as the event-causing entry.

The trigger requires access the event-causing entry. The precondition also may need access to this entry. Because actions modify the attributes of existing entries, access to the event-causing entry may be required. The reader will note that entries that are discovered by the FIND operation in a precondition may also be communicated to the action. This suggests that *local variables* are required within a Knowledge Source in order that information be communicated between the trigger, precondition and action. The values bound to local variables are referred to as the *local context* of the Knowledge Source. Given the fact that a Knowledge Source may be triggered by many, distinct, events, it is necessary, at this point, to distinguish between Knowledge Source instantiations—this will be considered in very much more detail in the next section, but here it need only be remembered—each instantiation has different values bound to its local variables (which suggests that the difference in bindings is what makes Knowledge Source instantiations different). In order to control local variables, a number of operations are required: they are the SET and VALUE operations. SET is the same as conventional assignment; VALUE performs a dereferencing operation on a variable, and therefore returns the value bound to it. In addition, it is sometimes useful to have an UNBIND operation which deletes the variable whose identifier it takes as an argument (this operation is useful when space is tight). Also, a predicate, BOUNDP is useful for determining whether a variable has a value bound to it at any particular time. The reader should note that these operations *only* apply to the variables which are bound locally to the particular

Knowledge Source instantiation: access to the local variables in other Knowledge Sources is *not* permitted (hence, we are assuming a form of *lexically scoped* régime for local variables). Other mechanisms are employed to access and set system-wide variables.

Finally, we come to actions. As has already been stated, actions cause changes to the blackboard state by either adding new entries, by updating the values stored in one or more of the attributes held in an existing entry, or by adding one or more attribute-value pairs to an existing entry. It should be noted that each operation counts as one event: thus the creation of a new entry counts as one event, as does the update of the value stored in one attribute, as does the addition of one attribute-value pair to an existing entry. The event-causing operations are the primary functions to be found in Knowledge Source actions— this is because they are just those operations which take the system towards the solution state. In addition, it is useful for actions to access ` and update external databases and data streams. Here, these last two possible operation classes will not be considered in more detail because we wish to concentrate on the blackboard system proper. Knowledge Source actions obtain their basic information via local variables, but it is also possible for them to declare and bind their own variables and to use the FIND operation to gather information which can be used in performing state-changing operations on the blackboard (we will not consider this in the specification that we present in the next Chapter).

3.3.4   Control

Control has been cited (Craig, 1988a, Craig, *in press*) as the most complex aspect of blackboard systems. Given the particularly large search spaces generated by the problems that blackboard systems solve, the analysis of only those regions which are of particular importance to the solution process is vital. This fact leads to control structures which are considerably more complex than those in other problem-solving systems (for example, the backchaining in MYCIN (Shortliffe, 1976), and forward chaining in production systems like OPS5 (Forgy, 1986).

In our interpretation of the blackboard architecture, control is a complex activity which is performed by a separate component called the *scheduler*. The scheduler operates in a manner similar to that found in many operating systems, and selects the Knowledge Source instances which are next to be executed. It should be noted that it is Knowledge Source *instances* and not Knowledge Sources themselves which are executed to cause changes to the global blackboard. In our view, it is the Knowledge Source instances which execute actions: hence, it is the case that they are executed to cause state changes. This view is held by many other workers in the field (e.g., Hayes-Roth, 1983, Nii, 1986a).

The need for distinguishing between instances of Knowledge Sources and Knowledge Sources proper was introduced in the last section where it was stated that Knowledge Sources contain local variables which can take different values (i.e., which can be bound to different values) at different times. This fact entails that the execution of two instances of the same Knowledge Source will cause different changes to the blackboard because the changes depend on the values bound to each of the instances local variables. Since the execution of Knowledge Source instances causes changes to the blackboard, it is therefore reasonable that the scheduler should act upon these instances. We will call Knowledge Source instantiations *KSARs*: this stands for *Knowledge Source Activation Record*.

A KSAR is created whenever a Knowledge Source is triggered by some change to the blackboard state. In other words, for each event, at least one Knowledge Source trigger will evaluate to *true*. All those Knowledge Sources whose triggers evaluate to *true* are used in the creation of KSARs—one KSAR for each Knowledge Source. Each KSAR contains the bindings of the variables that are local to the corresponding Knowledge Source (it is these, together with the time at which the KSAR was created that make each instantiation distinct from all others). In addition, each KSAR contains information that is useful to the scheduler (for example, the name of the abstraction level on which the corresponding Knowledge Source was triggered, the time the KSAR was created and other, problem-specific information). KSARs also contain the name of the Knowledge Source which they instantiate: this allows the system to access the precondition and action in that Knowledge Source.

The triggering process works as follows. The set of Knowledge Sources in the system is searched and each Knowledge Source's trigger is evaluated against the event. This amounts to checking the trigger for the event type it expects, the abstraction level or levels on which it expects the event to occur. Each trigger may require the execution of one or more problem-specific predicates: these predicates take the event-causing entry as an argument and inspect the values it has on selected attributes. It is possible to employ indexing methods to speed this process up, but the basic concept is that of a search of all the Knowledge Source triggers in the system. Trigger evaluation causes local variables to be bound, so leads to the creation of Knowledge Source Activation Records.

Although interpretations of the architecture differ, one point which they have in common is the fact that KSARs are created when events occur. These events make the triggers of some of the Knowledge Sources in the system *true*. When the triggers are true, KSARs are created and stored in a data structure. In the HASP/SIAP system (Feigenbaum, 1982) and in AGE (Nii, 1979), KSARs are stored in a LIFO stack; in other systems such as BB* (Hayes-Roth, 1986) and OPM (Hayes-Roth, 1979), a priority queue, or *agenda*, is used to store them. In our interpretation, we employ a two-level storage scheme for KSARs: this scheme is reminiscent of that used in BB* (1986). Here, when KSARs are created, they are placed in an unordered structure (it can be thought of as a set). Once the KSARs are in this structure, which we will call the *triggered list*, their preconditions are evaluated. Those KSARs whose preconditions evaluate to *true* are then placed in another structure called the *eligible list*. The eligible list contains only KSARs whose preconditions have evaluated to *true* at some time during the execution of the system. The preconditions of the KSARs in this list are repeatedly tested against the state of the blackboard: when a precondition evaluates to *false*, its KSAR is returned to the triggered list. The triggered list therefore represents the set of KSARs whose preconditions are either *false* or whose preconditions have not yet been evaluated. The reader should note that triggers, once *true*, may never become *false*: this is because triggers are dependent upon events—the fact that an event has occurred can never be falsified by a subsequent event or state. This process complicates the precondition evaluation process slightly because two structures must be searched during the evaluation process: the triggered and eligible lists. A further complication is that KSARs have to be removed from the eligible list and returned to the triggered list when their precondition becomes *false*. Preconditions can be falsified by blackboard states, and so it is not possible to state once and for all that a precondition will remain *true* once it has evaluated to that value. Furthermore, preconditions can involve unbounded computation, so precondition checking can be an expensive business: for this reason, some systems, for example BB*, allow the user control over when preconditions are checked.

Once the preconditions of all KSARs in the triggered and eligible lists have been checked, the eligible list is ordered. The ordering process is problem-dependent and will depend upon domain- and problem-specific attributes. In our specification, we will say no more about this process. However, once the eligible list has been ordered, a KSAR can be selected for execution (this is the scheduling process). Because the eligible list has been sorted, it is clear that the KSAR with the highest rating will be at one or other end of the eligible list—we will assume that it is the first element—so all that need be done to find it is to examine the first element (the *head*, in other words). The eligible list is then set to be its tail. The action part of the chosen KSAR is then executed to cause more blackboard changes. These changes cause events and the triggering and precondition evaluation processes continue.

The triggering, precondition evaluation and action execution processes continue in a cyclic fashion from the time the system is started until such time as an acceptable final state has been generated. This constitutes the main cycle of the blackboard system's interpreter. In order to differentiate between KSARs that have been created for the same Knowledge Source at different times, and in order to implement some control structures, counters are frequently associated with the main loop. One counter is incremented on each cycle, the other is incremented on each event and is reset to zero at the end of each cycle (i.e., when the action of the chosen KSAR has been executed). These two counters, the *cycle* and *event* counters, are used to timestamp each KSAR in the system. This allows KSARs to be identified on the basis of their temporal proximity (in terms of the number of cycles or events) to the current scheduling decision.

The system begins with the creation of the first entry in the blackboard database. The creation of this entry causes a NEW event to which some Knowledge Sources respond. The termination of the system's execution depends upon problem-specific factors: clearly, there must be some linkage between the problem-specific termination detectors and the basic interpreted. This is achieved by the use of a boolean-valued flag STOP: when STOP is set to *true*, the main interpreter cycle halts. Any Knowledge Source can terminate the execution of the system by setting STOP to *true*, but its use should be restricted to those Knowledge Sources which detect the fact that an acceptable solution has, indeed, been encountered.

The STOP flag gives a hint as to what the main interpreter loop should look like:

```
while not stop do begin
        evaluate-triggers;
        evaluate-preconditions;
        order-eligible-list;
        next-task := head(eligible-list);
        eligible-list := tail(eligible-list);
        execute-action(next-task)
    end
```

Note that the STOP flag is set from within the **execute-action** procedure.

We have now completed the informal specification of the blackboard architecture, and it is time to move on to a more formal presentation. The reader should note that we have given an operational description of a blackboard system interpreter which conforms to the author's interpretation of the metaphor. In the next chapter, we will investigate this interpretation using Z and we will see how the concepts outlined above can be given a more rigorous interpretation.

Before moving on, we need to say a few things about the differences between the interpretation given above and the formal specification: most of the points are of minor importance, but might be a source of confusion to some readers.

3.3.5   The Formal Specification

The careful reader will note that there are some differences between the statements of the above interpretation of the blackboard architecture and the formal specification that we present in the next chapter. Specifically, the most important differences relate to the role of preconditions and to the agenda used in the scheduler. In addition, local variables and trigger conditions need an initial word of explanation.

To begin with, we state above that Knowledge Sources contain an explicit state-based precondition. In the formal specification, we give a specification of Knowledge Source actions in terms of production rules, and we integrate the precondition with each production rule's condition-part (this is done simply by conjoining the two formulae). The distinction between the two approaches is, really, one of efficiency. If the Knowledge Source's precondition is conjoined with each of the rules in its action, that precondition will be repeatedly evaluated. Accuracy is not an issue, here, only runtime speed. We argue in the next chapter that the two approaches are identical in effect—if the precondition is not satisfied by the current blackboard state, the action will never be executed. It should be pointed out that the separation of the precondition can be viewed as a device for reducing the number of tests that a Knowledge Source must perform before it can have its action executed by the scheduler. Since we are interested in a *formal* specification, that is, a mathematical object, efficiency or other runtime issues are not in question, and we want the most faithful statement of the structure which is in agreement with our intuitions. Because there is very little difference, in the abstract, between testing once and testing a hundred times, we have chosen the latter.

Where the decision *does* have an impact is on the scheduler. Above, we discuss the use of a *triggered* list, and an *eligible* list. The reader will find that the eligible list is, in fact, a local variable that is used exclusively by the scheduler (and we say nothing in particular about the scheduler as a matter of policy—schedulers are, basically, application-specific, and there are a number of different, and equally viable approaches to scheduling, so we prefer not to impose constraints in this case). We still specify operations for the removal of KSARs from the triggered and eligible lists, and we specify operations for the removal of

KSARs from the eligible list. What we have not done in any detail is to specify a mechanism for determining *which* KSARs should be removed. One reason for this is that we have decided, effectively, to "bury" the eligible list in the scheduler (in fact, this decision was implied by the structure of the specification itself, and, since it turned out to have relatively pleasant consequences, we decided that we would retain it); another is that we have merged preconditions with the conditions that belong to the production rules in each Knowledge Source's action.

Given these decisions about the specification, we are *unable* to determine *before* action execution time which preconditions will not be satisfied, so we have, effectively, recast the scheduling problem a little: what our specification is actually saying is that scheduling should be performed at the level of the individual production rule, with account being taken of the general scheduling criteria which apply to the Knowledge Source as a whole. This is still, we argue, in general keeping with the informal specification that we have given above, but it also introduces some interesting new possibilities into the interpretation of Knowledge Sources. These possibilities relate to the introduction of parallelism into blackboard systems, and, in this case, the issues relate to preconditions *and* to action execution. We leave it as a research exercise to specify a control layer for the production rules in actions.

The position with local variables and triggers is considerably easier to explain. We have chosen to ignore local variables because they require us to define a syntax for a language in which we can define Knowledge Sources. It turns out that this exercise is not as simple as it might seem, and we have found that it is decidedly non-trivial in Z. In addition, the interfacing problems that are encountered when one engages in such an exercise are also fairly difficult. For these reasons, and because we are mainly interested in the fundamental interpretation mechanisms of the blackboard interpreter, we have decided to omit local variables. We leave it to the reader to specify the various operations we mentioned above (for example, the SET and VALUE operations) and to attempt to integrate them with the remainder of the interpreter specification.

With Knowledge Source triggers, our specification is couched, basically, in terms of table lookup. We represent the triggers as sets of mappings. Above, we described triggers in terms of event-based predicates, so this device may be a little surprising (actually, it is a technique that was employed in a slightly different form in BB1 (Hayes-Roth, 1985)). Using sets of tables, we are able to model disjunctive triggers (i.e., triggers that are satisfied by different event-types), the tables that appear as the elements of these sets representing a single (conjunctive) trigger (i.e., a conjunction of event-based predicates). Now, it is the case that we cannot handle negated predicates using this scheme. If we had adopted a more general scheme in which triggers could call arbitrary pieces of code, negation would have been easy to model: calling arbitrary code leads to difficulties in the specification, and it leads to "holes" in the system (specifically, there is no way of guaranteeing that triggers only access events), so we decided that the table-based method was the best from both angles (we had similar problems with arbitrary code in production rule conditions, although we adopted a somewhat different approach there). The limitation on negated trigger elements is no real limitation in practice: what one is interested in, when one specifies a trigger, are the reasons *why* a Knowledge Source should be triggered (i.e., positive reasons), and we tend to demote detailed testing of the event-causing entry to the precondition (which can contain negations). We have therefore lost nothing, and we have gained a simpler specification which is still adequate for our needs.

We believe that all of these simplifications remain within the informal specification that we have presented in this chapter. The points relating to preconditions and scheduling lead to issues that are very much research topics: before engaging in the formal specification exercise, we had our suspicions that something of this ilk might be in order. It is interesting to note that the formal specification exercise has given clear indications as to further research. With these thoughts behind us, we can now move on to the formal specification itself.

4

The Blackboard
Specification in Z

4.1 Introduction

In this Chapter, we present the formal specification of the blackboard
interpreter in the Z specification language. The specification is derived
from the English statement that concerned us in the last Chapter. The
specification deals with all aspects of the blackboard interpreter except

local variables and the issues that arise from their inclusion. We will spend considerable time on the specification of the blackboard database, on Knowledge Source triggering and on Knowledge Source actions: this is because they are relatively complex sub-systems and the effectiveness of the specification depends upon the facilities that they provide.

The Chapter is organised as follows. In the next section, we define the blackboard database and its abstraction levels. As an integral part of the section, we define the schemata that represent entries, and we define the various operations that can be performed on entries. The specification is based on the assumption that entries are, in fact, an integral component of the blackboard database. In section three, we define the event system. The event system is what provides the causal connection between blackboard modification and Knowledge Source triggering. Once we have defined the event system, we move on to the definition of the structures with which we will model Knowledge Sources: these turn out to be simple product types. Having defined the representation for Knowledge Sources, we have another short section in which we define our representation for Knowledge Source Activation Records (we model them as partial functions), and we define operations for their manipulation.

In the next section, we concern ourselves with Knowledge Source triggers: their representation and function. Triggers are the first part of the central functioning of the blackboard interpreter, and we are careful to explain what we are doing as we engage in the specification. Following the specification of triggers, we consider Knowledge Source actions, which we model as collections of production rules. The specification of actions also includes that of preconditions. In fact, we mix actions and preconditions, so that there is no separate precondition in a Knowledge Source: we have already argued for this approach in the last Chapter, and we present a further justification below. When we present this part of the specification, we will emphasise what we see as a limitation of Z: we need higher-order functions and relations, but they are not immediately available in Z. Of course, Z does provide them, but the proof methods that are available to us rapidly become more difficult than we would wish. Instead of engaging in a direct representation of production rule conditions and of Knowledge Source preconditions, we adopt an indirect route and impose constraints on any application-specific software that is supplied to perform these functions (indeed, it is the very fact that we want to be able to include user-defined code that led us to adopt the approach that we have taken).

Finally, the Chapter concludes with the specification of the outer loop, or the main cycle. The main cycle controls the actions of the blackboard. We include some initialisation schemata in our specification of the outer loop in order to make our specification more complete.

4.2   Entries and the Blackboard

In this section, we present the Z specification of the entries that represent elements of the emerging solution and of the blackboard database in which they are held. As we have said, entries are best regarded as complex structures similar to records or structures in programming languages like **Pascal** or **C**. We will give a top-level specification of entries in terms of their attributes and the values that are stored under attributes (we will often state this by saying that a value is stored "in" an attribute). We will define a number of operations over entries, and each will be given a complete specification.

The blackboard is the global database in which entries are stored. As we have seen, the blackboard is organised as a linear abstraction hierarchy: each level of the hierarchy is represented as an abstraction level. We will define operations to construct the blackboard and to access its contents. We will show that the specifications are correct by proving properties of them.

We begin the specification with a complete account of entries. Next, we define the abstraction level data type: this definition will involve the use of schemata developed in the course of the specification of entries. Finally, we will connect abstraction levels together into the global blackboard. As a final section, we will define the interface to the blackboard that is seen by all other system components: this interface generates blackboard events which are used in triggering Knowledge Sources.

Throughout the specification that we present in this Chapter, we will not be concerned with implementation issues. This is particularly important for the blackboard because it would be very easy to try to specify it and the entries it contains in such a way that they can easily be turned into code. We believe that this would make the specification more complicated and would not make for a specification which was easy to understand. Even though the correct functioning of the blackboard is essential (and, indeed, its efficient operation, particularly in terms of speed critically impacts upon the performance of the system), we have systematically ignored implementation biases: that is, we couch the specification *entirely* in terms of what facilities Z provides, and not in terms of other structures. As a result, we believe that the specification that we give below is quite simple and easy to understand.

4.2.1 Entries

As we have seen, entries are complex structures that reside on the blackboard. Each entry is composed of a set of attribute-value pairs. The attributes represent properties of the object that the entry represents; attributes are filled with values. This basic structure is reflected in our definition of the entry type. Before we can define the entry schema (the abstract data type that represents the entry in our specification), we need to define the following atomic types:

$$[ATTR, VAL]$$

Values of type $ATTR$ are attributes, and values of type VAL are the abstract values that fill attributes. We do not say what values are found in $ATTR$: they might be strings or **LISP** atoms, for example. Equally, we do not give any structure to VAL: this is because we want to keep the specification as abstract as possible. In an implementation, we would explect VAL to contain integers, reals, strings and so on: here, we do not need to go into such detail.

The schema defining the entry data type is:

$$
\begin{array}{|l}
\hline
\_ENTRY \rule{6cm}{0pt} \\
\hline
slots : ATTR \twoheadrightarrow VAL \\
knownslots : \mathbb{P}\, ATTR \\
\hline
knownslots = \mathrm{dom}\, slots \\
\hline
\end{array}
$$

The schema contains two variables, *slots* and *knownslots*. The first of these represents the attribute-value pairs that are to be found in a particular entry. The pairs are represented in terms of a *partial function* from values in *ATTR* to values in *VAL*.

The reason for making the function partial is that, for any given entry, that entry will not contain all possible pairs of attributes and values: indeed, as we will see, the attributes and values can change with time. The reason for making *slots* a function is that we have an abstract description which provides us with a very natural account of some of the operations that we want to perform on entries: in particular, the retrieval operation which fetches the value stored under a given attribute is extremely simple. We can naturally think of attribute-value representations in terms of functions, and this is the approach that we have adopted here.

The second variable in the schema, *knownslots*, is bound to the domain of *slots*. The ideas is that *knownslots* contains the identifiers of all those attributes that are currently in the entry. The type of *knownslots* is therefore a *set of ATTR*. We use *knownslots* to determine whether an attribute is present in a number of operations on entries. We could perform such a test directly, but it turns out to be quite convenient to have a separate variable. It should be noted that whenever an operation adds an attribute-value pair to *slots*, *knownslots* is updated automatically.

We will actually assume that the schemata $\Delta ENTRY$ and $\Xi ENTRY$ are defined in the conventional way. Since this is the first time that we introduce these schemata, we will write them out in full.

The $\Delta ENTRY$ schema is:

```
┌─ ΔENTRY ──────────────────────────────
│ ENTRY
│ ENTRY'
│
└───────────────────────────────────────
```

This expands to:

```
┌───────────────────────────────────────
│ slots, slots' : ATTR ⇸ VAL
│ knownslots, knownslots' : ℙ ATTR
│
└───────────────────────────────────────
```

The primed version ($ENTRY'$) represents the after state components, as we noted in the last Chapter. The inclusion of the two schemata $ENTRY$ and $ENTRY'$ serves to declare four variables. Note that there is no predicate in the Δ schema: in some cases, we will explicitly define the Δ schema and supply a predicate for it (this holds for the *Blackboard* schema in particular). The fact that there is no predicate entails that the state before and state after components of the $ENTRY$ schema are unrelated: we must supply a relation when we define operations that change the state of $ENTRY$.

The Ξ schema is:

```
┌─ ΞENTRY ──────────────────────────────────
│  ENTRY
│  ENTRY'
├────────────────────────────────────────────
│  slots' = slots
│  knownslots' = knownslots
└────────────────────────────────────────────
```

The signature is the same as $\Delta ENTRY$, but there is a predicate: the predicate states that the before and after states are identical. Notice that the two included schemata serve to introduce variables and that the predicate relates them. Since the Ξ schema states that the before and after states are the same, this schema is used by operations that cause no changes to the state of $ENTRY$.

Now that we have a state space, we need to define operations over entries. These operations are represented by schemata. The operations that we define are:

- An initialization operation.

- A creation operation (the difference between this and the initialization operation will be examined below).

- An operation to retrieve the value stored on some attribute.

- An operation to add a new attribute-value pair to an entry.

- An operation to modify the value stored under an attribute that is already in the entry.

We will give schemata for all of these operations and we will describe the schemata so that the reader can better understand them.

We clearly need to be able to initialize objects of type *ENTRY*. We will define two operations, one called *InitENTRY*, the other called *CreateENTRY*. The names are given to what might appear to be the *wrong* schemata: we call the *InitENTRY* operation that operation which creates an entry, and we call the operation that puts some initial attribute-value pairs into a new entry *CreateENTRY*. The reason for this is as follows. For *InitENTRY*, we follow the Z convention (Spivey, 1989) which associates the prefix *Init* with the operation on a type which creates or initializes it. In the case of entries, we will create an instance of *ENTRY* and then associate a name with it; only after these operations have been performed will we provide it with its initial attribute-value pairs. As far as the rest of the blackboard is concerned, an entry is only created when it has a name and a set of initial attribute-value pairs: the *InitENTRY* schema represents an operation which is hidden from the rest of the blackboard system.

With this in mind, we define the initialization operation as follows:

$$
\begin{array}{|l}
\_\mathit{InitENTRY} \underline{\hspace{8cm}} \\
\hline
\mathit{ENTRY} \\
\hline
\mathit{knownslots} = \varnothing \\
\end{array}
$$

This schema simply states that the result of initializing an object of type *ENTRY* is that the domain of *slots* is empty. If the domain is empty, the range is also empty, and therefore, *slots* is the empty function: in other words, *slots* is empty. This schema does not refer to the Δ or to the Ξ form of the *ENTRY* type because it is creating an initial state: the two other forms can be used only after an initial state has been defined.

Is this initialization a reasonable one? We can answer this by proving a result:

Theorem 1

$$\exists \, \mathit{ENTRY} \bullet \mathit{InitENTRY}$$

PROOF   We expand the schema in the statement of the theorem to:

$$\exists \, slots : ATTR \nrightarrow VAL; \; knownslots : \mathbb{P} \; ATTR \bullet$$
$$knownslots = \varnothing$$

Since $\varnothing$ is an element of $\mathbb{P} \, ATTR$, and

$$knownslots = \text{dom} \; slots$$

the assignment of $\varnothing$ to $knownents$ is equivalent to

$$\text{dom} \; slots = \varnothing$$

we have an empty function. $\square$

The creation operation actually loads attribute-value pairs into an entry: this schema takes the place of the initialization schema *InitEN-TRY* (even though we define the latter and refer to it—the reason for this is that there may be operations which require an entry which has no slots). In this case, we need to supply attribute-value pairs in order to load them: this will be the first instance of an input variable that we will have encountered. We have a choice in defining the creation schema: we can supply a function of type $ATTR \nrightarrow VAL$, or we can supply something that looks more like the graph of the function. We will adopt the latter approach because it is more interesting. We have:

$$AVL == ATTR \times VAL$$

and:

```
┌─ CreateENTRY ──────────────────────────────────────
│ ΔENTRY
│ avps? : ℙ AVL
├────────────────────────────────────────────────────
│ #slots' = #avps?
│ #knownslots' = #avps?
│ ∀ avp : AVL; a : ATTR; v : VAL |
│         avp ∈ avps? ∧
│         a = first(avp) ∧
│         v = second(avp) •
│     a ∈ knownslots' ∧
│     v ∈ ran slots' ∧
│     slots'(a) = v
└────────────────────────────────────────────────────
```

The type definition that appears before the schema serves to associate the name *AVL* with the set of all pairs of attributes and values. This definition is used to simplify the schema that follows: we will encounter *AVL* again when we refine the *ENTRY* type.

In the creation schema, there are two observations to be made about the signature. Firstly, it contains an instance of the Δ form of the *ENTRY* schema: this means that *CreateENTRY* changes the state. Second, the signature contains a variable *avps?* of type $\mathbb{P}\,AVL$—that is, it can be bound to sets of pairs of attributes and values. This definition of *avps?* means that it is bound to the *graph* of the functions:

$$ATTR \nrightarrow VAL$$

The predicate of the schema is complex. First, it asserts that the size of *slots* after the creation operation has terminated is the same as the cardinality of the set *avps?*. In other words, after the operation, *slots* has all and only the elements of *avps?*. The universally quantified formula asserts that the state after the operation is composed of *slots'* such that every attribute in *avps?* is correctly associated with its value. This is done by asserting that every component of *avps?* is projected onto its components (using *first* and *second*—the projections onto the components of a product), that all values of the first component of *avps?* is in the domain of *slots'* (via *knownslots*), and that the second component is in the range of *slots'*. Finally, it asserts that every second component of *avps?* is the image of its associated first component.

We employed the graph of the type of *slots* because it introduced quantification in schema predicates. An alternative would have been to give *avps?* the same type as *slots*: this would not have been as interesting, we believe. The remaining operations are less complex to specify.

The next schema specifies the operation which retrieves the value stored on an attribute in an entry. The operation has one input variable, *a?*, which represents the attribute. In order for the operation to suceed, the attribute named by *a?* must be known to the entry. If it is, *slots* is treated like a function and applied to *a?* to yield *v!* the output value. Clearly, this operation does not alter the state. The schema is:

```
┌─ GetAttr ─────────────────────────────────────
│  ΞENTRY
│  a? : ATTR
│  v! : VAL
│ ──────────────────────────────────────────────
│  a? ∈ knownslots
│  v! = slots(a?)
└───────────────────────────────────────────────
```

The add operation represented by *AddAttr does* alter the state of an entry (as does *ModAttr*, the next schema we will define. The add schema represents the operation of adding a wholly new attribute-value pair to an entry. The entry must first exist, and the attribute must not be known to the entry (in other words, the attribute must not be an element of *knownslots*). If the second condition is satisfied (we cannot, at this stage, test the first), a new mapping from the input attribute (represented by $a?$) to the input value (represented by $v?$) is added to *slots*:

```
┌─ AddAttr ─────────────────────────────────────
│  ΔENTRY
│  a? : ATTR
│  v? : VAL
│ ──────────────────────────────────────────────
│  a? ∉ knownslots
│  slots' = slots ∪ {a? ↦ v?}
└───────────────────────────────────────────────
```

The alteration of the state is performed by the last line of the predicate. The association of $a?$ with $v?$ is performed using a maplet ($\mapsto$): this maplet is converted to a set and united with the old value of *slots* to derive the new value (*slots'*). The test on the attribute is performed on the previous state of *ENTRY*, so it tests *knownslots*.

We have a result about *AddAttr*:

Theorem 2

$$AddAttr \vdash \# \operatorname{dom} slots' = \# \operatorname{dom} slots + 1$$

PROOF   We have:

$$\# \operatorname{dom} slots'$$

$$= \# \operatorname{dom}(slots \cup \{a? \mapsto v?\})$$
$$= \#(\operatorname{dom} slots \cup \operatorname{dom}(\{a? \mapsto v?\}))$$
$$= \#(\operatorname{dom} slots \cup \{a?\})$$
$$= \# \operatorname{dom} slots + \#\{a?\}$$
$$= \# \operatorname{dom} slots + 1$$

$\square$

Now that we have *AddAttr*, we can prove the following result:

Theorem 3

$$k = \#avps? \vdash (InitENTRY \wedge CreateENTRY) \equiv$$
$$(InitENTRY^+ \wedge (AddAttr^{\langle k \rangle}))$$

PROOF   The proof is by induction on $\#avps?$.
The left-hand side of the equivalence expands to:

InitENTRY $\wedge$ *CreateENTRY* _____

$\Delta ENTRY$
$avps? : \mathbb{P}\ AVL$

$knownslots = \varnothing$
$\#slots' = \#avps?$
$\#knownslots' = \#avps?$
$(\forall avp : AVL;\ a : ATTR;\ v : VAL|$
$\qquad avp \in avps? \wedge$
$\qquad a = first(avp) \wedge$
$\qquad v = second(avp) \bullet$
$\quad a \in knownslots' \wedge$
$\quad v \in \operatorname{ran} slots' \wedge$
$\quad slots'(a) = v)$

InitENTRY$^+$ expands to:

InitENTRY$^+$ _____

$ENTRY^+$

$knownslots^+ = \varnothing$

This is just a renamed version of *InitENTRY*: renaming is used to keep variables distinct.

The $\langle k \rangle$ superscript represents an operation that is related to iteration, but which also replaces all variables in the schema by new ones. The action on signature variables is, in the present case:

$$
\begin{array}{|l}
\hline
AddAttr^{\langle k \rangle} \\
\hline
knownslots_k, knownslots'_k : \mathbb{P} \; ATTR \\
slots_k, slots'_k : ATTR \nrightarrow VAL \\
a_k? : ATTR \\
v_k? : VAL \\
\hline
a_k? \notin knownslots_k \\
slots'_k = slots_k \cup \{ a_k? \mapsto v_k? \} \\
\hline
\end{array}
$$

(The schema is written out in full).

To make things work, the following identities are required:

$$knownslots_k = knownslots'_{k-1}$$

and

$$slots_k = slots'_{k-1}$$

Such that, for all i, $a_i? \neq a_{i+1}?$ and $v_i? \neq v_{i+1}?$. That is, the renaming is assumed to substitute fresh variable names for all input and output variables of the schema.

The action of $\langle k \rangle$ on the predicate is identical to iteration.

We continue with the proof proper.

Base Case (1). $\#avps? = k = 0$, so $avps? = \varnothing$. We have:

$$(InitENTRY \wedge CreateENTRY) \equiv InitENTRY^{+}$$

since $R^0 = \text{id}$. Clearly, $knownslots^{+} = knownslots'$. The proof of the equivalence is as follows.

(1a) $\Rightarrow$. $\#knownslots' = \#avps? = 0$ and $slots' = \varnothing$. The antecedent and consequent of the universal are both false. Since $knownslots^{+} = \varnothing$, the implication is proved.

(1b) $\Leftarrow$. Similar to (1a).

Base Case (2). $\#avps? = k = 1$, so $avps? = \{(a_1, v_1)\}$. We have:

$$(InitENTRY \wedge CreateENTRY) \equiv (InitENTRY^+ \wedge AddAttr)$$

This is because $R^1 = R$; we forget about renaming for convenience. The right-hand side is:

```
┌─ InitENTRY⁺ ∧ AddAttr ─────────────────────────────────
│  ΔENTRY⁺
│  a? : ATTR
│  v? : VAL
├────────────────────────────────────
│  knownslots⁺ = ∅
│  a? ∉ knownslots⁺
│  slots⁺′ = slots⁺ ∪ {a? ↦ v?}
└────────────────────────────────────────────────────────
```

($\Delta ENTRY$ must be identified with $\Delta ENTRY^+$ in $AddAttr$—we can do this informally.)

Because $knownslots^+ = \mathrm{dom}\ slots$, the predicate can be simplified to:

$$knownslots^+ = \varnothing\ \wedge$$
$$slots^{+\prime} = \{a? \mapsto v?\}$$

(since $\varnothing \cup A = A$).

We have:

$$(knownslots^+ = \varnothing\ \wedge$$
$$slots^{+\prime} = \{a? \mapsto v?\}) \equiv$$
$$(knownslots = \varnothing \wedge \#slots' = \#avps?\ \wedge$$
$$\#knownslots' = \#avps?\ \wedge$$
$$(\forall\ avp : AVL;\ a : ATTR;\ v : VAL|$$
$$avp \in avps?\ \wedge$$
$$a = first(avp)\ \wedge$$
$$v = second(avp)\ \bullet$$
$$a \in knownslots'\ \wedge$$
$$v \in \mathrm{ran}\ slots'\ \wedge$$
$$slots'(a) = v))$$

Now,

$$slots^{+'} = slots'$$

$$knownslots^{+} = knownslots$$

$$knownslots^{+'} = knownslots'$$

and:

$$slots^{+'} = \{a? \mapsto v?\}$$

We therefore have the two cases:
(2a) $\Rightarrow$.

$$
\begin{aligned}
(knownslots^{+} = \varnothing \wedge \\
slots^{+'} = \{a? \mapsto v?\}) \equiv \\
(knownslots^{+} = \varnothing \wedge \\
\#slots^{+'} = \#avps? \wedge \\
\#knownslots^{+'} = \#avps? \wedge \\
(av \in avps? \wedge a = first(av) \wedge v = second(av) \Rightarrow \\
a \in knownslots^{+} \wedge \\
v \in \operatorname{ran} slots^{+'} \wedge \\
slots^{+'}(a) = v))
\end{aligned}
$$

(after a step of universal elimination on the right).

Since $knownslots^{+'} = \operatorname{dom} slots^{+'} = \{a?\}$ and $a = a?$, and $\operatorname{ran} slots^{+'} = \{v?\}$ and $v = v?$, and because $avps? = \{(a?, v?)\}$, the implication is satisfied.

(2b) $\Leftarrow$. By substitution in the opposite direction.

Induction Step. Assume $\#avps? = k = n$, then:

$$(InitENTRY \wedge CreateENTRY) \equiv (InitENTRY^{+}(AddAttr^{\langle n \rangle}))$$

But $R^{n} = R^{n-1} \mathbin{;} R$, so:

$$
\begin{aligned}
(InitENTRY \wedge CreateENTRY) \equiv \\
((InitENTRY^{+}) \wedge \\
(AddAttr^{\langle n-1 \rangle} \mathbin{;} AddAttr))
\end{aligned}
$$

where all variables in $AddAttr^{\langle n-1 \rangle}$ are distinct from each other and distinct from those in $AddAttr$; and, furthermore, where:

$$knownslots'_{n-1} = knownslots$$

$$slots'_{n-1} = slots$$

$CreateENTRY$ adds n pairs (a_i, v_i) to $slots$, and $AddAttr^{n-1}$ adds $n - 1$ such pairs. Therefore, by the induction hypothesis, $AddAttr^{\langle n-1 \rangle}$ followed by $AddAttr$ adds n pairs. Because $\#avps? = n$, we are done. $\square$

The $ModAttr$ operation is similar. In this case, though, the operation alters the value that is stored under an *existing* attribute. For the operation to suceed, the attribute must already be present in the entry, and the old value must be over-ridden. The schema is:

$$
\begin{array}{|l}
\hline
\,ModAttr \\\hline
\Delta ENTRY \\
a? : ATTR \\
v? : VAL \\\hline
a? \in knownslots \\
slots' = slots \oplus \{a? \mapsto v?\} \\\hline
\end{array}
$$

where the $\oplus$ operator over-rides the previous mapping between $a?$ and its old value. Again, the check on the input attribute is performed on the before state of $ENTRY$, so it involves $knownslots$.

We can prove the following:

Theorem 4

$$ModAttr \vdash \#\,\mathrm{dom}\,slots' = \#\,\mathrm{dom}\,slots$$

PROOF   We first prove that $\mathrm{dom}\,slots = \mathrm{dom}\,slots'$:

$\mathrm{dom}\,slots'$

$$
\begin{aligned}
&= \mathrm{dom}(slots \oplus \{a? \mapsto v?\}) \\
&= \mathrm{dom}\,slots \cup \mathrm{dom}\{a? \mapsto v?\} \\
&= \mathrm{dom}\,slots \cup \{a?\} \\
&= \mathrm{dom}\,slots \qquad\qquad\qquad [\text{since } a? \in \mathrm{dom}\,slots]
\end{aligned}
$$

Thus:

$$\# \operatorname{dom} slots' = \# \operatorname{dom} slots$$

□

Finally, we will define an operation that we will not actually use below. We provide it because it may be of use when defining the details of the condition-evaluation process. This relates to Knowledge Source preconditions and actions: we will argue that we cannot give as complete a specification as we would like within this book. We can, though, define an operation which will be of use when refining the specification and when tailoring the specification that we give here to a particular application. The operation tests the value stored on a particular attribute of an entry. The schema is:

```
┌─ TestAttr ──────────────────────────
│ ΞENTRY
│ a? : ATTR
│ tval? : VAL
│ ────────────────────────────────────
│ a? ∈ knownslots
│ tval? = slots(a?)
└──────────────────────────────────────
```

The schema has an input value $tval?$ which contains the value to be tested. The predicate tests the identity of the value of $tval?$ with the value stored under $a?$. This schema provides the basic facility for testing attribute values: as we have stated, we do not make use of it below.

We will deal with the issue of naming entries below: this is because it is only of consequence when we have abstraction levels to deal with. As far as the specification of the $ENTRY$ type is concerned, it is possible to ignore naming issues altogether. In other words, we have just defined a data type and a set of operations that can be performed on it without needing to know whether the objects are named.

Before moving on to the specifiction of abstraction levels and of the blackboard, we will prove some results about entries. These results are mostly about the behaviour of compositions of operations on entries.

Theorem 5

$$CreateENTRY \,\natural\, ModAttr \equiv CreateENTRY^+$$

where the superscript on the right-hand side merely serves to individuate the instance of CreateENTRY. All components of CreateENTRY$^+$ are decorated with $+$.

PROOF   This result just states that if a newly created entry has one of its attribute-value pairs modified, the result is the same as creating the entry with a different set of attribute-value pairs (specifically, one which contains the attribute and its value after modification).

We write the conjunction of *CreateENTRY* and *ModdAttr* as:

```
┌─ CreateENTRY ⨟ ModAttr ──────────────────────────
│ ΔENTRY
│ avps? : ℙ AVL
│ a? : ATTR
│ v? : VAL
├────────────────────────────────────────────────────
│ (∃ slots* : ATTR ⇸ VAL; knownslots : ℙ ATTR •
│       #slots* = #avps? ∧
│       #knownslots* = #avps? ∧
│       (∀ avp : AVL; a : ATTR; v : VAL |
│           avp ∈ avps? ∧
│           a = first(avp) ∧
│           v = second(avp) •
│           a ∈ knownslots* ∧
│           v ∈ ran slots* ∧
│           slots*(a) = v) ∧
│           a? ∈ knownslots* ∧
│           slots' = slots* ⊕ {a? ↦ v?})
```

We expand the right-hand side to:

$$\begin{array}{|l}
\hline
\_\_\,CreateENTRY^+\,_____ \\
\quad ENTRY \\
\quad avps^+? : \mathbb{P}\ AVL \\
\hline
\quad \#slots^+ = \#avps^+? \\
\quad \#knownslots^+ = \#avps^+? \\
\quad (\forall\, avp^+ : AVL;\ a^+ : ATTR;\ v^+ : VAL \mid \\
\qquad\qquad avp^+ \in avps^+? \wedge \\
\qquad\qquad a^+ = first(avp^+) \wedge \\
\qquad\qquad v^+ = second(avp^+)\ \bullet \\
\qquad\quad a^+ \in knownslots^+ \wedge \\
\qquad\quad v^+ \in \mathrm{ran}\ slots^+ \wedge \\
\qquad\quad slots^+(a^+) = v^+) \\
\hline
\end{array}$$

To prove $\Rightarrow$, we want the following to obtain:

$$slots'(a?) = slots^+(a^+)$$

The only way to achieve this is to have:

$$avps^+? = (avps? \setminus \{(a?, v)\}) \cup \{(a?, v?)\}$$

where v is the value in the pair whose first component is $a?$, and $v?$ is the input variable on the left-hand side.

To prove $\Leftarrow$, we simply use the converse of the above:

$$avps? = avps^+ \setminus \{(a?, v?)\}) \cup \{(a?, v)\}$$

$\Box$

A similar argument gives the proof of the following theorem.

Theorem 6

$$avps? = avps^+? \vdash CreateENTRY \,\fatsemi\, AddAttr \equiv CreateENTRY^+$$

PROOF   (We use the same expansion as in the previous result.)
$\Rightarrow$: This time, we know that:

$$a? \notin knownslots^*$$

so:

$$avps^+? = avps? \cup \{(a?, v?)\}$$

$\Leftarrow$: We have:

$$avps? = avps^+ \setminus \{(a?, v?)\}$$

$\square$

The next result shows that we obtain the same effect as adding an attribute and then modifying its value as we do if we simply add it with the second value.

Theorem 7

$$\vdash AddAttr \,\fatsemi\, ModAttr \equiv AddAttr^*$$

PROOF   The composition of $AddAttr$ and $ModAttr$ is:

```
AddAttr ⨟ ModAttr
  ΔENTRY
  a? : ATTR
  v₁?, v₂? : VAL
  ∃ ENTRY⁺ •
      a? ∉ knownslots ∧
      slots⁺ = slots ∪ { a? ↦ v₁? } ∧
      a? ∈ knownslots⁺ ∧
      slots' = slots⁺ ⊕ { a? ↦ v₂? }
```

The $AddAttr^*$ schema is defined as:

```
AddAttr*
  ΔENTRY
  a? : ATTR
  v₂? : VAL
  a? ∉ knowslots*
  slots*' = slots* ∪ { a? ↦ v₂? }
```

The predicate of the consequent is then:

$$a? \notin knownslots^* \wedge$$
$$slots^{*\prime} = slots^* \cup \{a? \mapsto v_2?\}$$

We need to make the following identifications:

$$knownslots = knownslots^*$$

$$slots^* = slots$$

$$slots' = slots^{*\prime}$$

These are reasonable because we want the before state of $AddAttr^*$ to be the same as the before state of $AddAttr \,\mathring{;}\, ModAttr$, and we want the after states to be the same.

The proof is now that the two after states are the same. The states in question are:

$$slots' = slots^+ \oplus \{a? \mapsto v_2?\}$$

and:

$$slots^* = slots^* \cup \{a? \mapsto v_2?\}$$

The proof is thus:

$slots^{*\prime}$

$$\begin{aligned}
&= slots^* \cup \{a? \mapsto v_2?\} && [\text{Defn. } AddAttr^+]\\
&= slots^+ \oplus \{a? \mapsto v_2?\}\\
&&& [\text{By definition of the composite schema}]\\
&= (slots \cup \{a? \mapsto v_2?\}) \oplus \{a? \mapsto v_2\}\\
&&& [\text{By definition of } slots^+]\\
&= slots \cup \{a? \mapsto v_2?\}
\end{aligned}$$

The last step looks obviously true—it is, but we give a proof:

$$(slots \cup \{a? \mapsto v?\}) \oplus \{a? \mapsto v?\}$$
$$= (\mathrm{dom}\{a? \mapsto v?\} \lhd slots \cup \{a? \mapsto v?\}) \cup \{a? \mapsto v?\}$$

[By definition of $\oplus$]

$$= \{a?\} \vartriangleleft (slots \cup \{a? \mapsto v?\})$$
$$= (ATTR \setminus \{a?\}) \vartriangleleft (slots \cup \{a? \mapsto v?\})$$
$$= \text{id } ATTR \setminus \{a?\} \,\stupcolon\, (slots \cup \{a? \mapsto v?\})$$
$$= slots \cup \{a? \mapsto v?\}$$

The other direction is proved by noting that on the left-hand side, the *ModAttr* operation can have the same value bound to $v?$ as does the *AddAttr* operation. The proof is now complete. $\square$

The next result shows that the effect of modifying the same attribute twice is the same as modifying it with its latest value.

Theorem 8

$$ModAttr[a/a?, v_1/v?] \,\stupcolon\, ModAttr[a/a?, v_2/v?] \equiv$$
$$ModAttr^*[a/a?, v_2/v?]$$

where $S[x/a]$ is the schema that results from uniformly substituting its variable x for the variable a.

PROOF $\Rightarrow$: Assume that $v_1 \neq v_2$. The predicate of the composite schema is:

$\exists\, ENTRY^+ \bullet$
  $a \in knownslots \wedge$
  $slots^+ = slots \oplus \{a \mapsto v_1\} \wedge$
  $a \in knownslots^+ \wedge$
  $slots' = slots \oplus \{a \mapsto v_2\}$

We note the following identities:

$$slots^{+\prime} = slots'$$

$$slots^+ = slots$$

These are because we want to identify the before state of the composite on the left-hand side with the before state on the right-hand side; we also want to identify the after states.

We now expand:

$slots'$

$$= slots^+ \oplus \{a \mapsto v_2\}$$
$$= (slots \oplus \{a \mapsto v_1\}) \oplus \{a \mapsto v_2\}$$
$$= (slots^+ \oplus \{a \mapsto v_1\}) \oplus \{a \mapsto v_2\}$$
$$= slots'^+$$

The proof now reduces to:

$$(slots \oplus \{a \mapsto v_1\}) \oplus \{a \mapsto v_2\}$$
$$= slots \oplus (\{a \mapsto v_1\} \oplus \{a \mapsto v_2\})$$
$$\text{[Since } (f \oplus g) \oplus h = f \oplus (g \oplus h)]$$
$$= slots \oplus \{a \mapsto v_2\} \qquad\qquad\qquad \text{[Defn } \oplus]$$

and we are done.

The converse direction also rests on the above and on the observation that:

$$f \oplus \{a \mapsto b\} \oplus \{a \mapsto b\}$$
$$= f \oplus \{a \mapsto b\}$$

The proof of $\Rightarrow$ also rests upon this fact if $v_1 = v_2$. $\square$

4.2.2   Abstraction Levels

In this sub-section, we specify the abstraction level type which we will call *ABSLEV*. As we stated in the last Chapter, the blackboard is composed of a linear hierarchy of abstraction levels, and each entry resides on exactly one abstraction level. We can think of an abstraction level as being a small database in its own right. We can also think of it as representing a mapping from entry identifiers to entry structures. Retrievals from an abstraction level are performed on the basis of entry identifier for the most part (below, we will see an instance of where this is not the case). In order, therefore, to define the *ABSLEV* type, we need to define an entry identifier type:

[*EID*]

Again, this type is atomic for we do not care what the fine structure of an entry identifier is.

We define the abstraction level type as:

$$
\begin{array}{|l}
\underline{\quad ABSLEV \quad\rule{0pt}{0pt}} \\
\quad entries : EID \nrightarrow ENTRY \\
\quad knownents : \mathbb{P}\ EID \\
\hline
\quad knownents = \mathrm{dom}\ entries \\
\end{array}
$$

This schema is very similar to the one we defined for entries. The details of the operations that we define over the type are somewhat different, though. The *ABSLEV* type is defined in terms of a mapping from entry identifiers to entry structures: entry structures are of type *ENTRY*. We defined *ENTRY* in the previous sub-section, and its use here is an example of the way in which a datatype-defining schema can be used as a type in Z.

Abstraction levels must be initialized when the blackboard system is started. In order to initialize an abstraction level, we must ensure that it contains no entries. This immediately gives the definition of the operation:

$$
\begin{array}{|l}
\underline{\quad InitABSLEV \quad\rule{0pt}{0pt}} \\
\quad ABSLEV \\
\hline
\quad knownents = \varnothing \\
\end{array}
$$

As with *ENTRY*, this operation makes the domain of *entries* empty.

In order to put an entry on an abstraction level, we need an identifier for the entry and we need the entry structure. The entry structure should have been created using *CreateENTRY*. The operation to add an entry to an abstraction level is:

$$
\begin{array}{|l}
\underline{\quad AddEntry \quad\rule{0pt}{0pt}} \\
\quad \Delta ABSLEV \\
\quad eid? : EID \\
\quad e? : ENTRY \\
\hline
\quad eid? \notin knownents \\
\quad entries' = entries \cup \{eid? \mapsto e?\} \\
\end{array}
$$

In order to add an entry to an abstraction level, that entry should not already be there (this is the test performed on the first line of the predicate). We have couched this in terms of entry identifiers: in order to add a new entry to an abstraction level, the identifier associated with that entry should not already be in the domain of the abstraction level. We could define a stronger version in which we compare entry structures:

$$\forall\, e : ENTRY \mid e \in \text{ran } entries \bullet$$
$$e? \neq e$$

but this requires information about how to determine whether two entries are identical. This information is application-specific, and we do not have access to it when defining a domain-independent shell. We are reduced to considering entry identifiers only, even though this leaves open the possibility that some entry *structure* can appear many times on the same abstraction level (it also leaves open the possibility that the same structure can appear on more than one abstraction level). By the remark above, our approach is the best available to us, and we have to leave more complex tests until such time as we have detailed information.

We have the following result:

Theorem 9

$$AddEntry \vdash \#knownents' = \#knownents + 1$$

PROOF   First note that:

$$knownents = \text{dom } entries$$

Therefore, we have:

$$
\begin{aligned}
\# \,\text{dom } entries' &\\
&= \#\,\text{dom}(entries \cup \{\,eid? \mapsto e?\}) \\
&= \#\,\text{dom } entries + \#\,\text{dom}\{eid? \mapsto e?\} \\
&= \#\,\text{dom } entries + 1 \\
&= \#knownents + 1
\end{aligned}
$$

□

The *AddEntry* schema is the only one defined over abstraction levels that uses the $\Delta ABSLEV$ schema: all the others use $\Xi ABSLEV$. This is an imporant property when considering preconditions and refinements.

The next operation that we define returns an entire entry structure from the abstraction level. The schema is:

```
┌─ GetEntry ──────────────────────────────
│ Ξ ABSLEV
│ eid? : EID
│ e! : ENTRY
├──────────────────────────────────────────
│ eid? ∈ knownents
│ e! = entries(eid?)
└──────────────────────────────────────────
```

In order to retrieve an entry from an abstraction level, it is necessary that the identifier already be recorded as being one for a known entry. This enables the retrieval to take place, and it is also a logical precondition of the operation. The second line of the predicate binds the entry to the variable *e!*. Again, we see the usefulness of considering the database to be a function.

The next three operations, *GetEntryVal*, *AddEntryVal* and *ModEntryVal* are analogous to those that we encountered when defining the *ENTRY* type. These operations act upon entries in the abstraction level. The first retrieves the value stored on some attribute; the second adds an attribute-value pair to an entry; the third modifies the value that is stored on some attribute. In each case, the schema has an input variable which determines the name under which the entry is stored. The identifier is used to retrieve the entry in question. Thereafter, the operations that are to be performed are those we defined in the last sub-section. These schemata have interesting properties, so we will first define the *AddEntryVal* schema and then discuss it. The discussion emphasises properties of this schema that are common to all three.

```
┌─ AddEntryVal ──────────────────────────────────────
│ ΞABSLEV
│ eid? : EID
├────────────────────────────────────────────────────
│ eid? ∈ knownents
│ ∃ ΔENTRY | ENTRY = entries(eid?) •
│     AddAttr
└────────────────────────────────────────────────────
```

The first thing to notice about this schema is that it represents an operation that does not alter the state of the abstraction level. Clearly, the operation does alter the state of an entry because it adds an attribute-value pair. In order to see the difference, though, we need to examine the contents of the entry, and this is not part, we believe, of the abstraction level state: we consider, in other words, the abstraction level state to depend on the existence of an entry identifier and some entry structure only. This leads to the view that the range of *entries* is not affected by the addition of a new attribute-value pair: what matters is that the entry to which this modification has been performed is an element of the range of *entries*.

The second thing to notice is that the schema contains a reference to another schema in its predicate. The referenced schema is *AddAttr*, a schema that we defined above. In addition, there is the matter of quantification over a schema: one that seems a little strange at first sight.

The instance of *AddAttr* represents the operation that is to be performed. This operation depends upon two input variables, and upon $\Delta ENTRY$. $\Delta ENTRY$, as we have already seen, when it occurs in a signature, serves to declare variables. The variables that *AddAttr* declares are to be thought of as being added to the signature of *AddEntryVal*. Thus, the *AddEntry.Val* schema depends upon three input variables, and not just one. These variables are *eid?*, *a?* and *v?*. We can expand *AddEntryVal* to give:

$$
\begin{array}{|l}
\hline
\Xi ABSLEV \\
eid? : EID \\
a? : ATTR \\
v? : VAL \\
\hline
eid? \in knownents \\
(\exists \Delta ENTRY \mid ENTRY = entries(eid?) \bullet \\
\quad a? \notin knownslots \land \\
\quad slots' = slots \cup \{a? \mapsto v?\}) \\
\hline
\end{array}
$$

The explanation of the quantified occurrence of $Delta\,ENTRY$ can be explained by considering it as the introduction of a signature. The first expansion gives:

$$
\exists ENTRY;\ ENTRY' \mid ENTRY = entries(eid?)
$$

By expanding the component signatures, we obtain:

$$
\exists slots : ATTR \nrightarrow VAL;\ knownslots : \mathbb{P}\, ATTR; \\
slots' : ATTR \nrightarrow VAL;\ knownslots' : \mathbb{P}\, ATTR
$$

In other words, quantification over a schema is the same as quantifying over its signature. Expansion of Δ and Ξ forms yields the variables which they declare.

Now, quantifiers define schemata, and the part of the quantifier after the "|" is the signature of the schema over which quantification occurs. In the case above, we are most interested in where the occurrence of $ENTRY$ comes from, and in how we can bind it using a function. The occurrence of $ENTRY$ represents the variables, $slots$ and $knownslots$. The function $entries$ has the type $ENTRY$ as its range, and will therefore return one object of type $ATTR \nrightarrow VAL$ and one of type $\mathbb{P}\,ATTR$. We can completely expand the $AddEntryVal$ schema to obtain:

$\Xi ABSLEV$
$eid? : EID$
$a? : ATTR$
$v? : VAL$

$eid? \in knownents$
$(\exists\, slots, slots' : ATTR \nrightarrow VAL;$
$\qquad knownslots, knownslots' : \mathbb{P}\ ATTR\ |$
$\qquad\qquad ENTRY = entries(eid?)\ \bullet$
$\qquad a? \notin knownslots \wedge$
$\qquad slots' = slots \cup \{\, a? \mapsto v?\})$

(we have left the binding of $ENTRY$ intact in order to avoid notational
problems). The occurrence of $ENTRY$ after the vertical bar is the
one introduced as the quantified variable—that is, it is the $ENTRY$
that forms part of $\Delta ENTRY$. We thus have a complete account of this
schema, and we can see that it performs the task we expect. This
schema exemplifies all of the more unusual properties of the schemata
that we will see below; similar remarks apply to the schemata that we
define for the manipulation of the blackboard in the next sub-section.

The reader should note that quantification over $\Delta ENTRY$ effectively serves to hide it from all external observations of the schema.
We could have defined the $AddEntryVal$ schema without quantification
and then engaged in hiding: we have chosen to present the schema in
the way in which we have because it is, we believe, a more direct way
of doing things.

The results that we proved above in connection with $AddAttr$ still
hold good, and even carry over to $AddEntryVal$.

The $ModEntryVal$ schema is directly analogous to $AddEntryVal$:

___ $ModEntryVal$ _____
$\Xi ABSLEV$
$eid? : EID$

$eid? \in knownents$
$(\exists\, \Delta ENTRY\ |\ ENTRY = entries(eid?)\ \bullet$
$\qquad ModAttr)$

Expansion of this gives us:

$$
\begin{array}{l}
\Xi ABSLEV \\
eid? : EID \\
a? : ATTR \\
v? : VAL \\
\hline
eid? \in knownents \\
(\exists\, slots, slots' : ATTR \nrightarrow VAL; \\
\quad knownslots, knownslots' : \mathbb{P}\, ATTR \mid \\
\qquad ENTRY = entries(eid?) \bullet \\
\quad a? \in knownents \land \\
\quad slots' = slots \oplus \{a? \mapsto v?\})
\end{array}
$$

As can be seen, this schema is, indeed, very similar to the one obtained by expanding *AddEntryVal*.

Again, the results that we proved above in connection with *ModAttr* carry over to this case and remain valid. We can also extend them in an obvious way so that, for example:

$$ModEntryVal \vdash \#\operatorname{dom} slots' = \#\operatorname{dom} slots$$

obtains.

The composition results are also true because nothing alters except the slots in the entry in question. The effect of creating an entry on an abstraction level and then adding an attribute-value pair or modifying it is the same as creating an entry with the resulting value of *slots*, and also extends the function representing the entries on the abstraction level (and increases the cardinality of its domain by one).

$$
\begin{array}{l}
\underline{\ GetEntryVal\ } \\
\Xi ABSLEV \\
eid? : EID \\
\hline
eid? \in knownents \\
(\exists \Xi ENTRY \mid ENTRY = entries(eid?) \bullet \\
\quad GetAttr)
\end{array}
$$

We can expand this schema to give:

$$
\begin{array}{l}
\Xi ABSLEV \\
eid? : EID \\
a? : ATTR \\
v! : VAL \\
\hline
eid? \in knownents \\
(\exists\, slots, slots' : ATTR \nrightarrow VAL; \\
knownslots, knownslots' : \mathbb{P}\ ATTR \mid \\
\qquad ENTRY = entries(eid?)\ \bullet \\
\quad a? \in knownslots \land \\
\quad v! = slots(a?) \land \\
\quad slots' = slots \land \\
\quad knownslots = knownslots')
\end{array}
$$

Again, we have left the occurrence of $ENTRY$ intact where it is bound to the value of $entries(eid?)$. In addition, we have included within the quantifier the constraint imposed by $\Xi ENTRY$ in order to make as much explicit as possible.

These schemata show that schema references can be made at a variety of different points in a schema. It is important to expand schemata fully if they include features such as the ones discussed above: this is because one always wants to be sure that the schemata that we derive by various combining operations are correct.

As we have mentioned, all of the results that we can prove above entries carry over to abstraction levels: in other words, there is nothing above that invalidates any results that we can prove about entries. As we will see, the properties that can be proved for abstraction levels carry over to the entire blackboard. We will now turn our attentions to the specification of the blackboard database in its entirety. The specification depends upon the structures that we have defined for entries and for abstraction levels.

4.2.3   The Blackboard

In this sub-section, we will define the structures that represent the blackboard database. This specification will connect all aspects of the specfication thus far. The operations that we have defined over abstraction levels which inherit operations from entries will be used below: this serves to define an interface.

In order to define the blackboard, we need to identify abstraction levels. We will do this as follows:

$$LEVID == \mathbb{N}$$

$LEVID$ is the set of abstraction level identifiers. We identify these identifiers with the naturals because the latter have convenient properties: in particular, they are ordered, and we wish to make use of this property when defining the abstraction hierarchy. We use abstraction level identifiers to access the blackboard when performing various operations on abstraction levels and entries.

We now define the schema for the blackboard type:

```
┌─ Blackboard ─────────────────────────────────
│  levels : seq ABSLEV
│  numlevels : N
│ ─────────────────────────────────────────────
│  numlevels = #levels
└──────────────────────────────────────────────
```

The variable *levels* contains the abstraction levels. They are maintained in a *sequence* because this allows us to make use of the natural ordering over the natural numbers $\mathbb{N}$ in defining the abstraction hierarchy. An abstraction hierarchy defines its own ordering: the ordering is in terms of the relation "more abstract than": this ordering can be directly represented in terms of the naturals, and, since Z provides a sequence type, we make use of it. Strictly speaking, we should impose the condition that there be at least two abstraction levels on the blackboard (for otherwise, the hierarchy is somewhat redundant): we do not impose this condition because it is common during system development to build the blackboard up level at a time from a one abstraction level initial prototype.

The predicate of the *Blackboard* schema defines *numlevels* to be the number of abstraction levels on the blackboard (this is determined by the number of elements in the sequence *levels*). A constraint on the blackboard is that once the abstraction hierarchy has been defined, it may never change. We need to enforce this constraint in our specification, and we need to say what the number of abstraction levels is. We can obtain the latter from the length of the sequence *levels*, and we can set it by supplying a value to the initialization schema. We define the initialization schema as:

```
┌─ InitBlackboard ─────────────────────────────
│ Blackboard
│ num_of_levels? : ℕ
├──────────────────────────────────────────────
│ numlevels = num_of_levels?
│ (∀ i : 1 .. numlevels;  ABSLEV |
│         ABSLEV = levels(i) •
│   InitABSLEV)
└──────────────────────────────────────────────
```

Note that we use a device similar to the one we used in defining most of the operations over abstraction levels: we include a schema in the predicate of the *InitBlackboard* schema. The expansion of the above schema is:

```
┌──────────────────────────────────────────────
│ Blackboard
│ num_of_levels? : ℕ
├──────────────────────────────────────────────
│ ∀ i : 1 .. numlevels;  ABSLEV |
│         ABSLEV = levels(i) •
│   knownents = ∅
└──────────────────────────────────────────────
```

The value of *num_of_levels?* is supplied by the user.

We now have to ensure that any operation that alters the blackboard state cannot alter the number of abstraction levels. The key to this is the definition of the △*Blackboard* schema:

```
┌─ △Blackboard ────────────────────────────────
│ Blackboard
│ Blackboard'
├──────────────────────────────────────────────
│ numlevels = numlevels'
└──────────────────────────────────────────────
```

This schema constains the number of abstraction levels after a destructive operation to be the same as it was before. Thus, no destructive operation can alter the number of abstraction levels on the blackboard. We will provide no operations to change the number of abstraction levels.

$$
\begin{array}{|l}
\hline
\;\Xi Blackboard \underline{\hspace{6cm}} \\
\; Blackboard \\
\; Blackboard' \\
\hline
\; numlevels = numlevels' \\
\; levels = levels' \\
\hline
\end{array}
$$

Clearly, the Ξ *Blackboard* cannot alter the abstraction hierarchy in any way.

We may safely assume that once the abstraction hierarchy has been set up, it cannot be altered in any way, although entries can be added and modified, of course.

Sometimes, we will want to obtain complete entry structures from the blackboard. In order to do this, the name of the abstraction level on which the entry resides must be known, and the entry must reside on that abstraction level. For the second part, we can rely upon the operation we defined for abstraction levels; for the first, we need to operate on the blackboard.

We can define a schema called *KnownLevel*:

$$
\begin{array}{|l}
\hline
\;KnownLevel \underline{\hspace{6cm}} \\
\; \Xi Blackboard \\
\; lev? : LEVID \\
\hline
\; 1 \le lev? \le numlevels \\
\hline
\end{array}
$$

This schema is true when the input variable *lev?* represents a valid abstraction level identifier: a valid identifier is one that is in the range $1 .. numlevels$. The point of defining this schema is that it represents an operation that we will use a great deal. We could simply include its predicate in all the schemata that we define, but we may want to allow other components of a system to know what a legal or valid abstraction level identifier is. We will therefore conjoin this schema with the others that we define below: in each case, we will expand the result to be sure of its correctness. Note that we could have written the predicate as:

$$lev? \in 1 \mathrel{..} numlevels$$

but we prefer the notation that we have used because we believe that it is clearer.

The first operation that we define is the one to extract an entry from the blackboard:

```
┌─ GetENTRYBB ────────────────────────────────────
│ ΞBlackboard
│ lev? : LEVID
├──────────────────────────────────────────────────
│ ∃ΞABSLEV | ABSLEV = levels(lev?) •
│     GetEntry
└──────────────────────────────────────────────────
```

We define the interface schema as:

$$GetBBEntry \mathrel{\widehat{=}} KnownLevel \wedge GetENTRYBB$$

This schema represents the conjunction of the *KnownLevel* and *GetEN-TRYBB* schemata: it is one which tests the level identifier *lev?* to see if it is valid, and then extracts the entry which it returns. The first expansion is:

```
┌─ GetBBEntry ────────────────────────────────────
│ ΞBlackboard
│ lev? : LEVID
├──────────────────────────────────────────────────
│ 1 ≤ lev? ≤ numlevels
│ ∃ΞABSLEV | ABSLEV = levels(lev?) •
│     GetEntry
└──────────────────────────────────────────────────
```

Note that *lev?* is not repeated in the signature: it is identified as being common to the two component schemata. This expands to:

$$
\begin{array}{|l}
\hline
\Xi Blackboard \\
lev? : LEVID \\
eid? : EID \\
e! : ENTRY \\
\hline
1 \leq lev? \leq numlevels \\
(\exists \Xi ABSLEV \mid ABSLEV = levels(lev?) \bullet \\
\quad eid? \in knownents \wedge \\
\quad e! = entries(eid?)) \\
\hline
\end{array}
$$

This is precisely the operation that we want.

We will use similar techniques to define the other operations on the blackboard.

The next three operations add attribute-value pairs to entries, modify attribute-value pairs, and extract the value from an attribute-value pair. In each case, we rely upon the operation (schema) that the abstraction level type provides for us.

The next schema returns the value stored on a particular attribute in a particular entry:

$$
\begin{array}{|l}
\hline
\;GetBBVAL \underline{\hspace{4cm}} \\
\Xi Blackboard \\
lev? : LEVID \\
\hline
\exists \Xi ABSLEV \mid ABSLEV = levels(lev?) \bullet \\
\quad GetEntryVal \\
\hline
\end{array}
$$

The interface is defined by:

$$GetBBVal \mathrel{\widehat=} KnownLevel \wedge GetBBVAL$$

The full expansion of this schema (ignoring expansion of Ξ forms) is:

$\Xi Blackboard$
$lev? : LEVID$
$eid? : EID$
$a? : ATTR$
$v! : VAL$

$1 \leq lev? \leq numlevels$
$(\exists \Xi ABSLEV \mid ABSLEV = levels(lev?) \bullet$
  $eid? \in knownents \wedge$
  $(\exists \Xi ENTRY \mid ENTRY = entries(eid?) \bullet$
    $a? \in knownslots \wedge$
    $v! = slots(a?)))$

The *AddBBVAL* operation adds a new attribute-value pair to an entry. The abstraction level must exist, as must the entry:

___AddBBVAL___
$\Xi Blackboard$
$lev? : LEVID$

$\exists \Xi ABSLEV \mid ABSLEV = levels(lev?) \bullet$
  $AddEntryVal$

The operation is called *AddBBVal*, and we have:

$$AddBBVal \mathrel{\widehat{=}} KnownLevel \wedge AddBBVAL$$

This expands to:

$$
\begin{array}{|l}
\hline
\Xi Blackboard \\
lev? : LEVID \\
eid? : EID \\
a? : ATTR \\
v? : VAL \\
\hline
1 \leq lev? \leq numlevels \\
(\exists\, ABSLEV \mid ABSLEV = levels(lev?) \bullet \\
\quad eid? \in knownents \wedge \\
\quad (\exists\, \Delta ENTRY \mid ENTRY = entries(eid?) \bullet \\
\quad\quad a? \notin knownslots \wedge \\
\quad\quad slots' = slots \cup \{a? \mapsto v?\})) \\
\hline
\end{array}
$$

The final schema in this group is the one for modifying the value stored in an attribute of some entry on the blackboard. Its schema is:

$$
\begin{array}{|l}
\hline
\;ModBBVAL \underline{\hspace{5cm}} \\
\Xi Blackboard \\
lev? : LEVID \\
\hline
\exists\, \Xi ABSLEV \mid ABSLEV = levels(lev?) \bullet \\
\quad ModEntryVal \\
\hline
\end{array}
$$

By conjunction, we have:

$$
ModBBVal \; \widehat{=} \; KnownLevel \wedge ModBBVAL
$$

which expands to:

$\Xi Blackboard$
$lev? : LEVID$
$eid? : EID$
$a? : ATTR$
$v? : VAL$

$1 \leq lev? \leq numlevels$
$(\exists \Xi ABSLEV \mid ABSLEV = levels(lev?) \bullet$
    $eid? \in knownents \land$
        $(\exists \Delta ENTRY \mid ENTRY = entries(eid?) \bullet$
          $a? \in knownslots \land$
          $slots' = slots \oplus \{a? \mapsto v?\}))$

The next schema that we need to define is needed by the *Find* operation, amongst others. The *Find* operation creates a set which contains all those entries on the blackboard that satisfy some predicate. The way in which we specify *Find* requires that we have access to the entire blackboard contents: in other words, we map the predicate over *all* the entries on the blackboard. As part of the operation's definition, we need an operation which will return the set of all the entries on the blackboard. We can define a schema *BBContents* to do this:

___BBContents___
$\Xi Blackboard$
$conts! : \mathbb{P}(EID \times LEVID)$

$\forall l : 1 .. numlevels; \ ABSLEV \mid$
    $ABSLEV = levels(l) \bullet$
  $\forall e : EID \mid e \in knownents \bullet$
    $(e, l) \in conts!$

The schema actually returns a set of pairs, the first component of which is the entry identifier, and the second component of which is the identifier of its abstraction level. This structure is required because every time we want to obtain an entry from the blackboard, we have to give the name of the abstraction level on which it resides: this is forced on us by the way in which we have defined the access operations, and is a good thing because it makes the blackboard more secure in the sense that we cannot try to obtain an entry whose identifier exists but whose entry structure does not.

The *BBContents* schema is defined in the obvious way. It leaves the blackboard invariant. The output variable *conts!* is a set of entry identifiers whose elements are all the identifiers currently on the blackboard.

We can prove a result about the contents of a freshly initialized blackboard:

Theorem 10

$$InitBlackboard \land BBContents \vdash first(\!|conts!|\!) = \varnothing$$

PROOF   The conjunction of the two schemata gives:

$$
\begin{array}{l}
\rule{0pt}{0pt}\underline{InitBlackboard \land BBContents}\\[4pt]
\quad \Xi Blackboard\\
\quad conts! : \mathbb{P}(EID \times LEVID)\\
\quad num\_of\_levels? : \mathbb{N}\\[4pt]
\rule{5cm}{0.4pt}\\
\quad numlevels = num\_of\_levels? \land\\
\quad (\forall\, i : 1 .. numlevels;\ ABSLEV \mid\\
\qquad\qquad ABSLEV = levels(i)\ \bullet\\
\qquad knownents = \varnothing)\\
\quad \land\\
\quad (\forall\, l : 1 .. numlevels;\ ABSLEV \mid\\
\qquad\qquad ABSLEV = levels(l)\ \bullet\\
\qquad (\forall\, e : EID \mid e \in knownents\ \bullet\\
\qquad\quad (e, l) \in conts!))
\end{array}
$$

Using *first* $(\!|conts!|\!)$, we can re-write the second quantified formula as:

$$
\begin{array}{l}
\forall\, l : 1 .. numlevels;\ ABSLEV \mid\\
\qquad ABSLEV = levels(l)\ \bullet\\
\quad (\forall\, e : EID \mid e \in knownents\ \bullet\\
\qquad e \in first(\!|conts!|\!))
\end{array}
$$

This is the same as:

$$first(|conts!|) =$$
$$\bigcup\{l : 1 .. numlevels; \ ABSLEV$$
$$| \ ABSLEV = levels(l) \bullet knownents\}$$

Now, we know that:

$$knownents = \varnothing$$

so:

$$first(|conts!|)$$
$$= \bigcup\{l : 1 .. numlevels; \ ABSLEV$$
$$| \ ABSLEV = levels(l) \bullet knownents\}$$
$$= \bigcup\{l : 1 .. numlevels; \ ABSLEV$$
$$| \ ABSLEV = levels(l) \bullet \varnothing\}$$
$$= \varnothing$$

$\square$

The *Find* operation is used in Knowledge Source preconditions and actions. It examines the state of the blackboard and produces a set. The elements of the set are those entries which satisfy the predicate. The predicate is expressed in terms of attributes and values: it is satisfied when an entry has attributes whose values fall within the predicate. To define *Find*, we will represent the predicate by its graph. The graph is a set of attribute-value set pairs:

$$POSSVALS == ATTR \times (\mathbb{P} \ VAL)$$

$$PGRAPH == \mathbb{P} \ POSSVALS$$

The predicate which is an input variable to *Find* is of type *PGRAPH*. The output of the *Find* operation is represented by an output variable *ents* of type $\mathbb{P} \ EID$. We define the schema for the operation as follows:

```
┌─ BBFind ─────────────────────────────────────────────
│ Ξ Blackboard
│ conts? : ℙ(EID × LEVID)
│ ents! : ℙ EID
│ pred? : PGRAPH
├───────────────────────────────────────────────────────
│ ∀ ent : EID × LEVID;  e? : EID;
│                lev? : LEVID |
│          ent ∈ conts? ∧
│          e? = first(ent) ∧
│          lev? = second(ent) •
│      (∀ pv : POSSVALS;  a? : ATTR;  vs : ℙ VAL •
│      (∃ v! : VAL •
│            pv ∈ pred? ∧
│            a? = first(pv) ∧
│            vs = second(pv) ∧
│            GetBBVal ∧ v! ∈ vs)
│      ⇒
│      e? ∈ ents!)
└───────────────────────────────────────────────────────
```

This schema expands to:

$\Xi Blackboard$
$conts? : \mathbb{P}(EID \times LEVID)$
$ents! : \mathbb{P}\ EID$
$pred? : PGRAPH$
$v! : VAL$

$\forall\ ent : EID \times LEVID;\ e? : EID;$
$\qquad\qquad lev? : LEVID\ |$
$\qquad ent \in conts?\ \wedge$
$\qquad e = first(ent)\ \wedge$
$\qquad l = second(ent)\ \bullet$
$\quad (\forall\ pv : POSSVALS;\ a : ATTR;\ vs : \mathbb{P}\ VAL\ \bullet$
$\qquad pv \in pred?\ \wedge$
$\qquad a = first(pv)\ \wedge$
$\qquad vs = second(pv)\ \wedge$
$\qquad l \in 1\ ..\ numlevels\ \wedge$
$\qquad (\exists\ \Xi ABSLEV\ |\ ABSLEV = levels(l)\ \bullet$
$\qquad\qquad e \in knownents\ \wedge$
$\qquad\qquad (\exists\ \Xi ENTRY\ |\ ENTRY = entries(e)\ \bullet$
$\qquad\qquad\qquad a \in knownslots\ \wedge$
$\qquad\qquad\qquad v! = slots(a))))$
$\qquad \Rightarrow e \in ents!$

Notice that the expansion declares a variable $v!$ that we eventually will want to hide (we will also want, one way or another, to hide *conts*).

We define the *Find* operation in terms of a composition:

$$Find \,\hat{=}\, BBContents \,\mathbin{\raise.2ex\hbox{$\fatsemi$}}\, (BBFind \setminus (v!))$$

The operation $\mathbin{\raise.2ex\hbox{$\fatsemi$}}$ is *sequential composition*. In this case, it is warranted, even though it reduces the amount of non-determinism that is present in the specification.. In order to find the sequential composition, we check the output and input variables of the two schemata that are being composed in order to make sure that their types are conformal (equivalent). Next, we identify the state after components of the first schema with the state before components of the second, and we rename them. Finally, we hide all the variables that we have thus identified and/or renamed. These two operations yield:

$\Xi Blackboard$
$ents! : \mathbb{P}\ EID$
$pred? : PGRAPH$
$v! : VAL$

$\exists\ conts : \mathbb{P}(EID \times LEVID)\ \bullet$
$\quad (\forall\ l : 1\ ..\ numlevels;\ ABSLEV\ |$
$\qquad\quad ABSLEV = levels(l)\ \bullet$
$\quad\ (\forall\ e : EID\ |\ e \in knownents\ \bullet$
$\qquad\ (e, l) \in conts)\ \wedge$
$\quad\ (\forall\ ent : EID \times LEVID;$
$\qquad\qquad e? : EID;\ lev? : LEVID\ |$
$\qquad\ ent \in conts?\ \wedge$
$\qquad\qquad\quad e = first(ent)\ \wedge$
$\qquad\qquad\quad l = second(ent)\ \bullet$
$\quad (\forall\ pv : POSSVALS;\ a : ATTR;\ vs : \mathbb{P}\ VAL\ \bullet$
$\qquad pv \in pred?\ \wedge$
$\qquad a = first(pv)\ \wedge\ vs = second(pv)\ \wedge$
$\qquad l \in 1\ ..\ numlevels\ \wedge$
$\qquad (\exists\ \Xi ABSLEV\ |\ ABSLEV = levels(l)\ \bullet$
$\qquad\quad e \in knownents\ \wedge$
$\qquad\quad (\exists\ \Xi ENTRY\ |\ ENTRY = entries(e)\ \bullet$
$\qquad\quad a \in knownslots\ \wedge$
$\qquad\quad v! = slots(a))))$
$\qquad\Rightarrow$
$\qquad e \in ents!))$

Note that, because both schemata include $\Xi Blackboard$, we do not
have to hide the state after *BBContents* once we have identified it with
the before state of *BBFind* (this is because they are the same). The
resulting schema still contains $v!$, and we need to hide it. This leads
to another level of quantification. We do not give the full expansion
of the result, because it would be tedious in the extreme. The scope
of the existential quantifier which hids $v!$ is the entire predicate of
the expanded schema: in other words, the quantifier which binds $v!$ is
outermost, so the entire predicate is existentially quantified.

The result of the composition and hiding is a very large schema.

This schema is very economical to define using the schema calculus: the resulting expanded schema shows how a little work with Z schemata can go a very long way (this is one of the reasons we chose Z for the specifications in this book). We are correct in using sequential composition because, before the predicate can be applied, the blackboard's contents must be known: this is a strict dependency, and we cannot rely upon conjunction to give us the right order for the two component actions (the action of obtaining the blackboard's contents and the action of applying the predicate). Sequential composition reduces the non-determinacy in the specification, which is not, in general, a good thing: in this case, though, we are required to impose a strict ordering, so we have a justification for our approach.

We have now defined the blackboard and its contents. We can move on to the definition of the external interface which the blackboard presents to the rest of the system. This interface involves the definition of the *events* which drive Knowledge Source activation.

4.2.4   Events and the Blackboard Interface

In this sub-section, we define the event system and the external interfaces presented by the blackboard. Events are caused whenever a change occurs on the blackboard, and we define three standard types of event: a NEW, a MOD and an ADD event. Each of these is an event *type* because it is instantiated whenever an event occurs. A NEW event occurs whenever a new entry is added to the blackboard at some level of abstraction; an ADD event occurs whenever an attribute-value pair is added to an entry on the blackboard, and a MOD event occurs whenever the value that is stored in an attribute is altered (modified).

We need to define a new type for blackboard events. This type is called *BBEVENT*:

$$BBEVENT ::= new \mid mod \mid add$$

This type is composed of the three values *new*, *mod*, and *add*. To save a little work later, we will define a similar type for use in Knowledge Source actions:

$$ACT\_TYPE ::= new \mid mod \mid add$$

We need schemata that will cause the required event. In the case of the specification, what we want is for the event's type to be propagated across the system to the trigger-management component. We therefore define three schemata as follows:

```
┌─ MkNewEvent ──────────────────────────────────
│  ev! : BBEVENT
│ ┌──────────────────────────────────────────────
│  ev! = new
└───────────────────────────────────────────────
```

```
┌─ MkAddEvent ──────────────────────────────────
│  ev! : BBEVENT
│ ┌──────────────────────────────────────────────
│  ev! = add
└───────────────────────────────────────────────
```

```
┌─ MkModEvent ──────────────────────────────────
│  ev! : BBEVENT
│ ┌──────────────────────────────────────────────
│  ev! = mod
└───────────────────────────────────────────────
```

Each of the schemata has the same structure: it merely declares a variable $ev!$ and assigns a value to it.

The interface which the blackboard presents to the rest of the system is defined using these event-generating schemata. What we call an event is not a true event, but just the notification that an event of a certain type has occurred. It is important when performing blackboard operations for the event to be made available to other modules, some of which will merely ignore it—the Knowledge Source triggering module is the only one which actually uses the information. We define the interface in terms of the blackboard operations which we specified in the last sub-section, together with the event-generating schemata that we have just given. It turns out to be the case that the interface is extremely simple to define: we merely compose schemata, with one composition for each operation that we define for the interface. The one complication is caused by entry creation, an operation which we have not fully defined so far. We will give the schemata for the other operations and then return to entry creation.

We define the blackboard operations which cause the ADD and MOD-IFY events as

$$BBAddEvent \mathrel{\widehat{=}} AddBBVal \land MkAddEvent$$

$$BBModEvent \mathrel{\widehat{=}} ModBBVal \land MkModEvent$$

We expand $BBAddEvent$ once:

```
┌─ BBAddEvent ──────────────────────────────
│ ΞBlackboard
│ lev? : LEVID
│ ev! : BBEVENT
├────────────────────────────────────────────
│ 1 ≤ lev? ≤ numlevels
│ (∃ ABSLEV | ABSLEV = levels(lev?) •
│     AddEntryVal)
│ ev! = add
└────────────────────────────────────────────
```

We can see, therefore, that the interface schema performs the add operation and then causes the ADD event.

The entry creation operation is complicated by the fact that we need to create entry identifiers before we can add a newly created entry to the blackboard. The following schema gives the outline:

$$CreateBBEntry \mathrel{\widehat{=}}$$
$$\qquad NewEntryName \land$$
$$\qquad InitENTRY \land$$
$$\qquad CreateENTRY$$

In fact, we want to be sure that name creation (performed by *NewEntryName*) is performed before we create the entry; in addition, the above (complex) operation must be performed before we add the newly created entry to the blackboard and cause the NEW event. To complete the definition, we need a schema which will add a new entry to the blackboard, and one to generate entry identifiers.

We give with the first schema immediately:

__ *AddBBEntry* _____

$\Xi Blackboard$
$lev? : LEVID$
$eid? : EID$
$e? : ENTRY$

$\exists \Delta ABSLEV \mid ABSLEV = levels(lev?) \bullet$
       $AddEntry$

_____

Notice that we use the *AddEntry* schema from the sub-section on abstraction levels.

The last schema defines the operation for adding a completely new entry to the blackboard: its definition was easy. In order to generate entry names, we have to do a little more work. First of all, we need to define a process which will generate unique entry identifiers each time we need one. The following schema defines this process:

__ *EIDs* _____

$eids : \text{seq}_1\ EID$
$n : \mathbb{N}$

$n \geq 1$
$\neg\ (\exists m : \mathbb{N} \bullet m > \#eids)$

$(\forall i : \mathbb{N} \bullet$
       $(\exists e : EID \mid e = eids(i) \bullet$
            $(\forall j : \mathbb{N};\ e_1 : EID \bullet$
                $e_1 = eids(j) \wedge e = e_1 \equiv i = j)))$
$(\forall e : EID \bullet$
       $(\exists i : \mathbb{N} \bullet$
            $e = eids(i)))$

_____

This schema defines an infinite sequence of entry identifiers, each of which is unique. The second line of the predicate assures us that the sequence is infinite: it states that there is no greatest index into the sequence. The second quantified formula states that each identifier in the sequence is unique and that it has a unique index. The last quantified formula states that there is no entry identifier (element of

EID) which is not in the sequence. We could derive the last quantified formula from the second: we choose to give the last one explicitly in order to make proofs easier.

We now define:

$$
\begin{array}{|l}
\underline{\Delta EIDs} \\
EIDs \\
EIDs' \\
\hline
n' > n \\
eids = eids' \\
\end{array}
$$

This schema states that no operation can alter $eids$, the sequence of all possible entry identifiers. It also states that after $EIDs$ has been acted upon by a state-changing operation, the index into the sequence must necessarily be greater in value than it was previously. The idea behind this schema is that, when we have taken an identifier from the sequence (in order to give it to an entry structure), there are still the same names in the name sequence $eids$. The index n is an index to the next available entry identifier in the sequence: in other words, the Δ schema states that after an indentifier has been taken from the sequence, the next available identifier will be the next in the sequence—this means that we will always have a unique identifier for each entry.

With these two schemata, we can now define the operation which yields the next entry identifier:

$$
\begin{array}{|l}
\underline{NewEntryName} \\
\Delta EIDs \\
eid! : EID \\
\hline
eid! = eids(n) \\
n' = n + 1 \\
\end{array}
$$

This schema actually performs the operation of obtaining the next entry identifier. It increments the next pointer by one, so a fresh identifier is always available. The identifier is returned as $eid?$. This schema just makes good the promises that we made when defining the $EIDs$ and $\Delta EIDs$ schemata. All that remains is for us to define an initialization schema. Part of that schema will set n to one; the other part of it will generate all the identifiers in some order. We can write the schema as:

$$
\begin{array}{|l}
\_InitEIDs_____ \\
EIDs \\
\hline
n = 1 \\
(\forall\, e : EID \bullet \\
\quad e \in \mathrm{ran}\ eids \equiv \\
\quad (\exists_1\ i : \mathbb{N} \bullet \\
\quad\quad eids(i) = e)) \\
\end{array}
$$

This schema performs the correct initialization operation, even though we have not specified *how* to generate all the elements of *EIDs*. This is an important aspect of specification: we should be concerned with the what and *not* the how—in other words, we have specified what is to be done, but not how it is to be done.

We can now define the blackboard interface operation that creates entries. We call it *BBNewEvent*:

$$
BBNewEvent \;\hat{=}\;
$$
$$
((KnownLevel \wedge CreateBBEntry) \wedge AddBBEntry)
$$
$$
\wedge MkNewEvent
$$

This is, in fact, only a provisional definition because it suffers from problems that we need to remedy. In order to avoid problems with the lack of ordering of the components of *CreateBBEntry*, we redefine it as:

$$
CreateBBEntry \;\hat{=}\;
$$
$$
NewEntryName \wedge
$$
$$
((InitENTRY \wedge CreateENTRY) \setminus (e?)) \setminus (\Delta EIDs)
$$

The problem is that the original definition of *CreateBBEntry* allowed too much of the state to be visible to outside observers. In particular, parts of the definition of *EIDs* and the entry input variable $e?$ were visible: as we will see, they should not be visible because they represent either intermediate names for an object (as is the case for $e?$) or part of the state which should not be seen (without hiding, n' in $\Delta EIDs$

remains visible, and we prefer the user not to be able to see what the next entry identifier to be generated will be).

The following is the correct and complete definition of *BBNewEvent*:

$BBNewEvent \; \hat{=}$
    $CreateENTRY \; \S$
        $(NewEntryName \; \S$
            $(AddBBEntry \wedge KnownLevel))$

We should expect the resulting schema to be reasonably complex:

$$
\begin{array}{l}
\Delta EIDs \\
\Xi Blackboard \\
lev? : LEVID \\
avps? : \mathbb{P}\ AVL \\
\hline
\exists\ ENTRY\ \bullet \\
\quad \#slots = \#avps?\ \wedge \\
\quad \#knownslots = \#avps?\ \wedge \\
\quad\quad (\forall\ avp : AVL;\ a : ATTR;\ v : VAL\ | \\
\quad\quad\quad\quad avp \in avps?\ \wedge \\
\quad\quad\quad\quad a = first(avp)\ \wedge \\
\quad\quad\quad\quad v = second(avp)\ \bullet \\
\quad\quad\quad a \in knownslots\ \wedge \\
\quad\quad\quad v \in ranslots\ \wedge \\
\quad\quad\quad slots(a) = v)\ \wedge \\
\quad\quad\quad (\exists\ eid : EID\ \bullet \\
\quad\quad\quad\quad eid = eids(n)\ \wedge \\
\quad\quad\quad\quad n' = n + 1\ \wedge \\
\quad\quad\quad\quad (\exists\ \Delta ABSLEV\ | \\
\quad\quad\quad\quad\quad\quad ABSLEV = levels(lev?)\ \bullet \\
\quad\quad\quad\quad\quad eid \notin knownents\ \wedge \\
\quad\quad\quad\quad\quad entries' = \\
\quad\quad\quad\quad\quad\quad entries \cup \{eid \mapsto ENTRY\}))
\end{array}
$$

With this schema, we have completed the definition of the blackboard and its contents.

4.3   Knowledge Sources

In this section, we will specify the basic Knowledge Source type. A Knowledge Source can be thought of as a structure which holds other structures of various types. Specifically, it is composed of:

- a trigger;

- a list of local variable declarations, and

- an action.

We need to define the Knowledge Source structure in such a way that these components can be accommodated and in such a way that we can extract them whenever necessary. We can model a Knowledge Source as a 3-tuple:

$$KS == (TRIGGER \times (LVARDECS \times ACTION))$$

where $TRIGGER$ is the triggering condition, $PRECONDITION$ is the state-based precondition, $LVARDECS$ is a list of variable names that are declared local to the Knowledge Source, and $ACTION$ is the Knowledge Source's action (a sequence of production rules).

Knowledge Sources are constructed by the user, and, once entered into the system, they cannot be altered (until the system terminates, that is—the user can *always* change Knowledge Sources during development, but we consider this action to be outside the scope of our system). We will assume that Knowledge Sources are constant objects, therefore.

We can define the access functions using axioms. To do this, we need to define projection functions from the product that represents the KS type onto the separate component types. The names that we give to these projection functions are not very mnemonic, but that does not matter, for we will define them only in order to define the access functions that will be used in the remainder of the specification. We begin with the projection function which enables us to access the trigger:

$$
\begin{array}{|l}
trig : KS \rightarrow TRIGGER \\
\hline
\forall k : KS \bullet \\
\quad trig(k) = first(k)
\end{array}
$$

To define the other two projections, we will need to project onto the second component of the *KS* type and then compose *second* with either *first* or *second* in order to obtain the object we require. The *second* of *KS* is *LVARDECS* × *ACTION*, so to obtain *LVARDECS*, we compose with *first*; to obtain *ACTION*, we compose with *second*. These facts immediately give us the definitions we need.

The function *klvars* gives the local variable declarations:

$$klvars : KS \rightarrow LVARDECS$$
$$\forall k : KS \bullet$$
$$\quad klvars(k) = first(second(k))$$

The function *kactn* gives the action-part:

$$kactn : KS \rightarrow ACTION$$
$$\forall k : KS \bullet$$
$$\quad kactn(k) = second(second(k))$$

With these definitions, we can move on to the definition of the projection functions which we will use below:

$$ks\_trigger : KS \rightarrow TRIGGER$$
$$\forall k : KS \bullet$$
$$\quad ks\_trigger(k) = trig(k)$$

$$ks\_localvars : KS \rightarrow LVARDECS$$
$$\forall k : KS \bullet$$
$$\quad ks\_localvars(k) = klvars(k)$$

$$ks\_action : KS \rightarrow ACTION$$
$$\forall k : KS \bullet$$
$$\quad ks\_action(k) = kactn(k)$$

KSARs need to contain the identifier of the Knowledge Source whose triggering caused them to be created. Knowledge Source actions have to be accessed via KSARs, so the identifier is needed to perform that access. This entails that we need a set of Knowledge Source identifiers:

$[KSID]$

and we need a structure in which to hold Knowledge Sources. Since we are assuming that we will never dynamically alter the Knowledge Sources in the system, we can use a total function from Knowledge Source identifiers to Knowledge Source structures to represent this structure. We therefore define the global variable KSs:

$$
\begin{array}{|l}
\hline
KSs : KSID \rightarrow KS \\
\hline
\mathrm{dom}\, KSs \neq \varnothing \\
\end{array}
$$

For any Knowledge Source identifier, ks, we have $KSs(ks)$ as the structure which represents the Knowledge Source. Composition of this function with the access functions allows us to extract Knowledge Source components whenever we want. For robustness, we need to know whether a Knowledge Source is present in the system, so we can define the relation:

$$
\begin{array}{|l}
\hline
known\_ks : KSID \leftrightarrow (KSID \rightarrow KS) \\
\hline
\forall\, ksid : KSID \bullet \\
\quad known\_ks(ksid) \equiv ksid \in \mathrm{dom}\, KSs \\
\end{array}
$$

With these definitions, we are able to continue the specification and are able to integrate the Knowledge Source components into one structure and to relate them to KSARs.

Two things must be noted about the above definition of a Knowledge Source. The first is that we do not have a component to represent preconditions. As will be seen, this is because we include preconditions in the condition-part of each of the production rules that are in a Knowledge Source action. We have, therefore, no need for an explicit representation. The second thing is that we allow local variables to appear in Knowledge Sources. What we do not do, in this specification, is to provide any schemata for their manipulation: we have argued for this omission elsewhere, and do not repeat it here.

4.4 KSARs

In this section, we define the operations that can be performed on KSARs (Knowledge Source Activation Records). In addition, we will define some additional structures that are useful in the blackboard system.

We begin with the types for KSARs. A KSAR records information that is used when making scheduling decisions. The information is recorded in an attribute-value form. We will, therefore, define the following atomic types:

$$[KSARATTR, KSARVAL]$$

to stand for KSAR attribute names and the values that they can contain. We have defined both types as atomic. For KSAR attributes, this is reasonable enough, for we consider them only to be names. For the values that are to be stored in KSARs, this seems a little unreasonable. What we are doing is, in effect, a refusal to state precisely what can legally be stored in a KSAR: in fact, one would expect a variety of types, ranging from integer and floating point numbers to pointers and symbols to be stored there. In many respects, the actual values that are stored in KSAR attributes is application-specific: in a system that used the blackboard control architecture (Hayes-Roth, 1985), Knowledge Source and KSAR identifiers would be stored, as well as entry identifiers and attribute names. In our specification, as will be seen, we require the storage of Knowledge Source, entry and abstraction level identifiers, as well as various items of numerical information. We prefer, since we are presenting a relatively abstract specification, to avoid the detailed definition of the *KSARVAL* type.

The attributes that are present in a KSAR will vary with time. This immediately suggests that we define KSARs as partial functions from *KSARATTR* to *KSARVAL*. We therefore have:

$$
\begin{array}{l}
\underline{\quad KSAR \quad\rule{3cm}{0pt}} \\
\quad ksarslots : KSARATTR \nrightarrow KSARVAL \\
\quad known\_ksarslots : \mathbb{P}\ KSARATTR \\
\underline{\quad\rule{3cm}{0pt}} \\
\quad known\_ksarslots = \mathrm{dom}\ ksarslots
\end{array}
$$

this type is our standard for KSARs. We also need the two standard schemata for dealing with KSARs:

```
┌─ ΔKSAR ──────────────────────────────────
│ KSAR
│ KSAR'
│
└──────────────────────────────────────────
```

and:

```
┌─ ΞKSAR ──────────────────────────────────
│ ΔKSAR
├──────────────────────────────────────────
│ ksarslots' = ksarslots
│ known_ksarslots' = known_ksarslots
└──────────────────────────────────────────
```

When creating KSARs, we need to initialise their attribute-value pairs (initialise their slots, in other words). In order to do this, we need the following schema:

```
┌─ InitKSAR ───────────────────────────────
│ KSAR
│ initslots? : KSARATTR ↠ KSARVAL
├──────────────────────────────────────────
│ dom initslots ≠ ∅
│ ksarslots = initslots?
└──────────────────────────────────────────
```

This schema works very much as we would expect. The variable *initslots?* is bound to a set of maplets $\{slot \mapsto slotval\}$. This set must not be empty (therefore, its domain must be not equal to $\emptyset$). If this condition is met, *ksarslots* is bound to the value of *initslots*, which happens on the last line of the predicate.

To obtain the value stored in a given attribute of a KSAR, we use the following schema:

```
┌─ GetKSARSlot ─────────────────────────────
│ ΞKSAR
│ slot? : KSARATTR
│ val! : KSARVAL
├──────────────────────────────────────────
│ slot? ∈ known_ksarslots
│ val! = ksarslots(slot?)
└──────────────────────────────────────────
```

To add a new attribute-value pair, we have the operation:

```
┌─ AddKSARSlot ──────────────────────────────────────────
│ ΔKSAR
│ slot? : KSARATTR
│ val? : KSARVAL
├────────────────────────────────────────────────────────
│ slot? ∉ known_ksarslots
│ ksarslots' = ksarslots ∪ {slot? ↦ val?}
└────────────────────────────────────────────────────────
```

We can now give a result about *AddKSARSlot*:

Theorem 11

$$\vdash (InitKSAR \ ; \ AddKSARSlot) \equiv InitKSAR^*$$

PROOF   We begin by writing out the expansions of left- and right-hand sides.

```
┌─ InitKSAR ; AddKSARSlot ───────────────────────────────
│ ΔKSAR
│ initslots? : KSARATTR ↠ KSARVAL
│ slots? : KSARATTR
│ val? : KSARVAL
├────────────────────────────────────────────────────────
│ (∃ ksarslots⁺ : KSARATTR ↠ KSARVAL;
│         known_ksarslots⁺ : ℙ KSARATTR •
│     dom initslots? ≠ ∅ ∧
│     ksarslots⁺ = initslots? ∧
│     slot? ∉ ksarslots⁺ ∧
│     ksarslots' = ksarslots⁺ ∪ {slot? ↦ val?})
└────────────────────────────────────────────────────────
```

```
┌─ InitKSAR* ────────────────────────────────────────────
│ ΔKSAR*    .
│ initslots*? : KSARATTR ↠ KSARVAL
├────────────────────────────────────────────────────────
│ dom initslots*? ≠ ∅
│ ksarslots*' = initslots*?
└────────────────────────────────────────────────────────
```

For the equivalence to obtain, we must have:

$$ksarslots^* = ksarslots$$
$$ksarslots^{*'} = ksarslots'$$

So:

$ksarslots^*$
$$= ksarslots'$$
$$= ksarslots^+ \cup \{slots? \mapsto val?\}$$
$$= initslots? \cup \{slot? \mapsto val?\} \qquad\qquad [(1)]$$
$$= initslots^*? \qquad\qquad [\text{since } ksarslots^{*'} = initslots^*?]$$

where (1) is true because $slot? \notin \mathrm{dom}\, ksarslots^+$ implies $slot? \notin \mathrm{dom}\, initslots?$.

Thus:

$$initslots^*? = initslots? \cup \{slot? \mapsto val?\}$$

Hence:

$$initslots? = initslots^*? \setminus \{slot? \mapsto val?\}$$

$\Rightarrow$. Using (1), we have:

$$(\mathrm{dom}\, initslots? \neq \varnothing \wedge$$
$$ksarslots = initslots? \wedge$$
$$slots? \notin \mathrm{dom}\, ksarslots_1 \wedge$$
$$ksarslots' = ksarslots_1 \cup \{slot? \mapsto val?\}) \Rightarrow$$
$$(\mathrm{dom}(initslots? \cup \{slot? \mapsto val?\}) \neq \varnothing \wedge$$
$$ksarslots' = initslots? \cup \{slot? \mapsto val?\})$$

(where $ksarslots_1$ is an arbitary value for the bound variable with similar name). This is true, for if $slot? \notin \mathrm{dom}\,(initslots^*? \setminus \{slot? \mapsto val?\})$ and $\mathrm{dom}\, initslots? \neq \varnothing$, then $\mathrm{dom}(initslots? \cup \{slot? \mapsto val?\}) \neq \varnothing$.
$\Leftarrow$. Substituing, the right-hand side becomes:

$$\mathrm{dom}(initslots^*? \setminus \{slot? \mapsto val?\}) \neq \varnothing \wedge$$
$$(ksarslots^{*'} \setminus \{slot? \mapsto val?\}) = initslots^* \setminus \{slot? \mapsto val?\} \wedge$$
$$slot? \notin (\mathrm{dom}\, ksarslots^{*'} \setminus \{slot? \mapsto val?\}) \wedge$$
$$ksarslots^{*'} = (ksarslots^{*'} \setminus \{slot? \mapsto val?\}) \cup \{slot? \mapsto val?\}$$

(where $ksarslots_1$ is as above). The last conjunct becomes:

$$ksarslots^{*'}$$
$$= (ksarslots^{*'} \setminus \{slot? \mapsto val?\})$$
$$\cup \{slot? \mapsto val?\} \qquad = initslots^*?$$

The implication is true. To see this, assume:

$$slot? \in \mathrm{dom}(ksarslots^* \setminus \{slot? \mapsto val?\}$$

that is, that $slot? \in \mathrm{dom}\ initslots?$. But then:

$$ksarslots_1 \cup \{slot? \mapsto val?\}$$
$$= ksarslots_1$$
$$= initslots?$$
$$\neq initslots^*?$$

which is a contradiction. $\square$

Finally, we need an operation that will over-write the value of an attribute that is already present in a KSAR:

```
┌─ UpdateKSARSlot ──────────────────────────────
│ ΔKSAR
│ slot? : KSARATTR
│ val? : KSARVAL
├────────────────────────────────────────────────
│ slot? ∈ known_ksarslots
│ ksarslots' = ksarslots ⊕ {slot? ↦ val?}
└────────────────────────────────────────────────
```

From this schema, we have two results, one of which is analogous to ones that we have seen before.

Theorem 12

$$UpdateKSARSlot \vdash \mathrm{dom}\ ksarslots = \mathrm{dom}\ ksarslots'$$

PROOF   Assume $slot? \notin known\_ksarslots$, then:

$$\mathrm{dom}\ ksarslots' = \mathrm{dom}\ ksarslots \cup \{slot?\}$$

So:

$$
\begin{aligned}
\operatorname{dom} ksarslots' &= \operatorname{dom} ksarslots \cup \{slot?\} \\
&= \operatorname{dom}(ksarslots' \oplus \{slot? \mapsto val?\}) \\
&= \operatorname{dom} ksarslots \cup \operatorname{dom}\{slot? \mapsto val?\} \\
&= \operatorname{dom} ksarslots \cup \{slot?\}
\end{aligned}
$$

But, by the predicate, we have:

$$
\begin{aligned}
\operatorname{dom} ksarslots' &= \operatorname{dom} ksarslots \cup \{slot?\} \\
&= \operatorname{dom} ksarslots
\end{aligned}
$$

since $slot? \in \operatorname{dom} ksarslots.$ $\square$

Theorem 13

$$
\vdash (InitKSAR \wedge UpdateKSARSlot) \equiv InitKSAR^{+}
$$

PROOF   Similar to theorem 5. $\square$

In the specification of the various operations that concern KSARs, we will not make use of the last three schemata: they have been defined for the sake of completeness. Now, this is not to say that they will *never* be used—on the contrary, the scheduler function will have to make extensive use of them. For the operations that we define as part of our general specification, we make no use of these last three schemata: their use comes in the application-specific components that we are unable to specify (since we are concerned *only* with the general-purpose components that comprise the interpreter). In a sense, we are also being somewhat cavalier about our treatment of KSARs: we do not provide rugged specifications for them because we are only marginally concerned with their use. This is why we do not define schemata to denote error conditions. For the application-specific code, we would, of course, have to provide these schemata.

Below, we define a number of schemata that create and manipulate the KSARs which are to be inserted into the triggered list. A word of warning is required concerning the use of the type:

$$
KSARATTR \nrightarrow KSARVAL
$$

It might appear that our use of the above type circumvents the KSAR schemata that we have defined above. The reader should remember that the use of this type is to introduce new sets of attribute-value pairs into KSARs: the use of the partial function type in no way represents an entire KSAR.

4.5   Triggers and KSAR Creation

4.5.1   Triggers

In this sub-section, we specify the mechanisms by which Knowledge Sources are triggered, and we specify the nature of the triggers themselves. Our specification of triggers is rather less complex than we would like, because we are not going to define some of the facilities that we would prefer to include. This omission is made on the grounds of space and complexity of presentation.

The facilities that we are omitting are those which depend upon the ability to call arbitrary predicates from Knowledge Source triggers. The specification that we present only allows us to match specified attributes in triggers: the original source for this interpretation is the AGE system (Nii, 1979), although the triggering mechanisms in BB* are very similar. In our NNB system (Craig, 1987) and in the blackboard system specification in (Craig, *in press*), we allow triggers to call arbitrary pieces of code: this entails that triggers can inspect attributes of the entry that caused the triggering event and they can also bind local variables. The specification that we give allows attribute-matching only, but, as we have observed, this is very similar to the situation found in two other systems, so we feel that the slight loss of generality it tolerable. In any case, if variables are to be bound, the binding can occur when preconditions are evaluated: we will be specifying facilities that bind some of the information provided in a triggering event to KSAR attributes (in particular, we will be binding the identifier of the triggering entry, its abstraction level, and, optionally, the triggering attribute), so later access is not rendered impossible.

For our specification of Knowledge Source triggers, we are going to make the assumption that, in the case of NEW events, the newly created entry has already been added to the blackboard. This assumption allows us to assume that we can immediately access the entry via its identifier, and that it will remain on the blackboard for inspection by preconditions (thus, Knowledge Source-local variables can be bound to values contained in the entry). In the case of ADD and MODIFY events, the entry is, in any case, already present on the blackboard.

We will define the types we require for triggers and then discuss them. We begin the definitions with two primitive types:

$$[TATTR, TVAL]$$

$TATTR$ is the type which represents *Trigger ATTributes*. $TVAL$ is the set of trigger values. We are assuming (another!) attribute-value representation for triggers. It will come as no surprise to the reader, then, that the definition of the basic trigger type is:

$$TRIGGEREL == TATTR \nrightarrow TVAL$$

The definition of $TRIGGEREL$ is similar to that for $ENTRY$, and we will be using some of the standard techniques for handling partial functions.

Before going on, we need to make some observations about our representation of triggers and some constraints that we impose on the basic types.

We are interpreting triggers as sets of attribute-value pairs. A trigger evaluates to *true* if and only if all of the values it specifies are satisfied by the current event. Events have properties, some of which are possessed by all events. All events have a type (the values of the type are NEW, ADD, and MODIFY), and all events occur at *exactly one* level of abstraction (this is an immediate consequence of the fact that entries can reside on just one abstraction level). For ADD and MODIFY events, the event also mentions the attribute that was added or modified.

A Knowledge Source trigger refers to this information: the Knowledge Source can trigger when some conditions are true—the conditions are expressed in the form of the type and location of an event, and, depending upon the event type, on the attribute that has been modified or added. This formulation is related to the problem of focus-of-attention in blackboard systems: it is necessary to focus attention in the form of local problem-solving activity in order that only the most promising regions of the search space are explored. By concentrating on just one, or on just a few abstraction levels, Knowledge Sources can be written in such a way that the knowledge that they contain can be made highly situation-specific. Another reason for interpreting triggers in this way is to do with knowledge representation: if we assume that the sets of attributes that are permitted on distinct abstraction levels are disjoint, then we can see that the kinds of object that can be represented will vary between levels. Since the knowledge representation is abstraction level-specific, it is necessary that Knowledge Sources be able to interpret the information encoded at given levels of abstraction in order to make problem-solving moves. This suggests that Knowledge Sources be triggered on one or on only a few of the possible abstraction levels. This last point will be taken up again when we complete our definition of the trigger type.

The values that trigger attributes can take must range over entry identifiers, event types and abstraction level identifiers. That is, we could write the *TATTR* type as:

$$TATTR == ATTR \cup LEVID \cup BBEVENT$$

This definition suggests, correctly, that trigger attributes specify the event type and abstraction level identifier as well as the name of the attribute which caused an event. If we were to add a general facility for inspecting entry attributes, we would need to add the *VAL* type to the last definition. The addition of an inspection facility is not very difficult: it requires that we employ the value-extracting operation on the other attributes in the trigger. We can assume that the identifier of the event-causing entry is available to the trigger (the definition of the event system makes this explicit), so we could extract information. Such an extraction process does not gain us very much, however, for we cannot execute arbitrary predicates in triggers: we would be reduced to simple symbol-matching as our only comparison operation. For that reason, we have decided not to permit arbitrary attributes to appear in triggers. The definition of *TATTR* that we have given in this paragraph will, then, be adequate for our present needs.

We have observed that Knowledge Sources might be interested in events on more than one abstraction level. If they are interested in more than one level, it makes perfect sense for them to be interested in more than one event type. Knowledge Sources can be interested in different types on the *same* abstraction level, it should be pointed out: we can handle this using the scheme that we are adopting here. This has the consequence that we will need to store the event type that caused triggering in the KSARs which are thus created. It also has the consequence that the type we gave above for triggers is inadequate. If Knowledge Sources are to be triggered on more than one level, we can consider triggers to be composed of *sets* of trigger tables. This gives us the full type for triggers:

$$TRIGSPEC == \mathbb{P} \; TRIGGEREL$$

In words, we have the statement that a Knowledge Source trigger is composed of a set of trigger elements. Each trigger element defines a situation on the blackboard in terms of a few attributes.

Our interpretation of $TRIGGEREL$ is that the current event must have attributes which match *all* of the attributes in an element of $TRIGGEREL$.

The natural interpretation of the interpretation of $TRIGSPEC$ is that it represents a disjunction: it is satisfied when at least one of its elements is satisfied (below, we will ignore the case in which more than one element is satisfied, for this causes severe complications and is only possible in parallel implementations—our current specification deals only with the case in which triggers are evaluated as soon as events occur). We have to take into account the case in which a Knowledge Source is interested in *all* events that occur (a termination Knowledge Source is one example of this): this amounts to having a Knowledge Source whose trigger is always *true* (i.e., is satisfied by all events). We will define the perpetually satisfied trigger as the empty trigger. There is no need to take the case of the perpetually false trigger into account. If a Knowledge Source ever had such a trigger, it would never be executed.

In order to determine whether a trigger is satisfied by the current event, we need to access the attributes and values in an element of the trigger. We are going to assume that each trigger element has a standard structure (which is not an unreasonable assumption, given the above discussion). We will need to gain access to the attributes in a trigger element: this is done using the fact that a trigger element is a function. We do, though, need to define three constants: these constants are the names of the standard attributes that appear in triggers.

$$\boxed{event, level, attr : TATTR}$$

(Strictly speaking, we have defined three *variables*, but we have no other way of defining them, for we have not defined what a constant of type *TATTR* looks like. The fact that they are Z variables does not matter to us.)

We are now in a position to define the trigger evaluation schema. This schema makes the assumption that the triggers for Knowledge Sources can be obtained in some way, and that they are bound to one of its input variables (*trig?*). We note at this point that the schema will be employed within the scope of a quantifier ranging over all the Knowledge Sources in the system, so one trigger at a time is evaluated. The schema's predicate is a disjunction, with one disjunct each for the case of the empty trigger (which is always satisfied), for the case in which the latest event is a NEW event, and a disjunction for the other two event types. The schema is:

$$
\begin{array}{l}
\underline{EvalKSTrigger}\\
\quad trig? : TRIGSPEC\\
\quad ev? : BBEVENT\\
\quad lev? : LEVID\\
\quad a? : ATTR\\
\hline
\quad (trig? = \varnothing)\ \vee\\
\quad (ev? = newev) \Rightarrow\\
\qquad (\exists\, t : TRIGGEREL \mid t \in trig?\ \bullet\\
\qquad\qquad t(event) = ev?\ \wedge\\
\qquad\qquad t(level) = lev?)\ \vee\\
\quad (ev? = addev) \vee (ev? = modev) \Rightarrow\\
\qquad (\exists\, t : TRIGGEREL \mid t \in trig?\ \bullet\\
\qquad\qquad t(event) = ev?\ \wedge\\
\qquad\qquad t(level) = lev?\ \wedge\\
\qquad\qquad t(attr) = attr?)
\end{array}
$$

The structure of the schema is clear: it accounts for each possible kind of permitted trigger. The reader should note that in the case of a NEW event, the attribute variable a? is merely ignored.

We will use this schema when we create KSARs. Thus, we will not hide any of the inputs to *EvalKSTrigger* at this point (although we may wish to later). *EvalKSTrigger* will be composed with the KSAR creation schema: precisely what goes into a KSAR will depend upon the type of event that caused it to be created, so the reader can expect some further testing of the event type (this is particularly true for the empty trigger, since the information that is recorded in the KSAR will depend upon the event type—with triggers that specify event types, we know *a priori* what must be recorded). It is again emphasised that re-testing is not necessarily inelegant, for we are dealing with a mathematical model, and not implemented code, so time is not an issue.

Before moving on, it is important to note that there can be no possibility for error in event types. This is because we have defined the event type exhaustively. Had we allowed the user to define application-specific event types (as is permitted in AGE (Nii, 1979) or BB1 (Hayes-Roth, 1985)), there may have been the need to include an *undefined* type and to check for errors. Such a definition might take the form of a set:

$$[USERDEF\_EVENTS]$$

together with partitions which are mapped onto the three primitive blackboard modifying operations. We concentrate in our specification on just three event types for reasons of simplicity, although the reader might like to define additional structures to handle user-defined operation types and to map them onto the schemata that we have defined here.

4.5.2   KSAR Creation

We have defined KSARs as mappings from a set of KSAR attributes to a set of permissible values. Here, we define the operation which creates KSARs. This operation amounts to the setting of values for some special KSAR attributes. The special attributes are:

- Knowledge Source name (*ks_name*): the identifier of the Knowledge Source whose triggering has caused this KSAR to be created.

- *cycle_no*: the number of the interpreter cycle on which the KSAR was created. The interpreter is built around a main loop which invokes the triggering, scheduling and action-execution modules; the iterations of this loop are counted, and it is this that is referred to as the cycle number.

- *event_no*: the number of the event which caused the KSAR to be created: this is the number of the event in the cycle with number (i.e., event numbers are reset to zero at the end of each cycle).

- *event_type*: the type of the event which caused the KSAR to be created.

- *event_level*: the name of the abstraction level on which the creating event occurred.

- *event_entry*: the identifier of the entry whose creation or update caused the creating event.

- *event_attribute*: the identifier of the attribute whose addition or modification caused the creating event—this KSAR attribute is set only when the creating event is *not* NEW.

- *ksar_id*: the identifier of the KSAR. We will merely assume that all KSARs are assigned a unique name when they are created.

In addition to these attributes, we might want to define an attribute *ksar_name* to give KSARs unique identifiers. The identifier creation mechanism we used for entries can be replicated to provide unique identifiers in this case, also.

We will use the schemata we defined when we first specified KSARs. We omitted a schema for KSAR creation on the grounds that we wished to leave our options open until we had more information about what we wanted KSARs to contain when they were created. We will use the *InitKSAR* schema as a basis for our specification.

We will begin with a new schema:

```
┌─ AddKSARSlots ──────────────────────────────────
│ ΔKSAR
│ newksarslots? : KSARATTR ↛ KSARVAL
├──────────────────────────────────────────────────
│ ksarslots' = ksarslots ∪ newksarslots?
└──────────────────────────────────────────────────
```

We can now prove the following result:

Theorem 14

$$AddKSARSlots \vdash \# \operatorname{dom} ksarslots' \geq \# \operatorname{dom} ksarslots$$

PROOF   By definition,

$$ksarslots' = ksarslot \cup newksarslots?$$

So,

$$\# \operatorname{dom} ksarslots$$
$$= \# \operatorname{dom} ksarslots + \# \operatorname{dom} newksarslots?$$

Since $\# \operatorname{dom} newksarslots \geq 0$,

$$\# \operatorname{dom} ksarslots' \geq \# \operatorname{dom} ksarslots$$

□

The creation schema merely inputs values for the attributes listed above. We will assume that they have been defined as constants. We then have:

InitKSARSlotVals _____

$crslots, newksarslots! : KSARATTR \nrightarrow KSARVAL$

$ksid? : KSID$

$cycno?, evno? : \mathbb{N}$

$ev? : BBEVENT$

$lev? : LEVID$

$a? : ATTR$

$crslots =$

$\{ ks\_name \mapsto ksid?,$

$cycle\_no \mapsto cycno?,$

$event\_no \mapsto evno?,$

$event\_type \mapsto ev?,$

$event\_level \mapsto lev? \}$

$(ev? = newev \Rightarrow newksarslots! = crslots) \vee$

$(ev? = addev) \vee (ev? = modev) \Rightarrow$

$newksarslots! =$

$crslots \cup \{ event\_attribute \mapsto a? \}$

We can now define the KSAR creation schema:

$$CreateKSAR \;\widehat{=}\; InitKSAR \;\fatsemi\; InitKSARSlotVals \;\fatsemi\; AddKSARSlots$$

We have used sequential composition here because we are specifying the order in which these operations take place. We can expand the definition to give:

$$
\begin{array}{l}
\underline{\quad CreateKSAR \quad}\\[4pt]
ksarslots, ksarslots', ksar! : KSARATTR \nrightarrow KSARVAL\\
crslots : KSARATTR \nrightarrow KSARVAL\\
ksid? : KSID\\
cycno?, evno? : \mathbb{N}\\
ev? : BBEVENT\\
lev? : LEVID\\
a? : ATTR\\[4pt]
\hline\\[-6pt]
\exists\, ksarslots^+, known\_ksarslots^+,\\
\qquad newksarslots^+ : KSARATTR \nrightarrow KSARVAL \bullet\\
\quad known\_ksarslots = \varnothing \wedge\\
\quad crslots =\\
\qquad \{\ ks\_name \mapsto ksid?,\\
\qquad\quad cycle\_no \mapsto cycno?,\\
\qquad\quad event\_no \mapsto evno?,\\
\qquad\quad event\_type \mapsto ev?,\\
\qquad\quad event\_level \mapsto lev?\ \} \wedge\\
\quad ((ev? = newev \Rightarrow\\
\qquad\quad newksarslots^+ = crslots) \vee\\
\qquad (ev? = addev) \vee (ev? = modev) \Rightarrow\\
\qquad\quad newksarslots^+ =\\
\qquad\qquad crslots \cup \{\ event\_attribute \mapsto a?\ \}) \wedge\\
\quad (ksarslots^+ =\\
\qquad\quad ksarslots \cup newksarslots^+ \wedge\\
\quad known\_ksarslots^+ = \mathrm{dom}\, ksarslots^+)\\
\quad \wedge\\
\quad (ksarslots' = ksarslots^+ \wedge\\
\quad known\_ksarslots' = \mathrm{dom}\, ksarslots'\\
\quad ksar! = ksarslots')
\end{array}
$$

This schema looks forbidding, but a little simplification shows that it is what we required.

We are therefore in a position to use the KSAR created by the above schema in the rest of our specification. In particular, we can add it to the control database that contains newly triggered KSARs and KSARs whose preconditions have yet to be satisfied (i.e., to the *triggered list*). We will specify the control databases below, and will make use of *CreateKSAR* when we do so.

4.6   Knowledge Source Actions

In this section, we are going to specify the components of Knowledge Source actions (henceforth, simply *actions*). The reader will remember that it is the action that causes changes to the state of the global blackboard database. Our model of a Knowledge Source action is as a set of production rules: this model is becoming relatively standard (it is to be found in AGE (Nii, 1979), CAGE (Nii, 1989), BB1 (Hayes-Roth, 1985) and NBB (Craig, 1987)), so we adopt it. The production rule representation has advantages over the other primary candidate (programming language procedures): principally, it has the advantage that the action is decomposed into relatively small, independent components that can easily be read, understood and updated by people. In addition, the use of production rules poses some interesting problems from the point of view of their formal specification.

4.6.1   Conditions

As we discussed above (Chapter 3), the condition-part of a production rule (which we will abbreviate to *condition*) and the precondition of an entire Knowledge Source are very similar in operation. Both examine the blackboard state. In our specification of the blackboard architecture, we have decided to omit preconditions (although we will, of course, need a third component when we specify CASSANDRA Knowledge Sources because of the need for handling communications in a safe manner). The reason for this is that the rules in the action can perform exactly the same checks as those performed by a precondition: we may view the precondition as being an efficiency-improving device because it removes the overhead of performing the same checks in all the rules in an action. We can think of the precondition as being an applicability test which is performed before rule conditions are evaluated.

   Now, this decision quite clearly will impact on the way in which we create KSARs, and on the control databases into which they are placed.

In our "standard" interpretation, we place KSARs into a triggered list as soon as their trigger has evaluated to *true*; next, the precondition is evaluated, and if it is satisfied, the KSAR is placed in an eligible list where it is rated against scheduler criteria for execution. In the "non-standard" or "rational" interpretation that we adopt here, eligibility is a matter of rule-condition satisfaction. We would normally only rate those KSARs whose preconditions were satisfied by the current blackboard state. Now, we have a choice. We can do either of the following:

1. We can place all KSARs in a triggered list when they are created. Next, we can evaluate the conditions in their rules. Those KSARs whose rule conditions are satisfied are placed in an eligible list and rated against scheduler criteria. One or more KSARs are then executed to cause blackboard changes.

2. We can place all KSARs in a triggered list when they are created. The triggered list can be ordered against operative scheduler criteria, and one or more KSAR actions executed on this basis.

The second alternative is the one chosen for AGE (Nii, 1979) and for HASP/SIAP (Feigenbaum, 1982). In those systems, *all* KSARs that could be executed were then executed. We, on the other hand, are going to adopt the first alternative because it entails finer control over actions, *even though* it also entails a decoupling of rule condition and action. We believe that the second alternative needs to be backed up by mechanisms that we are not going to specify: in particular, it requires content-addressability for rules. Our choice has the advantages that the architecture is conceptually simpler, and that the specification does not become excessively complex.

We can become considerably clearer about these operations once we have explained our interpretation of production rules. The reader should note that the account we give here is considerably simpler than the one we would give if we were giving a specification of a system that relied entirely upon production rules—in particular, we need only specify a simple control mechanism for rules (although we have the option of extending this, should we desire).

We are going to consider production rules as being composed of a set C of conditions, and a sequence A of actions. Initially, our attention will focus on the conditions. We will assume that each condition is either a *positive* relation or a *negative* one: a *negative* relation has the form $\neg\ p$ where p is a positive relation (in other words, positive relations are un-negated). We will assume that if $C = \{c_i \mid 0 \le i \le n\}$ for some n, the interpretation of the condition is:

> C evaluates to *true* if and only if: for all i $(1 \le i \le n)$, c_i evaluates to *true*.

In other words, a condition is satisfied by the current blackboard state if and only if all of its components are satisfied by the current blackboard state. This implies that the interpretation of rule conditions is as a logical *conjunction*. That is to say:

C is *true* just in case
$$c_1 \wedge c_2 \wedge \ldots \wedge c_n$$
is *true*.

Below, we will define an operator which defines the *distributed conjunction* of a set (actually a sequence) of propositions.

Although it is well known that we can construct an adequate system for propositional calculus using only the connectives $\wedge$ and $\neg$, in practice it is extremely convenient to have disjunction $(\vee)$ at our disposal. It might be thought that disjunction is essential for the proper specification of rule conditions. Here, we are adopting a conjunction-based interpretation, so we need to show that disjunctions can be handled. Our interpretation amounts to the standard one that separate rules can be used to represent disjunctions. Although this is a common approach, it is, perhaps, worthwhile just to outline it, so that the reader is clear about what we intend.

Consider the rule:

$$(c_1 \wedge c_2) \vee (c_3 \wedge \neg\ c_4) \rightarrow A_1\ A_2$$

(We assume that negation binds tightest.) The actions A_1 and A_2 will be executed whenever $(c_1 \wedge c_2)$ is satisfied or whenever $(c_2 \wedge \neg\ c_4)$ is satisfied. The same effect can be obtained from:

$$
\begin{aligned}
c_1 \wedge c_2 &\rightarrow A_1\ A_2 \\
c_3 \wedge \neg\ c_4 &\rightarrow A_1\ A_2
\end{aligned}
$$

The two rules that we have created obviously have the same effect as the rule we gave at the start. Indeed, they are equivalent to it because of the way in which we interpret rules: we assume that if the condition of one rule is not satisfied, we merely pass to the next rule in the set and see whether it is satisfied. This amounts to a disjunctive interpretation for rules in a set of rules. Notice that *both* of the above rules may be executed if all of c_1, c_2, c_3 and $\neg\ c_4$ are *true*—this is because we are still assuming an *inclusive* interpretation of disjunction.

It needs to be stated that we cannot exclude negation from our interpretation. We need *at least* two primitive sentential connectives upon which to base our interpretation (unless we adopt a combined interpretation for a connective—we could always adopt joint denial (*NAND*) as our primitive, but we perfer to stay with the classical connectives). We need a way, therefore, of encoding negations in our condition elements. This poses a problem, for there is no obvious way of doing this in Z: we cannot use a free type, because free types do not automatically give us predicates for determining what the truth value of a particular expression is. In addition, we are dealing with operation schemata for the condition elements: although a schema determines a type, it is not clear how to extract the truth-value from the operation. Also, there is the fact that we very often want to bind variables as part of the condition-evaluation process. A careful examination of the types of the various schemata that we want to employ in conditions reveals that they have a number of different types: this entails that we require what amount to polymorphic types for condition elements, a feature which Z supports only through generic definitions. We could stipulate the *kinds* of condition element that we are going to support: it would then be up to the user to ensure that all application-specific conditions satisfied the constraints that we impose. We are, in short, faced with the problem of specifying a kind of interpreter for conditions. This is no mean task, and, before going into details, we will specify the basic mechanisms which we will use for evaluating the truth-value of rule conditions.

To begin with, we need to define a truth-value type. We believe that we cannot use the constants *true* and *false* provided by Z because they belong to the meta-language: what we believe that we are using is the object-level, and these constants do not belong there. In addition, Z does not provide an *undefined* truth-value, which we will need when we attempt the specification of the CASSANDRA architecture, so we define our own values:

$$CONDTV ::= ctrue \mid cfalse$$

The type $CONDTV$ is the type of truth-values that condition elements return. We can define a function $cnot$ to represent negation as follows:

$$cnot : CONDTV \rightarrow CONDTV$$

$$cnot(ctrue) = cfalse$$
$$cnot(cfalse) = ctrue$$

We can also define a conjunction function for $CONDTV$: this function is directly analogous to conjunction in a standard two-valued logic:

$$cand : CONDTV \rightarrow CONDTV$$

$$cand(ctrue, ctrue) = ctrue$$
$$cand(cfalse, ctrue) = cfalse$$
$$cand(ctrue, cfalse) = cfalse$$
$$cand(cfalse, cfalse) = cfalse$$

Because of the approach we are taking to disjunction, there is no need for us to define a disjunction operator.

When we come to specify the CASSANDRA architecture, we will need to extend the definition of $CONDTV$ to include a value for *undefined*: this extension will require the re-definition of the $cnot$ and $cand$ functions.

We will need a distributed $cand$ operation below (we call it $\backslash cand$) We define it as:

$$\backslash cand : \mathrm{seq}\ CONDTV \rightarrow CONDTV$$

$$\backslash cand(\langle\rangle) = ctrue$$
$$\backslash cand(\langle h\rangle \frown t) = cand(h, \backslash cand(t))$$

The definition of this operation is important in our account of rule conditions because we are going to specify their interpretation as a two-stage process. In the first stage, we obtain the truth-values of all the elements in the condition: because we are allowing variable binding to occur in condition elements, we are forced to treat condition elements as sequences of predicates, relations and assignments. In other words, we are forced to define conditions as:

$$CONDITION \ == \ \mathrm{seq}\ CondElem$$

with the understanding that the null sequence always denotes *ctrue*. Once we have evaluated a condition-part, we have a collection of truth-values (actually, values in *CONDTV*), so we expect the evaluation operation to have the basic type:

$$eval\_conds : CONDITION \ \to \ \mathrm{seq}\ CONDTV$$

In the definition of *eval_conds*, we will map the empty condition onto the value $\langle ctrue \rangle$ so that the *n*-way conjunction operator gives the correct results. We could define $\backslash cand$ in a slightly different way:

$$
\begin{array}{|l}
\hline
\backslash cand : \mathrm{seq}_1\ CONDTV \ \to \ CONDTV \\
\hline
\backslash cand \langle v \rangle = v \\
\backslash cand \langle h \rangle \ ^\frown t = cand(h, \backslash cand(t)) \\
\end{array}
$$

but that would entail slightly nastier inductive proofs. In addition, we need to specify the fact that the value of the empty sequence is just the identity on the last element: i.e., that

$$\backslash cand \langle v \rangle \ ^\frown \langle \rangle = cand(v, v)$$

Using the first version of $\backslash cand$, we can prove its correctness in the sense that we can prove that for any sequence, it reduces that sequence to a single truth-value:

Theorem 15 *For all* $\sigma : \mathrm{seq}\ CONDTV,$

$$\backslash cand(\sigma) = ctrue$$

or

$$\backslash cand(\sigma) = cfalse$$

PROOF   By induction on $\#\sigma$.

(1) $\#\sigma = 0$, $\sigma = \langle\rangle$, $\backslash cand\langle\rangle = ctrue$.

(2) $\#\sigma = 1$, $\sigma(\langle v\rangle)$, $\backslash cand(v, ctrue)$.

   1. if $v = ctrue$, $cand(ctrue, ctrue) = ctrue$.

   2. if $v = cfalse$, $cand(cfalse, ctrue) = cfalse$.

(3) (Induction step.) $\#\sigma = k$, $\sigma = \langle v\rangle \frown t$, $\#t = k - 1$.

$$\backslash cand(\sigma) = cand(v, \backslash cand(t))$$

Assume $\backslash cand(t) = ctrue$. Then, if $v = ctrue$,

$$\backslash cand(\sigma) = ctrue$$

otherwise:

$$\backslash cand(\sigma) = cfalse$$

If $\backslash cand(t) = cfalse$, then $\backslash cand(\sigma) = cfalse$. $\square$

We can define a reduction operation for conditions as follows. We evaluate the elements of the condition to obtain a sequence of truth-values. We then apply the distributed conjunction operator to give the final value for the condition as a whole. We can express this in an extensional form as:

$$\begin{array}{|l}
reduceCond : \operatorname{seq} CONDTV \rightarrow CONDTV \\
\hline
\forall c : \operatorname{seq} CONDTV \bullet \\
\quad reduceCond(c) = \backslash cand(c)
\end{array}$$

Note that we are expressing the fact that $reduceCond$ is a function by requiring that evey domain element maps to a *unique* range element. Note, also, that before applying $reduceCond$, we do not need to map the empty sequence onto $\langle ctrue\rangle$ because of our definition of $\backslash cand$.

Theorem 16 *For all σ: seq CONDTV,*

$$reduceCond\sigma = ctrue$$

or

$$reduceCond\sigma = cfalse$$

PROOF   By theorem 15. □

In order to go further than this, we need to make a number of assumptions, and we need to admit that there is a limit to what can be done. We need to assume that every element in a rule's condition outputs a value in *CONDTV*. This is because the blackboard interpreter needs a value which it can use to determine whether the condition element is satisfied by the current state of the blackboard. This assumption appears natural.

The limitation that we must admit is the following: we need to remember at all times that the software we are specifying is generic in nature. That is, we are specifying an interpreter, but one of a rather special kind. We cannot know *in advance* what the particular predicates that will be used by any application will be. That is to say, different applications (i.e., blackboard systems which use the interpreter that we are specifying) will be applied to different problems, and the objects which are required to solve these various problems will entail the use of different predicates and relations in conditions (we have set up the interpreter in such a way that there can only ever be three actions that can be performed, but we do not have this luxury for conditions). Whether the final system be implemented in **ADA**, **C**, **LISP**, or **Prolog**, the application-builder will have to supply his or her own predicates which will test the structures on the blackboard. These predicates cannot be anticipated when we perform the specification, and they represent external code that will have to be linked into the interpreter. Since we cannot tell what a particular application will require of its condition elements, we cannot reasonably expect to be able to give a complete specification of production rule conditions (if we admitted preconditions as separate Knowledge Source components, we would be forced into the same position, for a general precondition can call any predicate that is necessary).

Quite clearly, this concession imposes constraints on what we can do in our specification. Essentially, there are two paths that we can follow.

- The first approach is to add another interpreter to our blackboard system interpreter: this second interpreter is concerned with providing a language for expressing rule conditions. Such a language would provide the user with facilities for defining the relations and predicates that are to be used as condition elements. We might expect that this language be compiled down into the language used for implementing the blackboard system interpreter. The definition of an adequate language for rule conditions is not particularly difficult, and we could specify interpretation rules which would have to be followed when determining the truth-value of rule conditions.

- The second approach is to define an interface standard that *must* be met by *all* elements of a rule condition. This allows the user to introduce arbitrary code into the blackboard system. If we were thinking operationally, this approach has considerable advantages because it allows users to introduce code written in their favourite programming language, and it does not require the user to learn a new language and then to have to work around its inevitable limitations. In addition, this approach has the merit that it allows the user to interface the blackboard system to external databases and information sources. If we designed a special-purpose language for conditions, we would have to face the fact that, at some stage, we would have to accommodate this need.

We are going to follow the second path and give an interface standard. This standard needs to be such that any appropriate code can be used in a rule's condition. We do need safety factors, however: in particular, we require that the following obtain:

1. *No* condition element may alter the blackboard state: the blackboard is, therefore, a *read-only* structure.

2. *All* code that is used in condition elements must return a value that represents the satisfaction of the condition element given the blackboard state.

The first condition entails that all condition elements must include $\Xi Blackboard$ in their specification. The second entails that there must be a standard result variable, say *cval!*, which represents the result of evaluating the condition element: *cval!* must be of type $CONDTV$.

These are the weakest conditions that we can stipulate for user-defined condition elements. In some applications, it will be necessary for condition elements to access control databases. In these cases, they may not update any values they find there. We cannot know in advance which condition elements will need to access control databases, so we believe that we may only impose the condition on the blackboard.

With these constraints now stated, we are in a position to define the condition element schema in Z. We will first give the schema and then discuss it.

$$
\begin{array}{|l}
\hline
\quad CondElem \underline{\hspace{6cm}} \\
\;\; \Xi Blackboard \\
\;\; e? : EID \\
\;\; l? : LEVID \\
\;\; as? : \mathbb{P}(ATTR \times \mathbb{P}\; VAL) \\
\;\; res! : CONDTV \\
\hline
\;\; as? \neq \varnothing \\
\;\; 1 \leq l? \leq numlevels \\
\;\; \exists\, ABSLEV \mid ABSLEV = levels(l?) \; \bullet \\
\qquad e? \in knownents \;\wedge \\
\qquad \exists\, ENTRY \mid ENTRY = entries(e?) \; \bullet \\
\qquad\quad \exists\, avp : (ATTR \times VAL); \\
\qquad\qquad\quad a : ATTR; \; vs : \mathbb{P}\; VAL \mid \\
\qquad\qquad a = first(avp) \;\wedge \\
\qquad\qquad vs = second(avp) \; \bullet \\
\qquad\quad (\,a \in knownslots \wedge slots(a) \in vs \;\wedge \\
\qquad\qquad res! = ctrue\,) \;\vee \\
\qquad\quad (\,a \notin knownslots \wedge res! = cfalse\,) \;\vee \\
\qquad\quad (\,a \in knownents \wedge slots(a) \notin vs \;\wedge \\
\qquad\qquad res! = cfalse\,) \\
\hline
\end{array}
$$

The first thing to note is the basic similarity with the schema for *Find*. In this case, also, we define the operation in terms of the graph of a relation. The schema has three input variables, the first is the entry identifier, the second the abstraction level on which this entry resides, and the third is a set of pairs. The pairs are composed of a first element which is an attribute identifier (a value of type *ATTR*, in other words), and the second is a set of values (a set $\mathbb{P}\; VAL$).

The justification of the schema is as follows. Unless a condition element is performing a Find operation, it must *always* refer to a specific entry on the blackboard, and it must do so by name. That means that the name of the entry must be supplied to the condition element. Condition elements are intended to examine the blackboard and determine whether the value stored in an attribute (i.e., a slot) of the named entry has some property. Condition elements can, quite easily, be seen as relations between entry identifiers, attribute names and possible values. We have interpreted the test on the value stored in an attribute in terms of the set of all values which could be stored there and which would fall within the relation: in other words, the form of the test is such that we are, in fact, testing the value actually stored in the attribute to see whether it is in the extension of the relation.

It must be noted that this scheme only allows us to represent first-order relations. It might also be thought only to allow predicates (i.e., unary relation symbols). This is not the case because the definition given above is in terms of the *extension* of the relation that we are actually representing. We could define an additional schema which uses the following type:

$$CPOSSVAL == \mathbb{P}\,(\mathbb{P}\ VAL \times \mathbb{P}\ VAL)$$

```
┌─ RelCondElem ─────────────────────────────
│  ΞBlackboard
│  e? : EID
│  l? : LEVID
│  as? : ℙ(ATTR × CPOSSVAL)
│  res! : CONDTV
│ ──────────────────────────────────────────
│                 etc.
└────────────────────────────────────────────
```

If we consider an n-ary relation R, such that $R(x_1, \ldots, x_n)$, then we can consider the assignments that satisfy R as being partitioned into a set of values for $x_1, \ldots, x_{n-1}$, and a set for x_n. In the definition of *RelCondElem*, we give the sets of sets of values for the first $n-1$ arguments, and a set for x_n. We assume that the value that is actually stored in the slot corresponds to the value of x_n, and so we test on it. This test is identical to the one for *CondElem*, so we can see that the latter schema is equivalent. The difference between the two schemata is that *RelCondElem* explicitly provides the redundant values (even though they are held constant for each value set *vs*), whereas *CondElem* does not. By this argument, it can be seen that *CondElem* provides the facilities for representing *n*-ary relations, and not just predicates. It is still the case, however, that *CondElem* is restricted to first-order relations.

The final point is that the variable *res!* is used to communicate the result of the condition test to the rule condition evaluation mechanism. As we will see, conditions are represented as sequences of *CondElems* and sequences of truth-values are returned by the evaluation process. The truth-value return is performed using the result variable.

It should be emphasised that condition-elements typically test the values stored in attributes. This is the main way in which rule conditions interact with the contents of the blackboard. It might be objected that there is no provision for "link-chasing": that is to say, the above schema does not allow entry references to be followed so that solution islands can be explored. The reader should remember that we have chosen not to specify the structure of the *VAL* type: we have always had in mind the fact that the attribute name type should be a sub-type of *VAL* (i.e., $ATTR \subset VAL$).

In addition, we are not considering the case of condition-elements that represent tests on values proper (for example, if v_1 and v_2 are integers, we are not taking a relation like $v_1 \leq v_2$ into account). We argue that we *can* represent such relations using the *CondElem* schema, even though it involves a blackboard access: this is because one of v_1 and v_2 must be obtained from the blackboard (typically, both values would be), and this clearly opens the way for the above schema to be used. There will be, in general, relations that should be expressed, but which cannot be expressed in terms of the above. Such relations are application-specific and deal with external databases, for example. We could provide a general specification for such condition-elements, but we do not choose to do so. This is for two reasons. The first is that such an extension would complicate the specification greatly, and would obscure the points that we wish to make. The second is that, at this stage, we are ignorant of the interfaces that must be provided. What we can do, however, is to provide an invariant schema and require that *all* condition-elements that deal with external structures preserve this invariant. The invariant is:

$$
\begin{aligned}
&InvCondElem \;\widehat{=} \\
&\qquad \Xi Blackboard \;\wedge \\
&\qquad (\forall\, l : 1 \,..\, numlevels; \; \Xi Blackboard \mid \\
&\qquad\qquad ABSLEV = levels(i) \;\bullet \\
&\qquad\qquad \Xi ABSLEV \;\wedge \\
&\qquad\qquad (\forall\, e : EID; \; \Xi ENTRY \mid \\
&\qquad\qquad\qquad ENTRY = entries(e) \;\bullet \\
&\qquad\qquad \Xi ENTRY))
\end{aligned}
$$

The schema simply (!) states that the blackboard and all of its contents remain invariant under the externally-defined condition-element: that is, no externally-define condition-element may alter the blackboard or its contents in any way at all.

This invariant schema is only part of the issue, however, since, for any externally-defined condition-element schema Sc, we require a proof that:

$$Sc \Rightarrow InvCondElem$$

We can now prove three results about *CondElem*.

Theorem 17 *Provided that* dom *entries* $\neq \emptyset$ *for some abstraction level* $l?$, *then* $res! = cfalse$, *or* $res! = ctrue$

PROOF   Assume that $ent = levels(l?).entries$, which is reasonable by the definition of the schema and by the theorem statement. (Note that we use the dot notation for referencing schema variables: this operation gives access to the components of the signature of the schema in question—$levels(l?)$ has a schema as its value.)

By propositional calculus, we have:

- If $a \in$ dom ent and $ent(a) \in vs$, $res! = ctrue$.

- If $a \in$ dom ent, but $ent(a) \notin vs$, $res! = ctrue$.

- If $a \notin$ dom ent, $res! = cfalse$.

□

Theorem 18

$$\vdash (InitBlackboard \;\mathbin{\raise.3ex\hbox{$\scriptstyle\S$}}\; CondElem) \Rightarrow \neg \; CondElem$$

PROOF   This theorem merely states that any test of a condition-element will fail if it is applied to a newly initialized blackboard (i.e., one that contains no entries).

Since, for all i, $1 \leq i \leq numlevels$,

$$\text{dom } entries = \varnothing = knownents$$

we have:

$$e? \notin \text{dom } entries$$
$$= e? \notin knownents$$

so the predicate of *CondElem* is false. □

Theorem 19 *For any initialised blackboard that contains entries, and for all entries on the blackboard, the predicate of CondElem is satisfied.*

PROOF   For the predicate of *CondElem* to be satisfied, *res!* = *ctrue* or *res!* = *cfalse*.

The situations in which the predicate is false are the following:

1. There are no entries on the blackboard.

2. $e?$ is not an element of *knownents* in the abstraction level indexed by $l?$.

(1) is ruled out by the previous theorem. By that result, if the blackboard contains no entries, *CondElem* cannot be satisfied.

By the schema for *CondElem*, the abstraction level identifier must be valid. In addition, the schema requires that *as?* be non-empty. There remains only the case in which the specified abstraction level is empty (*knownents* = $\varnothing$), which is a reasonable demand.

For the schema to be true, there must be entries on the specified abstraction level, and so *CondElem* binds *res!* to either *ctrue* or *cfalse*.

In both of these cases, the predicate as a whole is satisfied, and so is true. □

Now we are in a position to define the condition type for production rules as:

$$CONDITION == \text{seq } CondElem$$

(this is the definition we gave above). It can be noted here that this choice of representation has interesting consequences. As we will see below, the schema that we define for the evaluation of conditions iterates along the sequence in index order (i.e., from least to greatest index value). Given the invariant that all conditions must satisfy (*InvCondElem*, that is), there is no reason at all why some other order cannot be used—we could, in fact, represent objects of type *CONDITION* as sets of *CONDELEM* to emphasize this fact. The most interesting consequence of this fact is that condition elements can be evaluated in parallel. Now, we have chosen to give a representation which implies sequential execution because Z is not yet equipped with explicit representations of parallel constructs and because we notionally intend the blackboard system to execute on a conventional, serial, processor. This observation is worth remembering: indeed, a careful examination of the specification which we are giving might lead to the discovery of more opportunities for parallelisation.

Now we can define the operation that evaluates a rule's conditions and returns a sequence of truth-values (elements of *CONDTV*). This operation is simple to define, and is exactly the operation that one would expect:

$$
\begin{array}{|l}
CondVal : CONDITION \rightarrow \text{seq } CONDTV \\
\hline
\forall c : CONDITION \bullet \\
\quad c = \langle\rangle \Rightarrow CondVal(c) = \langle ctrue \rangle \\
\quad c \neq \langle\rangle \Rightarrow \\
\quad\quad (\forall i : 1 .. \#c \bullet \\
\quad\quad\quad CondVal(c)(i) = c(i).res!)
\end{array}
$$

The reduction to a single truth-value is achieved by composition with the reduction function:

$$\frac{EvalConds : CONDITION \rightarrow CONDTV}{\begin{array}{l} \forall c : CONDITION \bullet \\ \quad EvalConds(c) = reduceCond(CondVal(c)) \end{array}}$$

We can prove that *EvalConds* yields a value of either *ctrue* or *cfalse* for all conditions.

Theorem 20 *For all c: CONDITION,*

$$EvalConds(c) = ctrue$$

or

$$EvalConds(c) = cfalse$$

PROOF

$$\begin{aligned} EvalConds(c) &= (reduceCond \circ CondVal)(c) && \text{[by definition]} \\ &= reduceCond(CondVal(c)) && \text{[by definition of composition]} \end{aligned}$$

If $c = \langle \rangle$, $CondVal = \langle ctrue \rangle$.

$$\begin{aligned} reduceCond\langle ctrue \rangle &= \backslash cand(\langle ctrue \rangle) \\ &= \backslash cand(\langle ctrue \rangle \frown \langle \rangle) \\ &= \backslash cand(ctrue, \langle \rangle) \\ &= cand(ctrue, ctrue) \\ &= ctrue \end{aligned}$$

Let $\#c = k + 1$, and let $CondVal(c) = \sigma$, $\#\sigma = k + 1$.

$$\sigma = \langle v \rangle \frown t$$

$$\begin{aligned} reduceCond\sigma &= reduceCond\langle v \rangle \frown t \\ &= \backslash cand(\sigma) \\ &= \backslash cand(\langle v \rangle \frown t) \in \{\ ctrue, cfalse\ \} \end{aligned}$$

□

We can now show that the invariant obtains across the evaluation of an element of *CONDITION*, provided that we make the appropriate assumptions.

Theorem 21 *Provided that each user-defined condition element satisfies the invariant CondElem, the evaluation of the condition of each production rule leaves the blackboard invariant.*

PROOF   The proof is by induction on the length of the condition.
Case 1: The rule condition is empty. Then the blackboard is trivially invariant.
Case 2: $\# conditions = 1$. By the statement, we have an invariant blackboard since the condition respects the invariant. We have:

$$condition \Rightarrow InvCondElem^1$$

which is:

$$condition \Rightarrow InvCondElem$$

Case 3: $\# conditions = n$, $n > 1$. Assume that $conditions_i$ $(1 \leq i < n)$ respect the invariant, then:

$$condition_1, \ldots, condition_{n-1}, condition_n \Rightarrow$$
$$InvCondElem^{(n-1)} \wedge InvCondElem$$

Since $InvCondElem$ is idempotent, i.e.,

$$InvCondElem \ \text{\textcommabelow{9}} \ InvCondElem \equiv InvCondElem$$

we have:

$$InvCondElem^{(n-1)} \equiv InvCondElem$$

So,

$$InvCondElem^{(n-1)} \wedge InvCondElem$$
$$\equiv InvCondElem \wedge InvCondElem$$
$$\equiv InvCondElem$$

Which leaves the blackboard invariant for all condition elements in any rule. $\square$

4.6.2   Rule Actions

The situation for rule conditions is complicated by the fact that we have to consider the impact if user-defined code. All we can do in that case is to make stipulations and hope that they will be respected (there is nothing to prevent a user from ignoring our requests). With actions, we are, once again, in full control. For us, the valid actions are those which cause blackboard events: that is, the NEW, ADD, and MODIFY events. This means that our specification need only take these three actions into account—this eases our work considerably, although we do have to remember to include KSAR creation and events.

In order to make our specification of rule actions a little more complete, we will have to define our notion of time. When KSARs are created, they are time-stamped. Part of the concept of time in our blackboard system is the number of events that occur within a given interpreter cycle. Each time an action causes an event, the event counter is incremented: the value of the counter forms part of the creation time of the KSARs which are created as a response to that event. The other counter is the interpreter cycle: it is incremented each time a complete Knowledge Source action is executed (i.e., when all the rules whose conditions are satisfied by the current blackboard state have had their actions executed). The cycle counter represents the number of times the interpreter has executed the loop composed of triggering applicable Knowledge Sources (thereby creating KSARs), matching the rule conditions in all triggered Knowledge Sources (actually KSARs, as we will see), and executing one or more actions. When a KSAR is created, the number of the cycle on which it was created is recorded in it. The cycle counter provides a concept of recency within the interpreter, and, in some schedulers, detailed information about the triggering event is recorded, correlated with the event number within the cycle, and is used to make control decisions.

We define these two counters in the obvious way.

```
┌─ CYCLECOUNT ────────────────────────────────
│ cycno : ℕ
├──────────────────────────────────────────────
│ cycno ≥ 0
└──────────────────────────────────────────────
```

$$\begin{array}{|l}\hline \text{\_\_} EVCOUNT \text{_____} \\ \quad evno : \mathbb{N} \\ \hline \quad evno \geq 0 \\ \hline \end{array}$$

We are going to assume that there is no *a priori* limit on the values that each of these two counters can take.

We define two initialisation schemata:

$$\begin{array}{|l}\hline \text{\_\_} InitCYCLECOUNT \text{_____} \\ \quad CYCLECOUNT \\ \hline \quad cycno = 0 \\ \hline \end{array}$$

Cycle counters can only be initialised once: this is when the interpreter is started.

$$\begin{array}{|l}\hline \text{\_\_} InitEVCOUNT \text{_____} \\ \quad EVCOUNT \\ \hline \quad evno = 0 \\ \hline \end{array}$$

The event counter *must* be re-initialised on every interpreter cycle: this we will do by definition of an increment schema for the cycle counter which also resets the event number. We can define a reset schema for the event counter:

$$\begin{array}{|l}\hline \text{\_\_} ResetEVCOUNT \text{_____} \\ \quad \Delta EVCOUNT \\ \hline \quad evno' = 0 \\ \hline \end{array}$$

The increment schemata are very much as we would expect:

$$\begin{array}{|l}\hline \text{\_\_} IncCYCLECOUNT \text{_____} \\ \quad \Delta CYCLECOUNT \\ \hline \quad cycno' = cycno + 1 \\ \hline \end{array}$$

$$\begin{array}{|l}
\hline \textit{IncEVCOUNT} \underline{\hspace{4cm}} \\
\Delta EVCOUNT \\
\hline
evno' = evno + 1 \\
\hline
\end{array}$$

The combined schema for incrementing the cycle count and setting the event counter to zero is:

$$NextCycle \;\hat{=}\; IncCYCLECOUNT \wedge ResetEVCOUNT$$

We need two enquiry schemata: they allow us access to the cycle and event counts:

$$\begin{array}{|l}
\hline \textit{CycleNo} \underline{\hspace{5cm}} \\
\Xi CYCLECOUNT \\
cycle! : \mathbb{N} \\
\hline
cycle! = cycno \\
\hline
\end{array}$$

$$\begin{array}{|l}
\hline \textit{EventNo} \underline{\hspace{5cm}} \\
\Xi EVCOUNT \\
event! : \mathbb{N} \\
\hline
event! = evno \\
\hline
\end{array}$$

We now have a record of time within the blackboard system at runtime. This allows us to record times in newly created KSARs.

Now, we need to say a few words about the scope of actions. In particular, we need to give a justification for the fact that this section contains considerably more material than would be expected for a task as simple as interpreting the actions in a production rule: the comments at the start of this section lead one to believe that everything is simple. When actions are executed, they cause blackboard events. Each event is located on the blackboard (on a particular—and unique— abstraction level, and within a particular and unique entry) and it is located at a particular time (as defined by the event and cycle counters). This information is of considerable use to the scheduler in any particular blackboard system, because it can support control decisions (the scheduler may be adopting a control regime which prefers some blackboard regions to others—"region" in this context has to be interpreted in a spatio-temporal sense). Indeed, this information is stored in KSARs at creation time. Now, we need to record this information when events occur, so we need to include it in the account we give of action execution. In this particular specification, we have chosen to include KSAR creation and addition to the *triggered* list as part of action execution. We need not have done this, and we could have kept the operations separate: however, at some stage in the specification, we would have had to integrate action execution with KSAR creation and insertion into the triggered list. One very good reason why we should want to include all of these operations in a single module is that they can be viewed as being logically connected: in a sense, they are operations that are performed together as a single operation at the macroscopic level (events "magically" cause KSARs to appear on the triggered list).

We approach the specification as follows. To begin, we will define the basic operation of executing an action in a production rule. This will require that we specify the type we need for rule actions. The action specification involves what would be a disjoint union in another language, and so we need to be a little careful about what we are doing. Once we have the action execution schemata in place, we will integrate the execution of an action with the creation of a set of KSARs and their inclusion in the triggered list. Once we have defined all of this, we can finish the specification of rule actions (which will involve a proof by induction). That will complete our account of actions, and we will be free to specify how rule conditions are linked to actions, and how to interpret the action-part of a Knowledge Source.

When we discussed the event system, we defined three event-causing actions: *BBNewEvent*, *BBAddEvent*, and *BBModEvent*. These actions cause alterations to the blackboard, and they also cause the requisite event. We know that any particular action that can be executed from within a Knowledge Source is one of these event-causing actions, so we naturally come to the conclusion that an action can be defined as:

___ *RuleAction* _____

acttype? : ACT_TYPE

$(acttype? = new \Rightarrow BBNewEvent) \vee$
$(acttype? = add \Rightarrow BBAddEvent) \vee$
$(acttype? = mod \Rightarrow BBModEvent)$

_____

We have called this schema *RuleAction* because it represents the primitive operation which is directly executed in the action-part of a production rule (the set of production rules constitutes the action-part of a Knowledge Source, it should be remembered). Note that we have added a new input variable to enable discrimination between the primitive event-causing actions.

At this point, it is, perhaps, worth reflecting on what we are doing. The schema above looks very much as if it represents *all* of the event-causing operations at the same time: this is, indeed, true. It is true because we are trying to produce a *model* of the blackboard interpreter, and, within the interpreter, any action that occurs within a rule can be exactly one of these primitives. Thus, we would expect any rule action to exhibit one of these behaviours if we had no knowledge about which particular one it is. In effect, *acttype?* tells the action to behave in one way as opposed to another. To us, this seems eminently reasonable.

We can now define the action type for production rules:

$$RULEACT == \text{seq}_1\ RuleAction$$

Note that we require actions to have at least one element: we do not allow *no-ops*, therefore. Each element of a *RULEACT* sequence is a complete schema. This fact must be remembered, as must the fact that each of the component actions in *RuleAction* makes available the following information:

- *ev!*, the event type;

- *lev?*, the abstraction level on which the event occurs;

- *eid!*, the identifier of the entry (newly created in the case of *BB-NewEvent*);

- *a?* and *v?*, the attribute name and value in the cases of the ADD and MODIFY operations.

In addition, the event-causing routines also provide access to the set of attribute-value pairs in the case of a NEW event. From this, it can be seen that *all* the information required to create a KSAR is provided, now that that event and cycle counters have been defined. We can move on to a definition of the triggering process, therefore.

In order to find those Knowledge Sources which are triggered by an event, we need access to the data listed above, and we need access to the Knowledge Source triggers themselves. Before we do anything else, we need to declare the global triggered list:

$$
\begin{array}{|l}
\hline
\_\ TriggeredList\ \_\! \\
\ triggered\_list : KSARSet \\
\hline
\end{array}
$$

Initially, the triggered list is empty:

$$
\begin{array}{|l}
\hline
\_\ InitTriggeredList\ \_\! \\
\ TriggeredList \\
\hline
\ triggered\_list = \varnothing \\
\hline
\end{array}
$$

We assume that the Δ and Ξ forms of *TriggeredList* are defined (they are standard).

The basic triggering operation is given in the following schema:

$$
\begin{array}{|l}
\hline
\_\ FindTriggeredKSs\ \_\! \\
\ cycno?, evno? : \mathbb{N} \\
\ ev? : BBEVENT \\
\ lev? : LEVID \\
\ a? : ATTR \\
\ ksars! : KSARSet \\
\hline
\ \forall\, ksid : KSID \mid known\_ks(ksid) \bullet \\
\quad (\exists_1 ks : KS;\ trig : TRIGSPEC \mid \\
\qquad\qquad ks = KSs(ksid) \wedge trig = ks\_trigger(ks) \bullet \\
\qquad\qquad (\exists\, ksar! : KSARATTR \nrightarrow KSARVAL \bullet \\
\qquad\qquad EvalKSTrigger \wedge CreateKSAR \wedge \\
\qquad\qquad ksar! \in ksars!)) \\
\hline
\end{array}
$$

This schema can be thought of as iterating over the Knowledge Sources in the system, extracting the trigger and evaluating it. If the trigger is satisfied by the current event, a KSAR is created and added to a set (which is eventually to be included in the triggered list). We can define the latter operation quite simply:

$$
\begin{array}{l}
\underline{\quad AddTriggeredList \quad\quad\quad\quad\quad\quad\quad\quad\quad\quad\quad} \\
\Delta\, TriggeredList \\
ksars? : KSARSet \\
\hline
triggered\_list' = triggered\_list \cup ksars?
\end{array}
$$

We have the following result:

Theorem 22

$$AddTriggeredList \vdash \#triggered\_list' \geq \#triggered\_list$$

PROOF   Immediate (see proof of theorem 2). □

So far, all is well and good. We can trigger Knowledge Sources when an event occurs, and we have the ability to add newly created KSARs to the triggered list. We can combine these two operations into a sequential one:

$$
\begin{array}{l}
TriggerAndAdd \;\widehat{=} \\
\quad\quad\quad (FindTriggeredKSs \,\fatsemi\, AddTriggeredList) \\
\quad \wedge\, IncEVCOUNT
\end{array}
$$

Notice that we need to define a sequential composition: this is because we do not want either *ksars?* or *ksars!* to be visible to the outside world. The operation is sequential because we need to find the triggered Knowledge Sources before we can add them to the triggered list. The event counter can be incremented either before the triggered Knowledge Sources have been found and added to the triggered list, or after this has been performed: it makes no difference. We also know that the composite schema formed from *RuleAction* and *TriggerAndAdd* is the operation that we need to perform in order to execute an action and create the KSARs that are caused by the event it generates. In fact, for every action in the sequence, we the operation that we require is precisely that one. There is a problem, however: we need to make a connection between elements of the sequence of actions and the actions themselves.

$$
\begin{array}{|l}
\hline
\_ ExecuteAction _____ \\
rule\_action? : RULEACT \\
\hline
\forall\, act : 1\,..\,\#rule\_action?\, \bullet \\
\quad RuleAction \wedge TriggerAndAdd \\
\hline
\end{array}
$$

The reader should note that we have not been bothered about the possibility that there exist local variables: indeed, we have been assuming that local variables are bound and unbound by some process that we do not care to specify. In order to complete the specification, it is necessary to include these operations. We feel that this amounts to the partial design of a language for rules, and, as we have stated above, we do not wish to engage in this exercise. The provision of local variables is, we consider, part of the specification of the interface between user-defined code and the facilities that we provide. Clearly, in the case of rule actions, there is a conflict because the purpose of binding local variables is to provide a means of communication between the elements of the condition and the actions that are eventually to be executed. We have given a complete account of the actions that we permit, and so we *should*, so it would appear, give a complete account of the interactions between local variables and actions, but we have not done so. To do so would require an abstract syntax for actions, and that we have not done: instead, we have concentrated upon the mechanisms which support action execution. In a strongly platonic sense, we do not need to bother about variables at all, for all actions that can ever be executed are already, in some sense of that word, supplied with the required values. We leave it as an exercise for the reader to integrate the local variable structures with actions and rule conditions in order to provide a more detailed specification.

One way to do this is to define each of the most basic blackboard changing schemata to have inputs which are variables or constants. The current set of variable bindings is also made available to the schemata. In each schema, before an input variable is used, it is checked to see whether it is bound to a variable or to a value: if it is bound to a variable, that variable is de-referenced to obtain its true value. The true value is then used in the operation. If the input is bound to a value, then all is as before.

4.6.3   Executing Rules

We may now move on to the question of how rule actions come to be executed in the first place. As we know, once the conditions of a rule have been satisfied by the current state, the actions in that rule may be executed to cause blackboard changes. We also know that some of the condition elements in a rule represent what we would otherwise wish to be a separate precondition which determines the applicability of the Knowledge Source in the present blackboard state. We have, however, integrated the precondition with each rule in the Knowledge Source action. This integration gives us great power, and it can cause us some problems. The power that we now have is that each rule can be considered as an independent unit: once we know which rules are applicable, they have all the necessary information bound in them and can be executed in any order we wish (this is taken to include the possibility that we might want to execute some actions repeatedly). The problems are connected with the amount of testing of the blackboard state that is required. It is known that precondition testing in systems such as BB* is expensive, and facilities are provided in that system to reduce the overhead (the user can, for example, state that the precondition be tested only on every n^{th} cycle). In our system, every time a rule's condition is tested, the precondition is evaluated in full: furthermore, that test is performed for *every* rule in a Knowledge Source action. In other words, we do not have the luxury of saying that preconditions be tested only once in a while. As should be clear, preconditions can fail to be satisfied: in our specification, precondition testing entails executing rule preconditions, and, because of the way we have set up our conditions, we can never tell whether it is the precondition that has failed or some more specific test. This is the price we must pay for a simpler specification.

We need to make these observations about preconditions and rule conditions explicit, lest the reader think that the specification that we present is optimal. We are fully aware of its limitations, but are willing to pay for them for the gain in clarity and simplicity. We also need to state that we do not anticipate anyone taking our specification and turning it into a working system: we are only providing an abstract specification in order to show the major points in a precise fashion (although we will say in the Appendix how to refine the specification).

With these remarks behind us, we turn to the job of specifying the process by which rule conditions are tested against the blackboard state and rule actions executed. When a KSAR is created, one of its attributes records the Knowledge Source whose triggering caused the KSAR to be created. This entails that Knowledge Sources can be accessed from KSARs. We define a function to perform this operation:

$$
\begin{array}{l}
ksar\_ks : KSAR \rightarrow KS \\
\hline
\forall\, ksar : KSAR \bullet \\
\quad \mathrm{dom}\, ksar \neq \varnothing \Rightarrow \\
\quad \exists_1\, ks : KS \bullet \\
\qquad \exists_1\, ksslot : KSARATTR;\ ksid : KSID \bullet \\
\qquad\quad ksslot \in \mathrm{dom}\, ksar \wedge ksid = ksar(ksslot) \wedge \\
\qquad\quad ksid \in \mathrm{dom}\, KSs \wedge KSs(ksid) = ks
\end{array}
$$

We can now define a function which gives us access to the action of a Knowledge Source from each of its KSARs:

$$
\begin{array}{l}
ksar\_action : KSAR \rightarrow PRRULE \\
\hline
\forall\, ksar : KSAR \bullet \\
\quad ksar\_action = ks\_action(ksar\_ks(ksar))
\end{array}
$$

where $PRULE$ is the type of production rules:

$$PRULE == (CONDITION, RULEACT)$$

For the rule type, we assume the two projection functions $rule\_condition$ and $rule\_action$. The action in a Knowledge Source is simply:

$$KS\_ACTION == \mathbb{P}\, PRULE$$

When testing rule conditions, the aim is to find those actions which can be executed to cause blackboard changes. We can avoid the use of a separate list of eligible actions—that is, actions which may be executed because their Knowledge Source's precondition has been satisfied. This is because the satisfaction of a rule's condition immediately determines the fact that the action may be executed. Of course, a scheduler will need more information to work on than this, so we must make that information available: this can be done by collecting all those KSARs which contain satisfied rule conditions into a new set. Here again, we can make a distinction between producing a *model* of a system and producing executable code: in the model, it makes no difference at all how many times the conditions in a rule are executed to determine the blackboard state; equally, the creation of new sets from old costs nothing. In the approach to scheduling that we are going to adopt, we will allow ourselves the luxury to create sets as we see fit and to "re-execute" rule conditions if the need arises.

Once a Knowledge Source trigger has been satisfied, there is nothing that the system can do to alter that fact: once an event has occurred, it remains a fact that it *has* occurred. Thus, once a KSAR has been created in the triggered list, it can only be removed if it is scheduled for execution. Now, we know that all rule conditions have a prefix that represents the precondition of the entire Knowledge Source of which they form the action. Thus, we will evaluate all conditions of all rules that comprise a Knowledge Source action. Those that are satisfied will be eligible for execution. However, we do not want to execute them immediately because we want the scheduler to decide which actions are the most appropriate given the state of the blackboard and of the solution-finding process. We will therefore create an intermediate structure for the scheduler to operate on: this intermediate structure will allow access to each KSAR in the triggered list, and it will allow access to the Knowledge Source whose action is mentioned by the structure. The main part of the structure will contain those rules from the Knowledge Source action whose conditions are satisfied by the current blackboard state.

We define this structure as:

$$SCHED == (KSARID \times KSID \times KS\_ACTION)$$

with the stipulation that for any object of type *SCHED*, the third component is an improper subset of the action of the Knowledge Source identified by the second component. We assume that the necessary projection functions are defined and that they are: *sched_ksar*, *sched_ksid*, and *sched_action*. The constraint that we impose on objects of type *SCHED* is therefore:

$$\forall s : SCHED \bullet$$
$$sched\_action(s) \subseteq ks\_action(KSs(sched\_ksid(s)))$$

We can define a type:

$$SATIS\_RULE == \mathbb{P}\ SCHED$$

and a schema:

```
┌─ SchedulableKSARs ──────────────────────────────
│ Ξ TriggeredList
│ executable! : SATIS_RULE
├──────────────────────────────────────────────────
│ ∀ ksar : KSAR | ksar ∈ triggered_list •
│     ∃ action : KS_ACTION; s : SCHED |
│         action = ksar_action(ksar) ∧
│         s ∈ executable! •
│         ∀ rule : PRULE | rule ∈ action •
│             EvalConds(rule_condition(rule)) = ctrue
│         ⇒
│                 rule ∈ sched_actions(s)
└──────────────────────────────────────────────────
```

The schema defines what it is for a Knowledge Source action to be a candidate for scheduling: this is merely that some of its rules have conditions that are satisfied by the current state of the blackboard.

When a KSAR is selected for execution, it must be removed from the triggered list:

```
┌─ DeleteTriggeredKSAR ───────────────────────────
│ Δ TriggeredList
│ ksar? : KSAR
├──────────────────────────────────────────────────
│ triggered_list' =
│     triggered_list \ { ksar? }
└──────────────────────────────────────────────────
```

This deletion is performed because we do not want repeatedly to execute the same KSAR.

For *Delete TriggeredKSAR*, we have the following result.

Theorem 23

$$Delete\,TriggeredKSAR \vdash$$
$$\#triggered\_list' \leq \#triggered\_list$$

PROOF   Immediate. $\square$

To execute a rule's action, we simply need the following:

```
┌─ ExecuteRules ─────────────────────────────────
│ rules? : RULE_ACTION
├─────────────────────────────────────────────────
│ ∀ rule : PRULE;  rule_action₁ : RULEACT |
│     rule ∈ rules? ∧
│     rule_action₁ = rule_action(rule) •
│   (ExecuteAction ⨾ DeleteTriggeredKSAR)
│          ⨾ NextCycle
└─────────────────────────────────────────────────
```

The value of *rules?* is determined by the scheduler function, which we can assume to be a function:

$$schedule : SATIS\_RULE \rightarrow SCHED$$

The selector functions must be composed with *schedule* in order to extract the rules to be executed. Note that the schema given above increments the cycle counter and resets the event counter: these operations should be performed *after* all of the actions have been executed.

We obtain the following (trivial) result.

Theorem 24   *1. ExecuteRules* $\vdash cycno' = cycno + 1$

    2. ExecuteRules $\vdash evno' = 0.$

PROOF

1. Immediate.

2. Immediate.

□

We also have the following results about events and triggering.

Theorem 25 *ExecuteRules causes blackboard events.*

PROOF   By expansion of *ExecuteRules*, we have:

$$\forall rule : PRULE; \; rule\_action? : RULEACT \mid$$
$$rule \in rules? \land rule\_action? = rule\_action(rule) \bullet$$
$$(\forall act : 1 .. \#rule\_action? \bullet$$
$$RuleAction \land TriggerAndAdd)$$

where *RuleAction* expands to:

$$(acttype? = new \Rightarrow BBCreate \land ev! = newev) \lor$$
$$(acttype? = add \Rightarrow BBAddAttrib \land ev! = addev) \lor$$
$$(acttype? = mod \Rightarrow BBModify \land ev! = modev)$$

□

Theorem 26 *An action is schedulable if and only if its Knowledge Source has triggered.*

PROOF   The only schedulable actions are those whose KSARs are in *triggered_list* (see schema *SchedulableKSARs*). KSARs can only be added to *triggered_list* by *TriggerAndAdd*, which is defined in terms of *FindTriggeredKSs*. □

We have now completed the core of the blackboard system specification. All that need be done is to specify the main loop.

4.7   Main Loop

The main loop begins execution when the blackboard system is started. It terminates whenever a suitable solution has been found: we do not know when this might be. As we have seen, the operations in the main loop, that is:

1. trigger Knowledge Sources,

2. create KSARs,

3. select one KSAR to be executed, and

4. execute the selected KSAR's action to cause new events,

have all been specified. In fact, they are all part of the condition-matching and action-execution processes. All that need be done is to collect everything together. This involves initialising the counters, and creating a control database that the scheduler can work on. Essentially, all that needs be done is a little schema composition and wrapping in a quantifier. This can be done quite readily. The only major problem is termination, and for this we are going to define a variable and two schemata.

We first define a type:

$$TermVal ::= can\_terminate \mid must\_continue$$

┌─ *TerminationTest* ─────────────────────────
│ *terminate* : *TermVal*
│
└───

┌─ *InitTerminateTest* ───────────────────────
│ *TerminationTest*
│ ─────────────
│ *terminate* = *must_continue*
└───

┌─ *SysCanTerminate* ─────────────────────────
│ *TerminationTest*
│ ─────────────
│ *terminate* = *can_terminate*
└───

This schema defines a predicate which is true whenever the termination flag (*terminate*) is set to the termination value (*can_terminate*). To set the flag, we need:

MakeTerminate _____
$\Delta\,TerminationTest$
$termval?\,:\,TermVal$

$terminate' = termval?$

The value of the termination flag can be set by the scheduler when it determines that the system must halt (either with an acceptable solution or in failure), or it can be set by a Knowledge Source action. We have not included the latter possibility in our definition of Knowledge Source primitive actions because of the choice which we allow: to add it would not be too difficult, but, for the present interpreter, we feel that the scheduler is the best place for termination to be decided. This is because we have resisted the inclusion of user-defined actions (and for very good reasons!) In addition, we made the ruling that the _only_ primitive actions which could occur in a Knowledge Source were those which caused blackboard events: clearly, termination does not cause any _blackboard_ events, although it does cause an event (termination) which is significant for the interpreter as a whole (clearly, it _is_ significant when the system decides to halt). In addition, it should be noted that the system is intended to terminate abnormally if the triggered list becomes empty (this is because there are no Knowledge Sources which can make a contribution to the solution).

Now that we have a termination test, we can define the outer loop:

BBOutLoop _____
$\Delta\,Blackboard$

$\forall\,n:\mathbb{N}\mid n = cycno\,\bullet$
$\qquad\neg\,SysCanTerminate \Rightarrow$
$\qquad\qquad ExecuteRules$

This loop requires a little initialisation so that there are some KSARs in the triggered list. We proceed to do this.

$InitSys \;\widehat{=}$
$\qquad(InitCYCLECOUNT \wedge InitEVCOUNT$
$\qquad\qquad InitBlackboard \wedge InitTriggeredList);$
$\qquad\qquad\qquad BBNewEvent \wedge TriggerAndAdd$

The final schema that we define is *BBSystem*:

$$BBSystem \; \hat{=} \; InitSys \; ; \; BBOutLoop$$

We have taken the position that all Knowledge Sources have already been created and that they are in *KSs*. We have also assumed that the number of abstraction levels on the blackboard has been fixed before we execute the system (perhaps by some configuration tool that we prefer not to specify).

With the definition of the outer loop and of the initialisation schema, our specification of the blackboard system is complete.

4.8   Blackboard Invariants

In this section, we investigate the various invariants that are required. The primary invariants are:

1. No entry can reside on more than one abstraction level.

2. Each event occurs at exactly *one* level of abstraction.

There are two versions of the first invariant. The first of these is given in the following theorem. The second interpretation is very much stronger, and can only be proved once the set of attributes that are possible for each abstraction level is known. The second interpretation states that *no entry* can reside on more than one abstraction level in the sense that two entries are identical if and only if their attributes are the same (or equivalent) and the values which fill those attributes are the same (or equivalent): the hedge "or equivalent" is intended to allow equivalence relations of various sorts to be included.

The reading that we prove in the next theorem reduces entry identity to identity of names: two entries are considered to be identical if and only if they have the same identifier. We cannot prove the much stronger version without knowledge of the attributes and their possible values, and without knowledge of what it is for two attributes or values to be the same. The reason for this is that we can assume that two abstraction levels have different attribute sets (i.e., the set of attributes which can appear in entries on one level is different from the set of attributes which can appear in entries on the other). It is possible for the two sets to have a non-empty intersection (in NBB (Craig, 1987), for example, standard attributes—such as one to hold the identifier of the Knowledge Source which created the entry—were provided), and we also need to have knowledge about the status of that intersection. Once we have the information just demanded, it then becomes necessary to know when two attributes are the same. This problem reduces to (i) knowing the definitions of the attributes (i.e., the definitions of the properties they are intended to represent), and (ii) knowing the values that may possibly fill them. In addition, there is the problem that, on one abstraction level, several attributes may contribute to the definition of an attribute on another abstraction level (i.e., that an attribute on another abstraction level may be directly equivalent to the composition, say, of the elements of a set attributes that appear on another level). Once this information is available, a strong identity theorem can be proved: for the general case which concerns us, such a result is beyond our powers.

Theorem 27 *No entry can reside on more than one abstraction level.*

PROOF   The statement is equivalent to:

$$\forall\, e : EID \bullet$$
$$(\forall\, ABSLEV_1, ABSLEV_2 \mid$$
$$ABSLEV_1 \in \text{ran } levels \land$$
$$ABSLEV_2 \in \text{ran } levels \land$$
$$ABSLEV_1 \neq ABSLEV_2 \bullet$$
$$knownents_1 \cap knownents_2 = \varnothing)$$

We concentrate on entry creation. If the creation operation were to produce duplicate entry identifiers, there would be at least two calls on *BBNewEvent* that involved the same element of *EID*.

Since the entry identifier generator schema, *NewEntryName*, has $n' = n + 1$ in its predicate, for some $m > n$, we would have:

$$eids(m) = eids(n)$$

We will prove that:

$$eids(m) = eids(n)$$

if and only if $m = n$.

Since the entry identifier generator schema has $n' = n + 1$, then for some $m > n$, we would have:

$$eids(m) = eids(n)$$

We will prove that:

$$eids(m) = eids(n) \qquad\qquad \text{[if and only if } m = n]$$

To do this, we concentrate on the composition:

$$NewEntryName \,\mathbin{\raise2pt\hbox{$\fatsemi$}}\, NewEntryName$$

which expands to:

$$\exists\, n^+ : \mathsf{N} \bullet$$
$$n^+ = n + 1 \wedge$$
$$enm! = eids(n) \wedge$$
$$enm! = eids(n^+) \wedge$$
$$n' = n^+ + 1$$

which implies that $n' > n$, and that

$$n \neq n^+ \neq n' \Rightarrow eids(n) \neq eids(n^+)$$

The proof is, therefore, that for $k \neq l$, $eids(k) = e'$, $eids(l) = e'_1$, $e' = e'_1$.

We argue by contradiction, and give an outline predicate calculus proof based upon the above assumptions.

$$\exists\, e : EID \mid e = eids(k) \wedge$$
$$(\forall j : \mathsf{N};\ e_1 : EID \bullet$$
$$(e_1 = eids(j) \wedge e = e_1) \equiv (i = j))$$

(by the generator schema). So, by universal elimination and by the definition of $\equiv$:

$$e' = eids(k) \wedge e'_1 = eids(l) \wedge e'_1 = e' \Rightarrow k = l \qquad\qquad [(1)]$$

(Note that the second, third and fourth premisses can be conjoined to form the antecedent of (1).)

$$\neg\,(e' = eids(k) \wedge e_1' = eids(l) \wedge e_1' = e')$$

from which, by Modus Tollendo Tollens with $k \neq l$ (the first premiss), we obtain:

$$\neg\,(e' = eids(k) \wedge e_1' = eids(l) \wedge e_1' = e') \qquad\qquad [(2)]$$

So, by $\wedge$-introduction with the antecedent of (1), we obtain:

$$\neg\,(e' = eids(k) \wedge e_1' = eids(l) \wedge e_1' = e') \wedge$$
$$e' = eids(k) \wedge e_1' = eids(l) \wedge e_1' = e'$$

which is a contradiction.

We need to prove that, given: $k \neq l$, $e' = eids(k)$, $e_1' = eids(l)$, and from

$$\exists\,e : EID \mid e = eids(k) \bullet$$
$$\forall j : \mathsf{N};\ e_1 : EID \bullet$$
$$e_1 = eids(j) \wedge e = e_1 \equiv i = j$$

that $eids(k) = eids(l)$

We now expand the proof of this using Lemmon's (1965) natural deduction rules:

$(1)\, k \neq l$ [A]

$(2)\, e' = e_1'$ [A]

$(3)\, e' = eids(k)$ [A]

$(4)\, e_1' = eids(l)$ [A]

$(4)\, \exists\,e : EID \mid e = eids(k) \bullet$
$\qquad (\forall j : \mathsf{N};\ e_1 : EID \bullet e_1 = eids(j) \wedge e = e_1 \equiv i = j)$ [A]

$(5)\, e' = eids(k) \wedge e_1' = eids(l) \wedge e_1' = e' \equiv k = l$
$\qquad\qquad\qquad\qquad\qquad\qquad\qquad\qquad\qquad$ [Assumption and UE]

$(6)\, e' = eids(k) \wedge e_1' = eids(l) \wedge e_1' = e' \Rightarrow k = l$
$\qquad\qquad\qquad\qquad\qquad\qquad\qquad\qquad\qquad$ [By definition of $\equiv$]

$$(7) \neg\, (e' = eids(k) \wedge e'_1 = eids(l) \wedge e'_1 = e) \hspace{2cm} \text{[MT 1, 6]}$$

$$(8)\, e' = eids(k) \wedge e'_1 = eids(l) \wedge e'_1 = e \hspace{2cm} \text{[$\wedge$I 2, 3, 4]}$$

$$(9) \neg\, (e' = eids(k) \wedge e'_1 = eids(l) \wedge e'_1 = e)\, \wedge$$
$$e' = eids(k) \wedge e'_1 = eids(l) \wedge e'_1 = e \hspace{2cm} \text{[$\wedge$I 7, 8]}$$

$$(10)\, k = l \hspace{2cm} \text{[RAA]}$$

We derive a contradiction on line (9) and this allows us to assert that $k = l$, as desired.

We have it that all identifiers are unique.

Therefore, $e' = e$ if and only if $k = l$.

Because the creation of two entries on different abstraction levels necessarily requires two calls on the identifier creation operation, we know that the indices into the name sequence (*eids*) will be distinct, and since we know that distinct identifiers have distinct indices in *eids*, the two calls will generate different names. It is therefore impossible for the same identifier to appear on distinct abstraction levels (and it is, indeed, impossible for it to appear twice on the same abstraction level).

Note that the only place in our specification where new entries are added to the blackboard is in *BBNewEvent*: this justifies our concentration on the entry identifier generation process. In addition, it should be noted that no operations move an entry from one abstraction level to another. □

Corollary 1 *Every blackboard event is associated with one and only one abstraction level.*

PROOF   This is a direct consequence of the uniqueness of entry identifiers. Since each event is associated with only one entry, and since that entry appears occurs on only one abstraction level by the previous theorem, any events associated with that entry by means of ADD and MODIFY operations, must necessarily be associated with one and only one abstraction level.

For the case of entry creation (a NEW event), the previous theorem gives the desired result. □

5

CASSANDRA

5.1 Introduction

In this Chapter, we give an informal account of the author's CASSAN-DRA architecture (Craig, 1988). As with the blackboard architecture, which we described in informal terms in Chapter 3, this description will serve as the basis for the formal specification which follows in the next Chapter. Again, as with Chapters 3 and 4, the formal specification of the CASSANDRA architecture will closely follow the informal specification given here.

The CASSANDRA architecture is an attempt to remedy what the author sees as some of the shortcomings of the blackboard architecture: these shortcomings are outside the scope of this book, so we ignore them here. In addition, it is one form of distributed problem-solving architecture. Distributed problem-solving (Gasser, 1989) is a sub-field of Artificial Intelligence in which the solution of problems is physically or logically distributed across a number of spatially separated problem-solvers. The problem-solvers communicate information amongst themselves until a solution is discovered. The CASSANDRA architecture attempts to be a disciplined architecture with which to construct distributed systems. As a consequence, there is no central scheduler in a CASSANDRA system: control is distributed across level managers. The distribution of control leads to a number of problems related to co-ordination: the architecture accepts this, but provides facilities for global control to be performed as a problem-specific exercise. As will be seen, a great deal of the structure in a blackboard system is decentralised, especially when control is an issue. This leads to the conclusion that the CASSANDRA architecture is essentially a distributed one.

This property of the architecture is of interest in formal specification: CASSANDRA systems exhibit natural parallelism, but the Z language is intended for sequential programs—this would seem to be a limitation. The full solution is that the parallel components of a CASSANDRA system should be specified using a notation such as CSP (Hoare, 1985) or CCS (Milner, 1980, 1989), and the sequential component should be specified using Z (Spivey, 1988, 1989) or VDM (Jones, 1980, 1986). The approach we adopt here is to specify the basics of the CASSANDRA architecture in Z: as will be seen, there is a set of core components which are necessary for any CASSANDRA system. These core components are connected to form a parallel, distributed program. The approach we adopt here is reminiscent of programming languages such as **Concurrent PASCAL or Modula**.

The nature of the eventual formal specification does not impact upon the subject matter of this Chapter, but it is worth considering while reading the informal specification. A CASSANDRA system (and a blackboard system, for that matter) is capable of considerable parallelisation, and the current specifications in Z can only hint at where this may occur (for example, in those components which are specified in a non-deterministic way): this remains an exercise for the future. As was the case with Chapter 3, here we will present a complete, informal specification of the CASSANDRA architecture and will move on to a formal treatment in the next Chapter. Because we have the luxury of informality, issues relating to parallelism can be treated relatively easily. Because of its close ties with the blackboard architecture, many of the constructs used in CASSANDRA systems should be familiar to the reader, so we will not define or justify them in detail here: if the reader does not feel sufficiently familiar with the older architecture, it is recommended that Chapter 3 should be re-read before going any further.

The organisation of this Chapter is as follows. First, we introduce the *level manager* construct. This is the CASSANDRA analogue of the abstraction level, and contains a database in which are stored the partial results generated by the solution-finding process. Level managers are the main component of CASSANDRA systems and also represent the unit of distribution, be it logical or physical. Next, the communication mechanisms (*channels* and *ports*) are introduced. Channels and ports connect level managers and allow information to flow between them during the problem-solving process. There are constraints imposed upon channels and these will eventually be captured in our formal account. The discussion of channels and ports also includes a description of how level managers handle communication internally. This leads naturally to a discussion of the relationship between Knowledge Sources and communications: as will be seen, Knowledge Sources are not permitted to engage in unrestricted communications with other level managers.

Readers who are familiar with previous descriptions of the CASSANDRA architecture (e.g., Craig, 1988a, 1988b) may find one or two differences between those accounts and the one given here: this is because some minor corrections have been made to what we feel are small errors in the architecture. It should be emphasised that these corrections are minor and do not impact in any major way on the overall structure and intention of the architecture.

5.2   Level Managers

The major component that the CASSANDRA architecture introduces
is called the *level manager* (in older versions of the architecture, for
example, in Craig, 1988b, an additional component, the local matcher,
was included. The matcher has been omitted since our view of the
matching process has changed from an essentially pattern matching
view to one that is much more procedural. The change is minimal: the
only thing that matters is that triggers and preconditions are matched
against entries in some way). Level managers are composed of the
followng components:

- A *local database.*

- A set of *local Knowledge Sources* (usually simply called *Knowledge
  Sources*).

- A *local scheduler* to make local control decisions.

- A set of *communications channels* for the transfer of information between level managers: they are usually referred simply as
  channels. Channels are required to be *uni-directional.*

- A set of *ports* to interface with the channels. The ports are the
  structures which are visible within the level manager: channels
  are invisible and are more properly part of the 'connection structure' which is imposed on a collection of level managers in order
  to configure them to solve a problem.

- A *port manager* which is charged with handling all communications between the level manager and other level managers in the
  system.

In this section, we will not be concerned with channels and ports. In addition, the relationship between channels, ports and Knowledge Sources
will be discussed below.

The level manager is intended to be a separate problem-solving
agent which is completely autonomous. A CASSANDRA system composed of only one level manager is as valid as one which contains ten

thousand. Level managers are autonomous because they each solve a separate sub-problem and contain expertise directly relevant to that sub-problem and to that sub-problem only, and because they are unable directly to inspect the state of other level managers. In order to gain information about the state of another level manager, a level manager must engage in communication. It is this second sense of autonomy that is most relevant to the current enterprise: as far as the specification is concerned, the knowledge that is contained in any particular level manager is a problem-specific matter. In this sense, a level manager builds an abstraction barrier around its internal state.

Level managers contain a *local database*. The local database contains entries that are very much like those found in conventional blackboard systems. The contents of a local database are entirely private to the level manager which contains it: the contents may not be directly inspected by any other level manager. In order for entries or attribute-value pairs to be made known to another level manager, an explicit request must be made to the level manager which can then decide to reply or to ignore the request. The entries in a level manager's local database are placed there by its local Knowledge Sources or by the port manager: they represent intermediate states in the problem-solving process. The entries in a local database can be connected to form a graph structure, as is the case with blackboard systems, but it is possible that the graph will span a number of level managers. The entries in the local database constitute part of the level manager's (invisible) local state.

The local database serves the same role in a level manager as does a single abstraction level in a blackboard system. In other words, partial results are stored there and can be inspected by all local Knowledge Sources. Entries can be updated by local Knowledge Sources using operations similar to ADD and MODIFY. The port manager can also perform a NEW operation and add entries to the local database. As is the case with blackboard systems, the basic operations on entries cause triggering events, but these events are local to the level manager in which they occur: the concept of a global event is not allowed in the CASSANDRA architecture, so, for example, the creation of a new entry in a local database cannot cause Knowledge Sources in other level managers to trigger. This, in turn, means that there is no *action-at-a-*

distance: in other words, whatever happens in one level manager can have no effect whatsoever on any other level manager unless it is explicitly communicated to other level managers using the communication mechanisms.

The entries in the local database have the same relationship with Knowledge Sources in the CASSANDRA architecture as they do in the blackboard architecture. The creation or modification of entries causes Knowledge Sources to trigger. Knowledge Sources are also assumed to have preconditions which examine the state of the local database. As will become considerably clearer below, the semantics of preconditions in CASSANDRA Knowledge Sources is somewhat different from that in blackboard systems: this is because of the need to engage in communications with other level managers. In this section, we assume that Knowledge Sources are interested only in the events and state within their level manager, and will return to the issue of the relationship between communications and Knowledge Sources below. Under this assumption, the behaviour of Knowledge Sources in the two architectures is identical. As was the case with our interpretation of the blackboard model, we assume that when a Knowledge Source in a level manager has been triggered, a KSAR is created for it. The KSARs in CASSANDRA systems play a rôle identical to that in the blackboard model: they are the unit of scheduling and it is the action in a KSAR that is executed to cause state changes (and further triggering events).

Since level managers are required to be totally independent modules, the above entails that each level manager be equipped with its own *local scheduler*. The local scheduler is concerned with scheduling KSAR execution within a single level manager. Each local scheduler controls the problem-solving activities within its level manager. This implies that the scheduling decisions that are made within a level manager depend, primarily, upon the internal state of the level manager and not upon a more global view of the entire system state: as we have stated, there is no global scheduler, so control *must* be performed at a local level. It is, of course, possible, for control decisions within a level manager to be made on the basis of some limited information about the global state of the system: this can be achieved by use of information gathered from the communications system. For the vast majority of the time, control decisions within a level manager will be made solely on the basis of the local state: this means that the local scheduler is a *purely local* version of the scheduler that is typically found in blackboard systems.

The local scheduler works in a manner that is directly analogous to the schedulers found in conventional blackboard systems. It maintains a database of KSARs, applies a problem-specific ordering function to them, then selects the KSAR with the best possible ratings against one or more scheduling criteria and executes it. As in our interpretation of the blackboard architecture, the model of the CASSANDRA architecture that we propose is such that there is a triggered list and an eligible list. These two lists play exactly the same rôle as in the blackboard architecture: once created, KSARs are placed in the triggered list until their precondition evaluates to *true*, at which point they enter the eligible list and are ordered by the scheduler's rating procedure.

As in our interpretation of the blackboard architecture, we are assuming that the local scheduler's control database (the eligible list, essentially) is maintained as an agenda: it is, of course, possible that another régime such as a LIFO stack or FIFO queue might be chosen if it is more suited to the needs of the problem under attack. Another assumption which we make is that the local scheduler only selects one KSAR at a time to execute: it is possible that it might select more than one, but we are assuming that each level manager is a strictly sequential program that generates new states in the solution graph one at a time—this seems to motivate the assumption that one KSAR at a time is chosen for execution.

Given that each level manager has its own, local, scheduler, it naturally follows that it has its own interpreter cycle. The cycle follows that of the conventional match-deliberate-execute pattern that is found in production and blackboard systems. During the match phase, preconditions are checked against the state of the local database and KSARs are moved between the triggered and eligible lists. During the deliberate phase, KSARs are rated against the operative scheduling criteria and the eligible list is ordered. During the act phase, one KSAR is selected for execution; its action is executed and events are caused and the triggered list is updated. As is the case with blackboard systems, the main cycle begins with the creation of an initial entry (thus causing an initial NEW event). Termination is effected by means of a STOP flag which halts the main cycle.

The actual main cycle is slightly more complicated than the one just given. This is because the communications mechanism has to be taken into account. It is assumed that messages passed along the communications channels cannot interrupt the main cycle and force it to enter an interupt processing state. The reason for this is that we do not wish to complicate the main cycle. Instead, the main cycle is modified so that the communications channels are inspected for new messages. When there are messages to be processed, the main cycle merely calls procedures to place them in the relevant places and also inspects a separate database that is held by the scheduler. This database is used to hold KSARs which are waiting for information from non-local sources: we will examine this database and the additional machinery required by the communications processor in the next two sections. As will become clear below, the logical place for the communications-related call is in the precondition evaluation part of the main cycle: the other parts of the main cycle are unaffected by the need for processing communications.

The level manager construct arose out of a need to distribute the abstraction levels of a conventional blackboard system. This, in turn, entailed that the degree of autonomy of each abstraction level be increased. In conventional blackboard systems, Knowledge Sources tend to be associated with one or two abstraction levels: it is typical for a Knowledge Source to be triggered on one level, and for its precondition to be satisfied by the contents of that same abstraction level; its action typically causes changes to the same abstraction level or to one that is very close in the abstraction hierarchy. The first of these two cases is handled by encapsulating Knowledge Sources within level managers: the second is accomodated by the communications mechanisms. Since the abstraction levels were considered to be physically distributed across an array of physical processors, it became clear that each level manager would need to have its own independent scheduler. The similarity with the abstraction levels found in conventional blackboard systems serves to explain why this section has been relatively brief: all of the relevant concepts have already been introduced in Chapter 3, so there is no need to go into details here.

5.3 Communications

In a distributed system it is clear that communications are an important aspect of the functioning of the system. This is also the case in distributed AI systems, and the CASSANDRA architecture is no different in this respect. In distributed AI systems, communication replaces the part played by the central memory within which resides the solution structure. Within a conventional AI system, a blackboard system, for example, there is effectively an infinite bandwidth in the communications medium: this is enshrined in the blackboard metaphor where it is stated that *all* experts may inspect and/or modify the emerging solution. With a distributed system, however, bandwidth is severely restricted and it becomes impossible for *all* experts to have access to every part of the solution. Effective use of available bandwidth remains an essentially open problem in distributed AI research (as it is in conventional distributed systems), but it is clear that they kinds of communication required by a distributed AI systems display considerably greater diversity than in the case of a conventional distributed system. As will be seen, the CASSANDRA architecture specification says nothing about *how* bandwidth is to be used, and is neutral about what is actually communicated between level managers: these aspects are considered to be problem-specific.

The CASSANDRA architecture provides communication channels (or more simply *channels*) between level managers. Channels are uni-directional and may be used to send information between two level managers which may be necessary for their effective operation. Channels can be considered to be directed arcs that connect level managers. They are private in the sense that messages sent along a channel cannot be intercepted by a third party. Since channels are uni-directional, if two level managers need to send and receive information, they must be connected by two channels. The reader may care to note that the existence of such loops may lead to a deadlock or to a livelock problem in an actual system: the avoidance of these two problems is considered to fall outside the scope of the architecture definition and it is, therefore, the responsibility of the user to prove that their system is free of deadlock and/or livelock. The architecture places no restrictions on the number of channels that a level manager may have. It does make the restriction that a level manager may not directly send information to itself along a channel.

Unlike a number of other proposals for concurrency (e.g., CSP (Hoare, 1985)), we assume that communications along a channel are *asynchronous*. This assumption is based upon the observation that physically distributed systems are denied the luxury of synchronisation: the latency of the physical link often prevents this. It is, of course, possible to introduce synchronisation across a physical link, but at the cost of extended periods of time during which the process enters and waits in the rendezvous state. The CASSANDRA architecture was initially conceived as an architecture for the construction or *real-time* knowledge-based systems, so it was decided that synchronisation should be abandoned in favour of a more flexible asynchronous scheme. Hence, no level manager may assume synchronisation when sending messages along channels. When we come to discuss the interactions between Knowledge Sources and communications, it will become clear that the fact that communications are assumed to be asynchronous causes one or two problems—these problems are considered to be slight enough to be tolerable in the final architecture.

One of the design considerations for the CASSANDRA architecture was that it should be incremental and modular. It should be incremental in the sense that the addition of new level managers should be as simple as possible, and it should be modular in the sense that each level manager represents, essentially, a unit of abstraction. As a unit of abstraction, the internal state of each level manager should be invisible to all other level managers in the system. In order to facilitate these aims, the architecture associates each channel with a *port*. Ports represent logical names for channels and are the representation of channels that is visible within a level manager. Since ports are a level manager's representation of channels, each port is invisible to external observers. This, in turn, implies that more than one port in the system can have the same name.

Since channels are uni-directional, ports are of two basic types. *Input* ports represent channels on which information flows into a level manager. *Output* ports represent channels on which a level manager sends information to one other level manager. Because of the strong constraints on communications, an input port cannot be used for sending information, only receiving it. Similarly, an output port cannot be used for the reception of messages. An attempt to violate these constraints lead to an error. Within these general constraints, the information sent to or received from ports can be of any type whatsoever: typically, it will consist of control messages or of entries that need to be added to the receiver's local database. In the formal specification that follows, the precise nature of the messages that travel along channels is irrelevant.

Associated with each port, there is some information that is of use to the level manager in which they reside. The port type is explicitly made available so that runtime checking is possible. Also, the name of the level manager at the "other end" of the channel is also made explicitly available: this allows messages to be selectively sent by the port manager—the information is therefore held in one, central, place and need not be distributed across the Knowledge Sources in a level manager.

The port manager is responsible for managing communications between level managers. Essentially, the port manager is charged with managing communication queues. When a message is to be sent by a level manager (or by one of its Knowledge Sources), that message is first directed to the port manager. The message must contain the name of the destination level manager, and the port manager maps the destination level manager identifier to the identifier of the port on which the message is to be sent. This mapping is performed so that the relationship between ports and level managers is encapsulated in the port manager itself: it is not necessary for the entire level manager to know of the mapping (and, thus, errors are reduced). When the port manager receives a message to be sent, it simply sends it along the appropriate channel. It may, optionally, place it on an output queue for later dispatch: this option is provided so that the architecture remains independent of the characteristics of any particular physical or logical implementation of the communications channels, but we do not specify this formally. As far as the port manager in the architecture is concerned, once it has been given a message to send, it merely sends it on the appropriate channel. When the message has been sent on the correct channel, the port manager attends to the next message (either input or output): no handshake mechanism is assumed.

It should be noted that the main source of output messages are the Knowledge Sources within a level manager. The scheduler may sometimes need to send messages—for example, messages stating that it is about to terminate with an acceptable local solution which needs to be incorporated within some larger solution. The possibility that level managers, schedulers and other non-Knowledge Source structures may need to send messages should be borne in mind—we refer to these as *service* messages—for they can sometimes be of use. Since the trend is for AI systems to be more explicit in their operations, it is expected that the majority of messages, perhaps including service messages, will originate from Knowledge Sources and this is considered in the next section.

When messages are received from the channels under the port manager's care, matters are a little different. On the input side, channels are associated with at least one input queue (in our Z specification, we only provide one queue). When a message is received, it is assumed that it is placed in the input queue by some low-level mechanism. With each input message is associated the identifier of its source: this amounts to the name of the input port on which it was received. The queue is required because of the assumption that level managers are sequential programs: the time required to process *all* messages as they are received would become excessive and would require either some form of interrupt mechanism or some form of multitasking within a level manager, and both of these assumptions violate the sequentiality assumption. Associated with each message in the input queue is the source identifier (the name of the port on which it was received) and the identifier of the object to which the message is destined. Normally, the destination object will be a Knowledge Source name, but it can also be used to provide a kind of store-and-forward mechanism for indirect routing between level managers. Although we have not assumed a broadcast mechanism, it is sometimes useful for a level manager to be able to send messages to more than one destination (for example, when announcing that it has found a solution in a competitive environment, or when announcing that it is about to shut down): the destination identifier method provides a simple (although rather inelegant) way of doing this.

In case the reader is concerned about how destinations are computed, the architecture makes a stipulation that each message that is sent can, optionally, include an additional identifier which denotes the destination. The destination can be thought of as a pair:

$$\langle level\text{-}manager\text{-}id,\ \ Knowledge\text{-}Source\text{-}id\rangle$$

The port manager passes this pair through as part of the message without change (it does not have access to the port mapping information held in the level manager to which the message will be sent). When the port manager receives a message with a destination pair, it locates the object to which the message is to be sent and hands the message to it. This mechanism is primarily used when Knowledge Source preconditions are requesting information from external sources. It should be noted that the interpretation of destination pairs is performed entirely by the port manager in the level manager to which the message is sent—this is another case of information hiding in the CASSANDRA architecture.

5.4   Knowledge Sources and Communication

In order to make progress towards a solution, the Knowledge Sources in a level manager must have access to their local database. This database contains the entries which represent the local state of the solution process. In addition, Knowledge Sources require access to non-local information, typically information that is held in other level managers. It is a major assumption of the CASSANDRA architecture that level managers are independent and that access to their local state by external agents is forbidded. The message-passing system is, therefore, used to perform this function. An analysis of Knowledge Source function quickly reveals that there are two basic operations that must be performed on non-local information: it must be inspected and it must be altered. The inspection is performed by Knowledge Source triggers and preconditions; the alteration is performed by Knowledge Source actions. This analysis also shows that there are potential problems if one were simply to allow Knowledge Sources to request information and to send update messages in an unconstrained and unstructured fashion. In this section, we examine the interactions between Knowledge Sources and the communications mechanism.

At this point, it is worth reminding the reader that this specification is about the *minimal* implementation of the CASSANDRA architecture: there may be aspects which appear necessary but which are not included in the specification. Our desire is to give a specification of what is *necessary* for a system to be called a CASSANDRA system, not to take into account all possible schemes and extensions. It is our stated opinion that a problem-solving architecture cannot be *fully* defined for so much depends upon the problem that is being solved. This caveat is necessary when dealing with the relationship between Knowledge Sources and communications.

The CASSANDRA architecture imposes restrictions on the behavious of its Knowledge Sources. In particular, triggers may only respond to events that are local to the level manager within which a Knowledge Source responds. Thus, triggers are excluded from accessing the communications mechanisms. It is not possible for a Knowledge Source trigger to be written in such a way that it could be paraphrased as stating "if a communication event has occurred".

Although communications are important in distributed problem-solving (particularly if one is using a speech act model (Searle, 1969) of inter-agent communications), the rôle of a trigger is to respond to a problem-solving event. In CASSANDRA systems, entries are the bearers of declarative knowledge and represent the state of the problem-solving process, and so triggering is restricted to the event-causing operations which can be performed on entries. In practice, this is not a problem for the port manager is able to create new entries in the local database directly: when the port manager creates a new entry, it causes a NEW event whose responsible Knowledge Source is **Port-Manager**, so all the relevant information is provided to Knowledge Sources and scheduling decisions can be made which take communications into account. Given this fact, it is not necessary for triggers to be concerned with the communications mechanisms directly. For this reason, it is a requirement of the architecture that triggers cannot explictly call any communications routines or request communications services.

In a conventional blackboard system, Knowledge Source actions alter the state of the blackboard database by creating and modifying entries: this is the way in which progress is made to the solution state. In CASSANDRA systems, this property must be retained. It is necessary, therefore, that actions be allowed to create entries and to modify them locally, and it is also necessary for them to do the same on a non-local basis. In order to create or modify a non-local entry, the communications mechanisms must be used. Non-local entry creation is a relatively simple matter: all that need be done is for the action to send a message containing the new entry to the relevant level manger whose port manager will add the entry to its local database, thus causing an event. In the case of entry modification, an action would need to have access to non-local state information, which is not permitted by the architecture. Rather than violate this constraint, the usual solution is to have the action send a message containing a description of the non-local operation it requires to be performed in the receiving level manager. A Knowledge Source in the receiving level manager responds to this request and performs the modification. This scheme leads to an increase in the number of Knowledge Sources in each level manager, but there is an identifiable tendency for Knowledge Sources to be smaller in more recent blackboard systems, so the CASSANDRA solution does not appear to be particularly out of step with current thinking.

There is often a need for an action to perform operations on the blackboard on a conditional basis: this is usually contingent upon the blackboard state at the time the action is executed. In terms of a distributed problem-solving system like a CASSANDRA system, this again seems to imply that Knowledge Source actions must be given access to non-local information, but, again, it is not so. The solution to this problem is to reduce the size of Knowledge Sources: where a large Knowledge Source would perform a sequence of conditional actions, the corresponding CASSANDRA system would have many Knowledge Sources, one for each conditional action. In this solution, the precondition of each of these smaller Knowledge Sources is used to test whether the operation is to be performed: if the precondition evaluates to *true*, the operation is performed, otherwise it is not. Again, this leads to an increase in the number of Knowledge Sources, but each Knowledge Source becomes more specialised and is more explicit in its operation.

The net result of these changes in the way in which Knowledge Sources are employed gives a big hint about the relationship between

Knowledge Sources and communications. Knowledge Source preconditions are essentially responsible for requesting information from non-local as well as local sources. Knowledge Source actions are responsible for causing local and non-local changes of state. Since we have avoiding the requirement that Knowledge Source actions need to inspect non-local states, it is clear that they do not need to request information from other level managers—preconditions can perform that operation—and they only need to send information when engaging in communications with other level managers. Thus, a Knowledge Source action need only call the message-sending primitive: if it makes an enquiry (i.e., makes a request to another level manager) an error should be raised.

In this scheme of things, a Knowledge Source action can never be deadlocked. This is because the message sending primitive always returns immediately (it only needs to hand the message over to the port manager which is a local structure in any case). If actions were able to send requests, they would have to wait for replies. This can lead to deadlocks because the level manager to which the request was sent may have terminated or may be engaged in infinitely many transactions with other level managers. In addition, there is the fact that communication requires an arbitrary time to complete a transaction. If an action made a request, it would have to wait for a reply before continuing: this would entail that its level manager could perform no other actions until the reply was received. This fact remains true even if many actions are executed at the same time (i.e., the case in which the local scheduler executes more than one KSAR at any time), for it is possible for all of the actions to make non-local requests at any time. If all of the actions made requests (which is not an unreasonable assumption), the level manager would still be unable to proceed. It is therefore safer to deny actions the possibility of making requests.

Since actions and triggers cannot make requests, it is clear that they must be made by preconditions. The semantics of triggers and actions is not made unduly complex by the existence of the inter-level manager communications mechanism (indeed, its presence does not impact upon the semantics of triggers in any way whatsoever). However, the semantics of preconditions does become slightly more complex when they are required to make non-local requests as well as perform local state examinations. The reason for this has to do with the time required for a reply to be sent in answer to a request.

Preconditions are charged with inspecting local and non-local states. In order to inspect non-local states, a precondition has to send a request message. That message requests the receiving level manager for some information, and that level manager has to send a reply message to the requesting precondition. This process naturally takes some time, and is unlike the normal mode of operation for preconditions: in a conventional blackboard system, each precondition has immediate access to the information that it requires since all that information is held in one address space. In conventional blackboard systems, the evaluation of a precondition is a sequential process and a truth-value can be determined in a conventional fashion. In the case of preconditions in CASSANDRA systems, the evaluation is no longer a sequential process, but, instead, depends upon the value returned by a parallel process. During the time in which a precondition is waiting for a reply to its request, a determinate truth-value cannot be assigned to it. It is necessary, therefore, for the precondition to be assigned the temporary truth-value *undefined*.

The rule for transferring a triggered KSAR to the eligible list is that its precondition must have evaluated to *true*. A KSAR's action can only be executed when the precondition is *true*. A KSAR may be transferred from the eligible to the triggered list when its precondition is *false*. When communication is an issue, these operations fail because preconditions may only be assigned the truth-value *undefined* while they are waiting for a reply: only after the reply has been received can the truth-value be reduced to either *true* or *false*. Thus any KSAR whose precondition is waiting for a reply cannot be moved from the triggered list, nor can it be considered for execution. In addition, any KSAR in this state cannot have its precondition re-evaluated. Therefore, the CASSANDRA architecture requires that any preconditions that are waiting for replies should be placed in a third scheduler list, called the *waiting list*. As soon as a precondition makes a remote request, the scheduler moves its KSAR into the waiting list. KSARs are only moved from the waiting list when all of their outstanding requests have been serviced. The list to which they are moved depends upon their final truth-value: if it is *false*, they are moved to the triggered list, if it is *true*, the KSAR is promoted to the eligible list.

In the specification that is presented in the next Chapter, it is assumed that each time the preconditions of all KSARs are evaluated the request-making process is repeated. In a realistic implementation, some other scheme would have to be adopted, of course (this corresponds to the option in BB* which allows the user to say how often preconditions are to be tested).

The scheme just described is complete in the sense that any situation that can be handled by conventional Knowledge Sources can also be handled in the presence of message-passing. The penalties that have to paid are an increase in the number of Knowledge Sources and the fact that some KSARs may never be executed because their preconditions never become *true* (they may have all predicates except the request ones *true*, and so are *almost true*). Here, it becomes crucial to distinguish between Knowledge Source instances and Knowledge Sources themselves. In the CASSANDRA interpretation, it is only particular *instances* of Knowledge Sources that become blocked by the communications mechanisms: it is not the Knowledge Sources themselves that can make no progress—it is always possible that events will occur which will allow progress in the face of such blockings. Thus, the distinction between instance and Knowledge Source shows how a level manager may still function, even if all of its current KSARs are waiting for replies. External events can still occur and cause internal, local database events, even when all of the current set of KSARs are in a waiting state. The penalty, in this context, is a long *waiting list*. Given this, it would seem to be the case that increased demand for communication bandwidth will merely serve to reduce the quality of the solution produced by any particular level manager and does not necessarily entail that a solution will not be found. This appears to be a saving grace of this method of communication.

6

CASSANDRA in Z

In the last Chapter, we presented a basic informal specification of the CASSANDRA architecture. The informal specification that we gave is basic in the sense that it defines all necessary components, but it relies heavily upon an understanding of the blackboard architecture and it does not contain any justifications (for the latter, the reader should consult Craig, 1988a). In this Chapter, we will turn the informal specification into a formal one. The Z specification that we give here requires a number of the constructs that we defined in Chapter 4, but, as we will see, they sometimes require modification in order to fit into the new architecture.

The most important "borrowings" concern Knowledge Sources and KSARs they are included in the CASSANDRA specification with a few slight modifications (for example, triggers cannot now mention abstraction levels, and actions can operate only on a single database). Preconditions now refer to non-local requests for information: they become explicit in the CASSANDRA architecture (they were included in rule conditions in the last Chapter), and they require a formal treatment. The event system can be borrowed intact, although there is a question as to whether we should allow for other event types: for example, events that relate to communications. Indeed, one of the problems with the current state of the architecture is that we feel that communications are not fully integrated into the architecture: it remains an open question as to whether events caused by communication with external level managers should be counted as full control events in the way that NEW or ADD are. Here, we will take the position adopted by Craig (1988a, Chapter 7): any events caused by acts of communication must be mediated by the standard events which are familiar from the blackboard specification.

In essence, then, this Chapter consists of the specification of a communications system and of the modification of schemata provided by the blackboard specification we undertook in Chapter 4. The modification task is not trivial and requires us to repeat large portions of the blackboard specification because the relationships between schemata are different.

Our specification covers all of the components of a level manager in CASSANDRA. We will, in fact, leave the specification of the level manager construct until the very end: this is because we will use it to connect all the other constructs into one unit, and we will also use it to perform a variety of hiding tasks. These tasks are necessary because we want the internal components of a level manager to be invisible to the outside world in order that modularity is enforced. The components that we will specify are:

- The local database and its entries.

- Ports, channels and communications (this requires that we define types to for input and output messages).

- Knowledge Source preconditions (these, it will be remembered, are the only components of a level manager that can issue requests for information to other level managers).

- Knowledge Source actions: actions can send information to other level managers, so there is a difference between actions in blackboard and in CASSANDRA systems.

- Finally, we specify the level manager construct proper: this will involve the integration of all other components and information hiding.

The reader should note that some few of the constructs that we actually require can be taken from the blackboard specification that we gave above. It needs to be pointed out that some modification is necessary in order to incorporate blackboard constructs into the CASSANDRA specification: most of the modifications are simple, and are therefore left as exercises for the reader.

Before we move on, it is necessary to say a few words about proofs. In the formal specification of the blackboard system, we gave a number of short proofs. In this Chapter, we will state relevant results, but we will not give proofs. We want the reader to be aware of some of the consequences of our decisions when defining schemata, but we do not wish to go into detail. This is because the CASSANDRA architecture will be less familiar to most readers than the blackboard architecture: we feel that the presentation of proofs would serve only to obscure the definition in many cases. The majority of the proofs are straightforward (in many cases, the reader can consult Chapter four in order to find analogous results). As a result, the reader will find a number of theorem statements, but no proofs, in sections 6.1 to 6.4; in the section on the level manager construct, we have, in addition, omitted all theorem statements (this is motivated by the fact that the proofs become very complex as we build up the level manager construct and define its schema).

6.1   Local Database, Entries and Events

In this section, we will give our specification of the local database that is in each CASSANDRA level manager. Each local database is similar to an abstraction level in the blackboard architecture, and contains entries with a similar representational vocabulary. The contents of each local database are private to its containing level manager, and at some stage, we will need to make sure that this is, indeed, the case.

Since the local database is unstructured in the sense that it does not contain abstraction levels, we have to alter our definition of the entry manipulation schemata to take this into account.

We begin with our basic type defintions.

The local database is represented by the type $DATABASE$. The database is a partial function from entry identifiers to entry structures. The fact that it is a *partial* function is justified by the fact that we want to be able to add new entries as and when we desire. We will give a formal definition of the types:

$[EID]$

$DATABASE == EID \nrightarrow ENTRY$

As in the blackboard specification, EID is the set of entry identifiers: this set is assumed to be infinitely large and that a unique identifier is associated with each entry. In the CASSANDRA arechitecture, however, we must *ensure* that entry identifiers are invisible to all level managers other than the one in which the entries reside: in other words, at some stage, we must ensure that all entry identifiers are *hidden.* For the time being, this will not be considered, and we will leave it as an open issue until we have completed the basic specification (a similar remark applies to KSAR identifiers).

In the above definition, the $ENTRY$ type was unspecified. We give it here (it should be familiar from the blackboard specification):

$[ATTR, VAL]$

$ENTRY == ATTR \nrightarrow VAL$

where $ATTR$ is the domain of attribute names, and VAL is the domain of values. Once again, we prefer not to specify VAL in detail.

Our specification of the local database is slightly different from the one we gave in Chapter 4. The reader might find the comparison of the two styles of interest. We define the local database as a state space:

```
┌─ LocalDB ─────────────────────────────────
│ db : DATABASE
│
└────────────────────────────────────────────
```

We assume that the Δ and Ξ schemata are defined as:

```
┌─ ΔLocalDB ────────────────────────────────
│ LocalDB
│ LocalDB'
│
└────────────────────────────────────────────
```

and:

```
┌─ ΞLocalDB ────────────────────────────────
│ ΔLocalDB
│ ──────────────
│ db = db'
└────────────────────────────────────────────
```

The intialisation schema for the local database is:

```
┌─ InitLocalDB ─────────────────────────────
│ LocalDB
│ ──────────────
│ dom db = ∅
└────────────────────────────────────────────
```

We can define a schema, *KnownEntry*, which is satisfied whenever the entry identifier it accepts as input is an element of the domain of the local database:

```
┌─ KnownEntry ──────────────────────────────
│ ΞLocalDB
│ e? : EID
│ ──────────────
│ e? ∈ dom db
└────────────────────────────────────────────
```

We need now to define the three basic operation schemata for the local database. These schemata specify the three operations which should be familiar from the blackboard specification.

$$
\begin{array}{|l}
\_AddAttr\_\!_____ \\
\Delta LocalDB \\
enm? : EID \\
a? : ATTR \\
v? : VAL \\
\hline
\exists\, e : ENTRY \bullet e = db(enm?) \mid \\
\quad db' = db \oplus \{\ enm? \mapsto (e \cup \{\ a? \mapsto v?\ \})\} \\
\end{array}
$$

We can prove the following:

Theorem 1

$$ AddAttr \vdash \# \operatorname{dom} db' = \# \operatorname{dom} db $$

$$
\begin{array}{|l}
\_ModAttr\_\!_____ \\
\Delta LocalDB \\
enm? : EID \\
a? : ATTR \\
v? : VAL \\
\hline
\exists\, e : ENTRY \bullet e = db(enm?) \mid \\
\quad a? \in \operatorname{dom} e\ \wedge \\
\quad db' = db \oplus \{\ enm? \mapsto (e \oplus \{\ a? \mapsto v?\ \})\} \\
\end{array}
$$

Using the definition of *KnownEntry*, we have the following definitions:

$$ DBAddAttrib \cong (KnownEntry \wedge AddAttr) \vee \neg\, KnownEntry $$

$$ DBModifyAttrib \cong (KnownEntry \wedge ModAttr) \vee \neg\, KnownEntry $$

Finally, we have:

```
┌─ CreateEntry ──────────────────────────────────
│ ΔLocalDB
│ enm? : EID
│ avpairs? : ENTRY
├────────────────────────────────────────────────
│ avpairs? ≠ ∅
│ db' = db ∪ { enm? ↦ avpairs? }
└────────────────────────────────────────────────
```

The interface schema (the robust version, in other words) is:

$$DBCreateEntry \hateq (\neg \, KnownEntry \wedge CreateEntry)$$
$$\vee \, KnownEntry$$

We can prove the following result:

Theorem 2

$$CreateEntry \vdash \# \operatorname{dom} db' > \# \operatorname{dom} db$$

We assume that the value of *enm?* in *CreateEntry* and in *DBCreateEntry* is generated in some way via an operation that creates new entry identifiers. The reader should also note that we require *avpairs?* to contain *at least one* attribute-value pair: in other words, entries *must always* be non-empty. We have no deletion operations, so we also require that operations on entries be *monotonic*.

All three of these schemata are similar to the ones we gave when specifying the blackboard architecture. The difference between these schemata and the ones in Chapter 4 is that the input variable that was bound to the abstraction level identifier is missing: this is an immediate consequence of the fact that there is only one database in a level manager. Similar theorems can be proved about these schemata, as we will see.

We have the following results concering addition and creation:

Theorem 3

$$\vdash (DBAddAttrib \, \semi \, DBModifyAttrib) \equiv DBAddAttrib$$

Theorem 4

$$\vdash (DBCreateEntry \mathbin{\raise0.5ex\hbox{$\scriptstyle \circ$}} DBAddAttrib) \equiv DBCreateEntry$$

Now we will define the basic event types. The event types are called *LMEVENT*:

$$LMEVENT ::= newev \mid addev \mid modev$$

We can define the three event schemata as follows:

┌─ *NewEvent* ─────────────────────────────
│ $ev! : LMEVENT$
├──────────────────────────────────
│ $ev! = newev$
└──────────────────────────────────

┌─ *AddEvent* ─────────────────────────────
│ $ev! : LMEVENT$
├──────────────────────────────────
│ $ev! = addev$
└──────────────────────────────────

┌─ *ModEvent* ─────────────────────────────
│ $ev! : LMEVENT$
├──────────────────────────────────
│ $ev! = modev$
└──────────────────────────────────

We can define the interface schemata for the local database. We are going to assume that there is a schema called *NewEntryName* which generates unique entry identifers (this is a schema that we will import from the blackboard specification). The schema that we define perform appropriate checks and cause appropriate events.

$$LDBCreate \mathrel{\widehat{=}} NewEntryName \wedge DBCreateEntry$$
$$\wedge\ NewEvent$$
$$LDBAdd \mathrel{\widehat{=}} DBAddAttrib \wedge AddEvent$$
$$LDBMod \mathrel{\widehat{=}} DBModifyAttrib \wedge ModEvent$$

Expansion of the above will show that they are the schemata that we require.

At this stage, we have a specification of the local database within a level manager. This specification contains all the essential features that we require, so it is an adequate model for our purposes. We can now move on to consider the communications facilities required by the CASSANDRA architecture.

6.2   Channels and Ports

In the CASSANDRA architecture, there is no global state, and level managers must communicate their results explicitly using communications mechanisms. All communications are in the form of message-passing over *channels*: a channel is a connection between two level managers and can only be used in one direction (that is, channels are *uni-directional*). The existence of a channel connecting two level managers means that the level managers are able to exchange messages, but they may do so only in one direction, so one level manager sees the channel as an input device and the other as an output device: any attempt to use a channel incorrectly leads to an error.

Within level managers, channels are not directly visible. They are, instead, represented by *ports*. In the original definition of the architecture (Craig, 1988a), ports were considered almost as *names* for channels. Certainly, if a channel is available to a level manager, it is known within the level manager via the existence of the corresponding port, and ports *do* represent channels as far as Knowledge Sources, KSARs and other level manager components are concerned, but the fact that ports have operations and restrictions associated with them implies that they are very much more than names. Below, we will give a specification for ports which makes their status and structure very much clearer.

The fact that communications play an important part in the operation of level managers entails that they impact on some of the internal structures. In particular, the execution cycle for some Knowledge Sources takes communication into account. Knowledge Sources in level managers have a precondition (this is very much in line with the classical blackboard architecture), but preconditions are concerned with communications. In the first complete definition of the architecture, preconditions could contain general predicates on the state of the local database: in the specification that we give here, this aspect of the precondition is consigned to rule conditions (we are assuming that Knowledge Source actions are composed of production rules), so preconditions take over a role that deals exclusively with communications.

In Craig (1988a), it is required that all communication acts that require a response be handled by preconditions: we follow this exactly, as we follow the prescription that Knowledge Source actions be able only to send information to other level managers. The restriction on actions entails that their semantics is the same as in the blackboard architecture, so we can adopt the specification that we gave in Chapter 4 (we need to make the stipulation that the conditions of the rules that compose an action *must not* be permitted to engage in *any* acts of communication with the outside world). In the 1988 specification, it was also stated that preconditions were 3-valued: that is, instead of evaluating to a truth-value in the set {*true, false*}, they evaluate to a truth-value in the set {*true, false, undefined*}, where the value *undefined* is taken to mean that there is no way of telling what the truth-value might be. The interpretation we gave is similar to one of Kleene's (1952). In addition to a change in interpretation for the connectives in a precondition, additional machinery was introduced to manipulate preconditions in CASSANDRA Knowledge Sources.

In this section, we are going to specify all those components of a level manager that are concerned with communications. This means that we will be giving a specification of Knowledge Source preconditions as well as the basic mechanisms that are needed to support communications. One fact which emerges is that we cannot make the specification as precise as we would like because there are aspects of the level manager which depend heavily upon the task to which it is assigned: this is both unfortunate and important. It is unfortunate because we would like to give a complete specification, and it is important because it forces us to be general, and it forces us to accept that there are limits to our method.

We begin the specification with the definition of some atomic types.

The types are:

$$[LMID, PORTID]$$

The type *LMID* represents the identifiers of all possible level managers: each level manager in a CASSANDRA system is associated with a unique identifier. This identifier is used to individuate the level manager in the system and is used extensively in communications: in effect, it serves as an address for communications.

The type *PORTID* represents all port identifiers. Each port in a level manager is associated with a unique identifier. All port operations use this identifier to address the port on which information is to be sent or received. The port identifier is, to all intents and purposes, the identifier of the corresponding channel. The channel is provided by the underlying communications mechanism and is invisible to the Knowledge Sources and other structures within each level manager. We will be assuming that channels are known *only* to the interface between the communications sub-system within each level manager and the underlying network mechanisms, and that a mapping is performed between ports and the channels that are provided by the network. We will come back to this point below. For the time being, it can safely be assumed that ports are the only communications structures which are accessible from within the application layer of a level manager.

Channels are uni-directional, so we associate a type with each port:

$$PORT\_TYPE == input \mid output$$

The *PORT_TYPE* determines which operations are permissible for a particular port. For example, if a port has type *input*, it may only be used to receive messages; if it has type *output*, on the other hand, any attempt to receive a message on it will cause an error. We can summarise this as follows:

input: If the port type is *input*, all operations connected with message output cause an error.

output: If the port type is *ouput*, all operations connected with message input cause an error.

Given the fact that each port has a type, and the fact that each port is associated with a channel that connects to another level manager, we can specify the type of the port structure. In the specification, we make use of an element of *LMID*: this represents the level manager at the "other end" of the channel. For input ports, the identifier represents the level manager which sends messages along this channel; for output ports, it represents the level manager which will receive the messages.

$$PORT == (PORTID \times PORT\_TYPE \times LMID)$$

A port is modelled by a triple. We define the obvious projection functions:

$$
\begin{array}{|l}
portid : PORT \rightarrow PORTID \\
\hline
\forall\, p : PORT \bullet \\
\quad portid(p) = first(p)
\end{array}
$$

$$
\begin{array}{|l}
port\_type : PORT \rightarrow PORT\_TYPE \\
\hline
\forall\, p : PORT \bullet \\
\quad port\_type(p) = first(second(p))
\end{array}
$$

$$
\begin{array}{|l}
port\_lm : PORT \rightarrow LMID \\
\hline
\forall\, p : PORT \bullet \\
\quad port\_lm(p) = second(second(p))
\end{array}
$$

Each level manager, quite obviously, needs more than one port, so we can define the type that we need to represent the ports in a level manager as:

$$PORTS == \mathbb{P}\ PORT$$

We define the ports as a set of ports. This causes us no problems. In fact, it is the correct definition because we do not want *a priori* to impose orderings on the ports in a level manager. We might want to define ports as the union of two sets of ports such that one set is the set of input ports in the level manager, and the other port is the set of its output ports. We can do this by the definition of a schema:

$$
\begin{array}{|l}
\underline{\;LMPorts\;}\rule{0pt}{0pt} \\
ports : PORTS \\
\hline
ports \neq \varnothing \\
(\forall\, iports, oports : PORTS \bullet \\
\qquad iports \subseteq ports \wedge .oports \subseteq ports \wedge \\
\qquad iports \cup oports = ports \wedge \\
\qquad (\forall\, op : PORT \bullet \\
\qquad\qquad port\_type(op) = output \Rightarrow op \in oports) \wedge \\
\qquad (\forall\, ip : PORT \bullet \\
\qquad\qquad port\_type(ip) = input \Rightarrow ip \in iports) \Rightarrow \\
\qquad oports \cap iports = \varnothing) \wedge \\
(\forall\, p : PORT;\ pt : PORT\_TYPE;\ lm : LMID\ | \\
\qquad port\_type(p) = pt \wedge port\_lm(p) = lm \bullet \\
\qquad (\exists\, p_1 : PORT;\ pt_1 : PORT\_TYPE;\ lm_1 : LMID\ | \\
\qquad\qquad pt_1 = port\_type(p_1) \wedge lm_1 = port\_lm(p_1) \bullet \\
\qquad lm = lm_1 \wedge pt = pt_1 \Rightarrow \\
\qquad p = p_1))
\end{array}
$$

This schema ensures that the ports used for input are distinct from those used for output. Notice that we need to define *iports* and *oports* as *improper* subsets of *ports*: this is because a level manager may only have input ports or it may only have output ports. In other words, it is not necessary that a particular level manager have both input and output ports. We also need the fact that *ports* contains only the two subsets *iports* and *oports*: this is because we do not want other types of ports to interfere with our definitions. We will return to the second universally quantified formula below when we come to discuss our specification of the ports that a level manager may have.

Quite clearly, we need to prove that the above definition is sound: i.e., we need to prove that it is true in all cases. The cases are:

1. *ports* is composed only of input ports;

2. *ports* is composed only of output ports;

3. *ports* contains both input and output ports.

We are going to assume that once the ports in a level manager have been set up, they remain constant for all time. This implies that we have no real use for the schema $\Delta LMPorts$. We can define the initialisation schema as:

$$
\begin{array}{|l}
\hline
\_InitLMPorts_____ \\
LMPorts \\
lmports? : PORTS \\
\hline
ports' = lmports? \\
\hline
\end{array}
$$

We need to prove some important results about initialization. In particular, we need to prove that the ports can be initialized correctly, for not any set of ports will do. In other words, we need to impose constraints on possible values of *lmports?*.

Theorem 5

$$\vdash \exists\, lmports? : PORTS \bullet InitLMPorts$$

We will assume two operations on ports: *portReceive* and *portSend*. The former produces messages, while the latter consumes them. For the schemata that follow, we will need types for messages. We are going to distinguish between two types of message: input messages and output messages. Input messages are messages that are received by a level manager from an external source (typically from other level managers). Output messages are those messages that a level manager sends to the external world (again, these will typically be to other level managers). These operations interface to the network, and we do not specify then further.

We will assume that there is a type:

$[DATA]$

which represents the data that is to be sent in a message. Usually, we will make no assumptions about what is sent, although, on occasion, we will need to examine a message's contents to ensure that certain information that is needed by the level manager is present. Since we do not need to know the structure of the data on all occasions, we have defined the type as atomic. This follows our general assumption that message contents are really the business of the application and not the architecture: it also relates to our assumption that the mechanisms that we are specifying here *must* be independent of the particular network architecture and the protocols that it supports.

6.2.1 Message Sending

We begin the specification of the communications component of the level manager with message-sending operations, and we define the output message type as follows:

$$OMSG ==$$
$$(PORTID \times (PORT\_TYPE \times (LMID \times$$
$$(LMID \times (DATA \times DESTINID)))))$$

The first component of type $LMID$ represents the identifier of the level manager to which the message is to be sent. The second component with that type represents the identifier of the level manager which is sending the message. The last component will be explained below, and the corresponding projection function will be explained there, too. We can summarise the interpretations of the component types (omitting the last for the present) as:

- $PORTID$ is the name of the port on which the message will be output.

- $PORT\_TYPE$ is the type of the port (this must *always* be *output*): this type is included only to allow extra checking.

- The first instance of $LMID$ is the name of the destination level manager.

- The second instance of $LMID$ is the name of the sending level manager.

- *DATA* is the data that comprises the message.

We will define the obvious projection functions:

$$
\begin{array}{|l}
\hline
omsgport : OMSG \rightarrow PORTID \\
\hline
\forall o : OMSG \bullet \\
\quad omsgport(o) = first(o)
\end{array}
$$

$$
\begin{array}{|l}
\hline
omsgport\_type : OMSG \rightarrow PORT\_TYPE \\
\hline
\forall o : OMSG \bullet \\
\quad omsgport\_type(o) = first(second(o))
\end{array}
$$

$$
\begin{array}{|l}
\hline
omsg\_destination : OMSG \rightarrow LMID \\
\hline
\forall o : OMSG \bullet \\
\quad omsg\_destination(o) = first(second^2(o))
\end{array}
$$

$$
\begin{array}{|l}
\hline
omsg\_originator : OMSG \rightarrow LMID \\
\hline
\forall o : OMSG \bullet \\
\quad omsg\_originator(o) = first(second^3(o))
\end{array}
$$

$$
\begin{array}{|l}
\hline
omsg\_data : OMSG \rightarrow DATA \\
\hline
\forall o : OMSG \bullet \\
\quad omsg\_data(o) = first(second^4(o))
\end{array}
$$

Where

$$second^2 = second \circ second$$
$$second^3 = second \circ second \circ second$$

and so on (in other words, the power just represents iteration).

For comparison, we define *IMSG*, the type of input messages, as follows:

$$IMSG == (LMID \times (LMID \times (DATA \times DESTINID)))$$

where:

[*DESTINID*]

is a set of *destination identifiers* (we will repeat this definition below when we come to discuss input messages). A destination identifier is intended to represent the name of the structure to which a message is to be directed: typically, destination identifiers will be interpreted as KSAR names. The reason for including destination identifiers in messages is that a particular message should be sent to some level manager component (say a KSAR) once it has been received from the network. Its main use is as follows.

When a Knowledge Source precondition makes a request, it sends a message to another level manager. That other level manager engages in some processing and, eventually, returns a message to the original, requesting, level manager (the one in which the Knowledge Source resides). When the message is received, the level manager must have information about where to send the message next: in this case, it is to be sent to a Knowledge Source instance (a KSAR, in other words). This information is encoded in the *DESTINID* component of the input message. The receiving level manager examines this component of the message and routes it accordingly.

The last component of *OMSG* is of type *DESTINID*: this component is the identifier of the structure within the sending level manager which is actually responsible for sending the message.

We can define a projection function so that receiving level managers can obtain the relevant information:

$$omsg\_sending\_structure : OMSG \rightarrow DESTINID$$
$$\forall o : OMSG \bullet$$
$$omsg\_data(o) = second^5(o)$$

In the *IMSG* type, there are two occurrences of the type *LMID*:
the first of these is the identifier of the sender of the message, and the
second is the identifier of the level manager to which the message should
be sent. The second occurrence of *LMID* has its value taken from the
sender component of *OMSG*.

As with *OMSG*, we prefer not to say anything about the contents
of a message's data: that is, we again impose no constraints upon the
structure of *DATA*.

We will define the projection functions for *IMSG* below. We considered it to be advisable to mention these facts about *IMSG* at this
point, so that the intentions behind the two types, *IMSG* and *OMSG*
would be clear.

We are now in a position to specify the communications operations.
Specifically, these are the operations which direct messages to ports.
We will also specify operations which will allow us to determine the
status of a port, to determine which level manager is at the other
end of a channel, which level managers are in communication with a
particular one, and so on. We will also define constraints on messages,
the most important of which is that a message cannot be sent to the
level manager which is sending the message (i.e., messages must always
be sent to *other* level managers). We will make one assumption which
might seem a little strange: we are going to assume that a level manager
can have *at least* one port which is connected to another level manager.
That is, assuming that *connects* is a two-place relation which denotes
the fact that two level managers may directly communicate with each
other, we have:

$$
\begin{aligned}
&\forall \, lm_1, lm_2 \bullet \\
&\quad connects(lm_1, lm_2) \Rightarrow \\
&\qquad (\exists \, p_1 : port \bullet \\
&\qquad\quad lmport(p_1, lm_1)) \land \\
&\qquad (\exists \, p_2 : port \bullet \\
&\qquad\quad lmport(p_2, lm_2))
\end{aligned}
$$

where *lmport* is a two-place relation that is true whenever its first argument is one of the ports in the second argument, and where lm_i, $i = 1, 2$,
is a level manager. The point is that we are merely allowing existential
quantification and *not* uniqueness. This implies that, for pair of level

managers i and j, there may be more than one port in level manager i which connects to level manager j, and that all of these ports can have the same type, if necessary. This assumption allows us to have level managers which engage in bi-directional communications (which requires that each have an input and an output port that is connected to the other level manager), and it allows us to have different channels connecting two level managers. We have already excluded the second alternative in our definition of *LMPorts* because it complicates matters considerably: this is the second universally quantified formula in the invariant of *LMPorts*.

We begin the specification of the interface to the ports in a level manager with a schema which determines the legality of an operation. This schema is particularly important for sending information to other level managers. We could choose to allow all receptions to occur automatically: in other words, we could adopt the position that a message that appears at an input port is automatically placed on an input queue which is inside the scope of the level manager. This avoids the need to engage in something akin to interrupt processing. We adopt this approach because it does not involve the specification of mechanisms at a level lower than we wish to provide.

$$
\begin{array}{|l}
\hline
\_\mathit{CorrectPortOp}_____ \\
\Xi \mathit{LMPorts} \\
\mathit{portid?} : \mathit{PORTID} \\
\mathit{porttyp?} : \mathit{PORT\_TYPE} \\
\mathit{portlm?} : \mathit{LMID} \\
\hline
\exists\, p : \mathit{PORT} \mid p \in \mathit{ports}\ \bullet \\
\quad \mathit{portid}(p) = \mathit{portid?} \land \mathit{port\_type}(p) = \mathit{porttyp?} \\
\quad\quad \land\ \mathit{port\_lm}(p) = \mathit{portlm?} \\
\hline
\end{array}
$$

We can use this schema to determine the conditions under which a send operation succeeds:

```
┌─ SendOpParams ─────────────────────────────
│ omsg? : OMSG
│ portid! : PORTID
│ porttyp! : PORT_TYPE
│ portlm! : LMID
├─────────────────────────────────────────────
│ portid! = omsg_portid(omsg?)
│ porttyp! = omsg_porttype(omsg?)
│ portlm! = omsg_portlm(omsg?)
└─────────────────────────────────────────────
```

The correct operation (in the sense that the parameters are correct) is:

$$CorrectSend \; \widehat{=}$$
$$\exists \, portid : PORTID;$$
$$porttyp : PORT\_TYPE; \; portlm : LMID \; \bullet$$
$$SendOpParams \; \wedge \; CorrectPortOp$$

We expand *CorrectSend* as follows:

```
┌─ CorrectSend ─────────────────────────────
│ ΞLMPorts
│ omsg? : OMSG
├─────────────────────────────────────────────
│ ∃ portid : PORTID; porttyp : PORT_TYPE;
│        portlm : LMID •
│   portid = omsg_portid(omsg?) ∧
│   porttyp = omsg_porttype(omsg?) ∧
│   portlm = omsg_portlm(omsg?) ∧
│   (∃ p : PORT | p ∈ ports •
│       portid(p) = portid ∧
│       port_type(p) = porttype ∧
│       port_lm(p) = portlm)
└─────────────────────────────────────────────
```

We will see that this expansion represents the operation we require when we come to specify the interactions between KSARs and message-sending.

Note that our definition allows us the freedom to impose the same constraints on the reception of messages as on their emission.

We can define the *SendMessage* schema as follows. The reader should note that the *sendPort* operation is assumed (it is an interface to the communications layer lower than the one which we are specifying):

$$SendMessage \; \hat{=} \; CorrectSend \land sendPort$$

For completeness, we can give an outline of *sendPort*:

```
┌─ sendPort ─────────────────────────────────────
│  omsg? : OMSG
├────────────────────────────────────────────────
│  comms_send(omsg_portid(omsg?), omsg?)
└────────────────────────────────────────────────
```

where *comms_send* performs the actual send operation over the network. Quite obviously not anything will do for *comms_send*, and so we have to impose some constraints upon it. This will also be the case for the message reception function which we shall see below. Once again, though, it is hard to see just *how* to impose such constraints and it is hard to see what form that they must take. The weakest assertions that we can make about *comms_send* are that it does not alter the port setup, nor does it alter the contents of *omsg?*. Of course, a complete specification of this function requires that we give a specification of the next level down in the communications system, and for present purposes, it is unnecessary to provide a complete specification of this function simply because we are not going to prove any deep results about it. This is an identical approach to the one that we will adopt for message reception.

6.2.2   Message Reception

The operation represented by *SendMessage* is the one that is used by level managers and Knowledge Sources to send information to other places in a CASSANDRA system. In order to describe the message reception structures in level managers, we need to introduce additional types. Specifically, we need to introduce types that model the messages that are received by level managers and a (FIFO) queue to hold incoming messages. We will define these types and then explain them and their utility in a CASSANDRA level manager.

We repeat the definition of the *input message* type, *IMSG* as:

$$IMSG == (LMID \times (LMID \times (DATA \times DESTINID)))$$

We will define some more projection functions over this type: these are the ones that we will use below.

$$
\begin{array}{|l}
\hline
sender\_lmid : IMSG \rightarrow LMID \\
\hline
\forall i : IMSG \bullet \\
\quad sender\_lmid(i) = first(i)
\end{array}
$$

$$
\begin{array}{|l}
\hline
destination\_lmid : IMSG \rightarrow LMID \\
\hline
\forall i : IMSG \bullet \\
\quad destination\_lmid(i) = first(second(i))
\end{array}
$$

$$
\begin{array}{|l}
\hline
imsg\_data : IMSG \rightarrow DATA \\
\hline
\forall i : IMSG \bullet \\
\quad imsg\_data(i) = first(second^2(i))
\end{array}
$$

$$
\begin{array}{|l}
\hline
internal\_destin : IMSG \rightarrow DESTINID \\
\hline
\forall i : IMSG \bullet \\
\quad internal\_destin(i) = second^3(i)
\end{array}
$$

Most of the projection functions are easy to interpret, we believe, so we do not explain them.

Messages of type *IMSG* record the identifier of the sending level manager and contain the identifier of the level manager that is to receive the message. In addition, messages contain data. Although we make the very general assumption that the underlying communications architecture will record the identifier of the sender and the receiver for its own use, our (redundant) inclusion of these two items of information is intended to provide an extra level of checking in a CASSANDRA system. Each level manager knows its own identifier, and can, therefore, check that each message that it receives is, in fact, correctly addressed: this is the first use of the destination component. The second use is that level managers might be required to engage in some kind of store-and-forward communications: although we would prefer this to remain at the level of the underlying communications system, its use cannot be ruled out as part of a problem-solving system. For example, some application-specific information in the message might indicate that it is to be broadcast to all level managers with the specific request that the destination level manager must, at all costs, receive the message. Such examples are, necessarily, application-specific, and we cannot examine them in detail here. What we are going to assume is that the destination level manager component in the message type is necessary for message verification and checking. We will consider this in more detail.

We want each level manager in a CASSANDRA system to be as secure as possible. This means that those messages which it *ought* to receive must be included in the set of messages which it *does* receive. Now, we already know that each port is connected to one and only one other level manager, and we know that the identifier of that level manager is known (because it is stored with the port). Each level manager also knows its own identifier, so it can check that the messages it has received have come along valid channels. Since we have imposed a uniqueness condition on ports (i.e., that there can be only one input port from each other level manager to which a particular level manager is connected, and similarly for output ports), we can make level managers check not only that they have received a correctly addressed message, but also that the use of the port is correct. We can, therefore, define two schemata, one to check addresses and one to check port use: we call the former *CheckMSGAddr*, and the latter *CheckInportUse*.

```
┌─ CheckMSGAddr ─────────────────────────────────
│ imsg? : IMSG
│ me : LMID
├──────────────────────────────────────────────
│ me = destination_lmid(imsg?)
└──────────────────────────────────────────────
```

The variable me is the identifier of the level manager. Note that me has no decorations: this is because we will hide it when we come to compose the level manager schema. All that $CheckMSGAddr$ does is to extract the second component of the message and test it against the level manager's identifier: clearly, if this test fails, the message has been addressed incorrectly, and some actions can be taken (either returning the message to the sender, or throwing the message away).

$CheckInportUse$ is defined as follows:

```
┌─ CheckInportUse ───────────────────────────────
│ imsg? : IMSG
├──────────────────────────────────────────────
│ ∃ s : LMID | s = sender_lmid(imsg?) •
│     ∃₁ p : PORT | p ∈ ports •
│         port_type(p) = input ∧
│         port_lm(p) = s ∧
│         LMPorts
└──────────────────────────────────────────────
```

(Notice that we have already hidden the sender by using an existential quantifier to restrict its scope.) The $CheckInportUse$ schema works as follows: the identifier of the sending level manager is extracted from the message. For this message to be valid, it must have been received on a port which is connected to the sending level manager: this port must have the type $input$, and it must be connected to the sender, s. If these conditions are met (or, rather, if there is such a port), then the message is assumed valid.

The point of this seemingly useless additional checking is quite simply that we *do not* want messages to be sent along channels other than those which have been *explicitly* defined for such communications. This point is made very clearly in the original CASSANDRA specification (Craig, 1988a, Chapter 4): here, we are merely taking that stipulation and making it a *formal* requirement.

Now, some readers might object that the assumption that we made above—that is, that if there exists an input port which is connected to the correct level manager, then all is well—is too strong. We agree with this, but would wish to observe that unless we specify the communications system in greater detail, this assumption is all that we can make. We could, for example, associate a queue with each input port and check each message in those queues to ensure that they were received on the corresponding port. Even here, there is room for doubt because a (malicious!) implementation might allow messages to be received on other ports, inspected for sender identifier, and then placed in the port queue for that sender identifier. At some stage, these queues would be merged to form a more general input queue: this operation costs us nothing to specify, but its complete implementation might turn out to be costly. Even if we adopted this multi-queue approach, given the level at which we are working, there is still no guarantee that ports will, in fact, be handled *exactly* as we might want to specify. We conclude that the specification that we have given above is *the most reasonable one* which we could give, when confronted by the different communications architectures that we are trying to accommodate.

The final point about input messages concerns the final component, which is of type *DESTINID*. This type represents *ultimate* destinations within a level manager. Now, an ultimate destination will, typically, be a KSAR. This is because messages are intended to be responses to queries raised by Knowledge Source instances (i.e., by KSARs). KSARs that request information enter a waiting state (see below for a specification) until the query has been answered satisfactorily. When a message is received by a level manager, it is important that it be directed to the object that requires it: in other words, if a KSAR makes a query and that query is answered, it is important that the response to the query be sent to the KSAR in question. This is the role of the *DESTINID* component in *IMSG*. If we wanted, we could define *DESTINID* as:

$$DESTINID == KSARID \cup SYSTEMID$$

where:

$$KSARID \cap SYSTEMID = \varnothing$$

and where:

$$[SYSTEMID]$$

is a set of identifiers for system components that need to engage in communication with other level managers. These components are somewhat application-specific, so we will be concerned below only with a subset of *DESTINID*:

$$DESTINID' == DESTINID \setminus SYSTEMID$$

This subset, we will simply refer to as *DESTINID*.

Finally, we observe that the component of type *DATA* is, essentially, opaque (as is the case for *OMSG*). In other words, we do not care to specify what might count as a legal value for *DATA* because the message-handling schemata rarely, if ever, examine items of this type (although we will see a couple of cases in which something of interest to us appears in the component of type *DATA*).

With output messages, we assumed that once a message was sent by the message-transmission primitive, it was gone for good. In other words, once a message had been sent by the level manager, the communications system took over management of the message and that the message was, effectively, gone from the level manager and was no longer amenable to further processing by that level manager (unless it had taken a copy). Now, we could adopt an identical approach in the case of input messages: we could assume that messages are received by the communications system and that they are stored there until the level manager makes an explicit request for a new message. This approach has some merits, but we do not adopt it: instead, we require all level manager components to access the message queue once on each iteration of the main cycle.

Our reasons for rejecting it have to do with the assumptions that we may reasonably make about the underlying communications system and have to do with the specification of operations over messages that are to be performed by level managers. Another reason is connected with the level at which we are aiming our specification.

The first reason is, quite simply, that we are assuming as little as possible about the communications system which level managers must use (indeed, we can see the simultaneous use of different communications architectures in some, very large, CASSANDRA systems). As will be seen below, we will need random access to input messages: this implies buffering. It is the case that not all communications architectures provide these facilities. We make the assumption that input buffering is performed, but we are trying to avoid any structures in our specification which make this property necessary (we can also assume output buffering, but, as we have seen, our primitives make no use of such a feature).

In other words, we are trying to reduce to a minimum the assumptions that we make about the communications architecture in order to allow CASSANDRA implementations on any architecture that might be available. Since we know the operations that level managers are to perform on input queues or buffers, we prefer to make them part of our specification: this also has the advantage that we have more under our control. We know, for example, that we will need a queue of input messages so that they can be directed to their ultimate destinations: we specify this component of the level manager so that we can be sure that the correct operations are performed on the queue.

Finally, we are aiming to produce a specification that can be implemented on a wide variety of hardware and which will work when layered on top of a variety of communication architectures. Although we do not want to specify an entire communications system (and that exercise would be interesting), we want to specify *enough* of the CASSANDRA architecture to make it portable. In addition, we are, of course, defining what amounts to a basic standard, so we are free to specify components which might "come for free" in some implementations. We feel free, therefore, to specify in detail *all of* those components whose behaviours need to have a complete and formal definition: the others, we may leave to one side.

On the basis of this argument, we will move on to give the specification of the queue that we will use to hold input messages. This queue is the primary database in which incoming messages are stored. Indeed, many operations are performed on the contents of this database, so its complete specification is of some importance to the overall specification of the level manager construct. The type of this database is *MSG_QUEUE* (we feel free to use this name to stand for the *input* message queue because we do not require an output queue):

```
┌─ MSG_QUEUE ──────────────────────────────
│  iqueue : seq IMSG
│
└──────────────────────────────────────────
```

We will assume that ΔMSG_QUEUE and ΞMSG_QUEUE are defined in the conventional fashion.

We can define an initialisation schema for MSG_QUEUE as follows:

```
┌─ InitMSG_QUEUE ──────────────────────────
│  MSG_QUEUE
├──────────────────────────────────────────
│  iqueue = ⟨⟩
└──────────────────────────────────────────
```

Given the definition of the message queue type, the initialisation schema should be obvious.

We are going to model the message queue type as a FIFO queue. This is not necessary, because we do not always require arrival time information to be represented explicitly in the input message queue. However, we adopt a FIFO discipline because it is relatively straightforward.

There are three schemata that we must define in order to provide an interface to the input message queue. These are:

1. An *enqueue* operation to add items (messages) to the queue.

2. A *dequeue* operation to remove items (messages) from the queue.

3. A predicate which is *true* whenever the queue is empty.

The predicate which we mentioned as (3) above is used in the definition of the dequeue operation: we will be engaging in a little schema composition, therefore. The definition of the queue-manipulating schemata is simple, and we give the three basic schemata with no further commentary.

```
┌─ Enqueue ────────────────────────────────
│  ΔMSG_QUEUE
│  imsg? : IMSG
├──────────────────────────────────────────
│  iqueue' = iqueue ⌢ ⟨imsg?⟩
└──────────────────────────────────────────
```

Theorem 6

$$Enqueue \vdash \#iqueue' = \#iqueue + 1$$

```
┌─ Delqueue ─────────────────────────────────────────
│ ΔMSG_QUEUE
│ msg! : IMSG
│ ────────────────────────────────────────────────
│ msg! = head iqueue
│ iqueue' = tail iqueue
└─────────────────────────────────────────────────────
```

Theorem 7

$$Enqueue \,\semi\, Delqueue \vdash \#iqueue' = \#iqueue$$

```
┌─ Emptyqueue ───────────────────────────────────────
│ MSG_QUEUE
│ ────────────────────────────────────────────────
│ iqueue = ⟨⟩
└─────────────────────────────────────────────────────
```

The *Delqueue* schema is not intended for unrestricted use: clearly, it can fail if the sequence denoted by *iqueue* is empty. We therefore define the interface schema:

$$Dequeue \,\hat{=}\, \neg\, Emptyqueue \wedge Delqueue$$

Expansion of this schema gives:

```
┌────────────────────────────────────────────────────
│ ΔMSG_QUEUE
│ msg! : IMSG
│ ────────────────────────────────────────────────
│ iqueue ≠ ⟨⟩ ·
│ iqueue' = tail iqueue
│ msg! = head iqueue
└─────────────────────────────────────────────────────
```

which is exactly what we require.

Theorem 8

$$Dequeue \vdash \#iqueue' = \#iqueue - 1$$

Theorem 9

$$Enqueue \, \fatsemi \, Dequeue \vdash \#iqueue' = \#iqueue$$

In order to assist encapsulation, we provide the following schema:

```
┌─ QueueLength ──────────────────────────────
│ ΞMSG_QUEUE
│ qlen! : N
├─────────────────────────────────────────────
│ qlen! = #iqueue
└─────────────────────────────────────────────
```

Such an operation may be useful in the construction of schedulers (for example, if the length of the input queue is below some threshold, the scheduler might concentrate on performing only local inference tasks).

We now have a queue in which to hold input messages, and we have some relatively simple checking operations. What we lack is any way of receiving messages from the outside world. As we were at pains to state above, we can only go so far in the specification of this component: we believe that we can only go as far as naming the function. What we can do, though, is to collect the appropriate schemata that we have defined above into an operation schema that is basic to each level manager. We define the operation using schema composition and quantification to be:

$$
\begin{aligned}
ReceiveIMSG \triangleq \\
\exists imsg? : IMSG \mid imsg? = receive\_msg \bullet \\
CheckInportUse \wedge CheckMSGAddr \wedge Enqueue
\end{aligned}
$$

We can expand this definition (with a slight re-arrangement) as:

```
┌─ ReceiveIMSG ──────────────────────────────────
│ ΞLMPorts
│ ΔMSG_QUEUE
│ me : LMID
├──────────────────────────────────────────────────
│ ∃ imsg? : IMSG | imsg? = receive_msg •
│     me = destination_lmid(imsg?) ∧
│     (∃ s : LMID | s = sender_lmid(imsg?) •
│         (∃₁ p : PORT | p ∈ ports •
│             port_type(p) = input ∧ port_lm(p) = s))
│     ∧ iqueue' = iqueue ⌢ ⟨imsg?⟩
└──────────────────────────────────────────────────
```

where *receive_msg* is a function of type

$$receive\_msg : \rightarrow IMSG$$

which represents the operation of receiving a message from the underlying communications system. The full schema inputs the message (which is hidden by existential quantification) and then checks what amounts to the header data; next it enqueues the message for future use.

Theorem 10

$$ReceiveIMSG \vdash \#iqueue' > \#iqueue$$

We now have an interface to the underlying communications system which allows us to send as well as to receive messages. When messages are received, they are placed in a FIFO queue for further processing. As we will see in the next section, this processing involves Knowledge Source preconditions.

6.3   Knowledge Source Preconditions

In CASSANDRA systems, the semantics of Knowledge Source preconditions are different from those in blackboard systems. This is primarily motivated by the fact that the precondition is the *only* part of a Knowledge Source that is permitted to send a request to another level manager and then to wait for a reply: this is done in order to obtain non-local information. Now, we have to be a little careful here because a number of errors can enter the discussion unless we make some distinctions. It is not, strictly speaking, the precondition of a Knowledge Source, but the precondition of a Knowledge Source *instantiation* that makes requests to other level managers. It should be remembered that many instances of the same Knowledge Source may be present in a blackboard system: each instance is created as a result of a different triggering event. This is also the case for Knowledge Sources in CASSANDRA systems: in other words, in CASSANDRA systems, Knowledge Source triggers respond to purely *local* events. When a Knowledge Source is triggered, a KSAR is created to record the Knowledge Source's instantiation. The precondition and action are evaluated in the context provided by the KSAR (which, it should be remembered, contains local variables that record information about the triggering event, amongst other things). Thus, it is, strictly speaking, the precondition of some KSAR that makes a request for information from another level manager.

This distinction is important because of the following. If it were Knowledge Sources proper that made non-local requests, it would be possible for *all* the Knowledge Sources in a level manager to be waiting for replies. When a non-local request is made, the KSAR making the request waits until a reply has been received. If it were Knowledge Sources that made requests, then, if all Knowledge Sources in a level manager made requests to other level managers, and if none of the expected replies had been received, all of the Knowledge Sources would be in a waiting state, and their level manager could make no progress towards a local solution state. Now, if we accept the fact that KSARs perform requests, it is still possible for all of the KSARs in a level manager to be waiting for replies. However, it is also the case that a new and purely local event can cause the creation of a new KSAR which does not have to enter a waiting state (because it does not make any non-local requests): this KSAR can be executed in order to cause further local events. The requirement that KSARs execute preconditions, helps to prevent the situation in which no progress can be made within a level manager. It should be noted that this fact about the internal structure of level managers does not, automatically, ensure that they *will* always make progress, but it serves to minimise the risk.

The distinction should be completely understood because it forms the basis of the specification that we present in this section. Here, we are concerned with the evaluation of preconditions. Specifically, we are interested in the interactions between the communications system (as represented by the port structure and input message queue that we specified in the last section) and KSARs. In addition to this interaction, we must take into account the fact that while a precondition is waiting for a reply to a non-local request, *it cannot be assigned a truth-value.* In other words, while preconditions are in a waiting state, it is not possible to determine whether they should be executed. We need to provide a model of the waiting state and show that preconditions have no truth-value.

For this section, we will be assuming the existence of a KSAR type (called *KSAR*) and a type to represent KSAR identifiers:

[*KSARID*]

The KSAR structure that we gave in the last Chapter is perfectly adequate for our needs, so we will assume it here.

From what has already been said about preconditions in CASSAN-DRA systems, it should be clear that they perform two functions:

1. Issue requests to other level managers for information.

2. Receive information as a reply.

When information is received from another level manager, a precondition may apply a predicate to it: if the predicate is satisfied, the precondition is satisfied, otherwise it remains in a waiting state. Now, this basic sketch can be extended very slightly: rather than simply test until data received from another level manager satisfies some predicate, a precondition may also evaluate to some value which indicates that it will no longer wait, and that it may be regarded as false. When this happens, the KSAR returns to its triggered state. If a precondition is satisfied, its KSAR can be promoted to an eligible list and therefore become a candidate for execution.

We can regard preconditions as being composed of pairs: the first component represents the request to be sent, and the second is a predicate. Before giving a definition, we need to be able to determine the value of a precondition. We therefore need:

$$PRECONDTV ::= pctrue \mid pcfalse \mid pcnoval$$

where the value $pcnoval$ denotes the value which all preconditions have while they are in the waiting state. Now it is a moot point as to whether a precondition evaluates to *undefined* while waiting or whether it simply has *no* truth-value. As the reader will see, we can remain neutral to this distinction in our specification.

Now, the definition of $PRECONDTV$ is necessary for the proper definition of the precondition type. This is because we define the second component to be a function:

$$PRECOND ==$$
$$(LMID \times DATA) \times (DATA \to PRECONDTV)$$

To simplify matters, we will define some projection functions.

$$
\begin{array}{|l}
\hline
precond\_enquiry : PRECOND \to (LMID \times DATA) \\
\hline
\forall p : PRECOND \bullet \\
\quad precond\_enquiry(p) = first(p) \\
\end{array}
$$

$precond\_enquiry$ is the message that is to be sent to the other level manager.

$$
\begin{array}{|l}
\hline
precond\_test : PRECOND \to (DATA \to PRECONDTV) \\
\hline
\forall p : PRECOND \bullet \\
\quad precond\_test(p) = second(p) \\
\end{array}
$$

The function $precond\_test$ yields the function which is applied to all messages that are received in reply to sending the first component of the precondition.

The next two functions are used to "unpack" the first component of a precondition. This unpacking is performed by the port interface in order to create a valid message of type $OMSG$.

$$
\begin{array}{|l}
\hline
precond\_enq\_dest : (LMID \times DATA) \to LMID \\
\hline
\forall ld : LMID \times DATA \bullet \\
\quad precond\_enq\_dest(ld) = first(ld) \\
\end{array}
$$

$$\begin{array}{|l}
\hline
precond\_enq\_msg : (LMID \times DATA) \rightarrow DATA \\
\hline
\forall\, ld : LMID \times DATA \bullet \\
\quad precond\_enq\_msg(ld) = second(ld) \\
\end{array}$$

We will allow each precondition to make several requests. This entails that we consider the actual precondition that is to be found in Knowledge Sources as a collection of primitive precondition structures. In fact, we will consider the Knowledge Source precondition to be a set of objects of type *PRECOND*:

$$\begin{array}{|l}
\hline
\_KS\_PRECOND_____ \\
\quad precond : \mathbb{P}\ PRECOND \\
\hline
\end{array}$$

(we assume the Δ and Ξ schemata are defined in the usual way). We will adopt the convention that if a precondition in a Knowledge Source is the empty set, that precondition represents the value *true*: that is, that the precondition is satisfied. This permits us to represent Knowledge Sources which do not engage in non-local communications: they are those Knowledge Sources whose precondition is $\varnothing$.

At this point, we are able to give a specification of the evaluation mechanism for preconditions. We are, though, faced with a choice: should we create a new KSAR for each element of a precondition? We believe, although we have no empirical evidence for this, that the answer should be negative. The argument for this negative position rests on the fact that preconditions can bind local variables: we do not know *a priori* where or how these variables will be used. Thus, each KSAR will be allowed to issue multiple requests. This position can pose problems, however, for a precondition may now enter a waiting state and remain there for an indefinite period: in fact, we believe that the chances that it *will* remain there indefinitely have now been increase considerably. However, we are forced to pay this price because of our ignorance of the variable-use pattern within the precondition and action.

In order to model the evaluation of preconditions, we need to give specification of what it is for a KSAR to be in a waiting state. We will do this by maintining a new database of KSARs: the contents of the database at any one time are those KSARs which are waiting for their precondition to be satisfied or falsified. We will define a function to help us in modelling the waiting KSARs:

$$
\begin{array}{|l}
ksarname : KSAR \rightarrow KSARID \\
\hline
\forall\, k : KSAR \bullet \\
\quad \exists_1 \, nm : KSARID \bullet \\
\qquad nm = ksar\_id(k)
\end{array}
$$

Note that this function assumes that there is an attribute, $ksar\_id$, stored in each KSAR.

Now, our model of the waiting state does not actually require that entire KSARs be stored in the waiting database. This is because the full information stored in a KSAR is not strictly necessary. In addition, we want to model the evaluation process in an explicit fashion. We will therefore define a new type for KSARs that are in the waiting state:

$$
\begin{array}{|l}
\_PCKSAR_____ \\
waiting\_ksar : KSAR \\
waiting\_preconds : KSPRECOND \\
false\_preconds : KSPRECOND \\
\hline
\mathrm{dom}\ waiting\_ksar \neq \varnothing
\end{array}
$$

(We will assume that the Δ and Ξ forms are defined as normal.)

The idea behind this definition is that the precondition should be easily accessible. It is therefore represented by $waiting\_precond$: this variable represents the entire precondition at any time. The variable $false\_preconds$ represents those parts of the precondition that have evaluated to $false$. When we come to specify the evaluation process, it will be seen that all preconditions that are satisfied by an input message are removed from $waiting\_preconds$; those that evaluate to $pcfalse$ are removed from $waiting\_preconds$ and added to $false\_preconds$. If a precondition remains undefined when it evaluates a message, it stays in $waiting\_preconds$. In other words, if a precondition is satisfied, it is removed from the KSAR: if it is not satisified (in the classical, two-valued, sense), it is retained in another part of the structure.

The justification for this approach is as follows. We assume that, once a message satisfies a precondition, that precondition will remain satisfied forever. This is a direct consequence of the fact that we are not permitting deletions within level manager local databases. It is the case that deletions may occur elsewhere and level managers may give different responses at different times—these, different, responses could cause precondition values to change, but we will ignore this because we can make the assumption that such changes will be notified via the local database and its associated Knowledge Sources. Now, in order to determine the value of a complete precondition (i.e., the set), we can say that once a precondition has evaluated to *true*, it no longer plays any part in the evaluation process. We are therefore concerned with the roles of those preconditions which have either no value or whose value is *pcfalse*. In the former case, we do not know what the value to be assigned to them will be, so we need to retain them for evaluation (in a simple fashion, we might consider them not to have been evaluated). When a precondition evaluates to *pcfalse*, we remove it from the *waiting_precond* set and add it to the set *false_preconds*: we do this for the following reasons. Firstly, because changes occur in the level manager from which the response comes, it is possible that that level manager, at some time in the future, will send another message which will satisfy the precondition. Second, the scheduler might have to make "last-ditch" decisions which are based on the number of unsatisfied and the number of false preconditions in a KSAR: such decisions might occur when no other progress is possible. We could have interpreted the precondition evaluation process in terms of a variable which records the value so far of the precondition: this does not seem appropriate because it does not permit such "worst-case" processing without other information being stored. In addition, a scheduler might wish to have available information about those preconditions which are false: the scheme that we adopt allows for this.

We now define the initialisation schema for *PCKSAR*:

```
┌─ InitPCKSAR ─────────────────────────────
│ PCKSAR
│ ksar? : KSAR
├──────────────────────────────────────────
│ waiting_ksar' = ksar?
│ waiting_precond' = ksar_precond(ksar?)
│ false_preconds = ∅
└──────────────────────────────────────────
```

where *ksar_precond* is a function which returns the precondition stored in the Knowledge Source associated with *ksar?* (it is defined as the composition of two functions—see Chapter 4).

Theorem 11

$$\exists\, ksar? : KSAR \bullet InitPCKSAR$$

Theorem 12

$$\text{pre } InitPCKSAR \vdash InitPCKSAR$$

It should be remembered that *only* those Knowledge Sources which have a non-empty precondition are entered into the waiting state. This complicates the KSAR creation process very slightly. We need to define a test:

```
┌─ WillWait ───────────────────────────────
│ Δ TriggeredList
│ ksarid? : KSARID
├──────────────────────────────────────────
│ ∃ ksar : KSAR | ksar ∈ triggered_list •
│     ksar(ksar_id) = ksarid? ∧
│     ksar_precond(ksar) ≠ ∅
└──────────────────────────────────────────
```

We now have a model for KSARs that are in the waiting state. We must now described the database in which they are stored within each level manager.

```
┌─ WKSARS ─────────────────────────────────
│ waiting : KSARID ⇸ PCKSAR
```

and we assume that the Δ and Ξ forms are defined by convention. We can also define an initialisation schema in the obvious fashion:

```
┌─ InitWKSARS ──────────────────────────────────
│  WKSARS
│ ────────────────────────────────────────────
│  dom waiting = ∅
└───────────────────────────────────────────────
```

There are three operations that we need to define for the waiting state:

1. Place a KSAR in the waiting state.

2. Remove a KSAR from the waiting state.

3. Find a KSAR in the waiting state so that its precondition evaluation function can be applied.

The first operation is simple:

```
┌─ SleepKSAR ───────────────────────────────────
│  ΔWKSARS
│  ksarid? : KSARID
│  ksarstruc? : PCKSAR
│ ────────────────────────────────────────────
│  waiting' = waiting ∪ { ksarid? ↦ ksarstruc? }
└───────────────────────────────────────────────
```

Theorem 13

$$SleepKSAR \vdash \#waiting' > \#waiting$$

The removal operation returns the KSAR only:

```
┌─ WakeKSAR ────────────────────────────────
│ Δ WKSARS
│ ksarid? : KSARID
│ ksar! : KSAR
├───────────────────────────────────────────
│ ksarid? ∈ dom waiting
│ (∃ k : PCKSAR | k = waiting(ksarid?) •
│          ksar! = precond_ksar(k))
│ waiting' = waiting \ { ksarid? ↦ waiting(ksarid?) }
└───────────────────────────────────────────
```

Theorem 14

$WakeKSAR \vdash \text{dom } waiting \neq 0$

Theorem 15

$WakeKSAR \vdash \#waiting' < \#waiting$

Theorem 16

$WakeKSAR \vdash ksarid? \notin \text{dom } waiting$

Theorem 17 *If waiting* $\neq \varnothing$,

$WakeKSAR \vdash \text{dom } waiting' \neq \varnothing$

The evaluation of the precondition is as follows. When a message arrives which is destined for a KSAR, that KSAR is extracted from the waiting list and each of its precondition elements is evaluated. If the element is satisfied, that element is removed from the set of precondition elements and evaluation continues until the set is empty (in other words, the process is reductive). If the precondition element's evaluation function returns a false value, the entire KSAR is removed. Part of the specification of the evaluation function is that it should return the undefined value when the message cannot be inspected by it (this can be made more concrete if it is assumed that messages are sets of attribute-value pairs). We can specify the basic evaluation mechanism as follows:

```
 ___ EvalPrecond _____
 |  Δ WKSARS
 |  imsg? : IMSG
 |  destination_ksar? : KSARID
 |_____
 |  ∃ mdata : DATA;  replm : LMID
 |          | mdata = imsg_data(imsg?) ∧
 |          replm = imsg_receiver(imsg?) •
 |       ∃ ksar : PCKSAR;  ksar' : PCKSAR' |
 |              waiting(destination_ksar?) = ksar •
 |          ∃ pc : PRECOND | pc ∈ waiting_precond •
 |          (∃ dpred : DATA → PRECONDTV |
 |                  dpred = precond_test(pc) •
 |              precond_eqn_dest(precond_enquiry(pc))
 |                      = replm ∧
 |              (dpred(mdata) = pctrue ∧
 |              waiting_precond'
 |                      = waiting_precond \ { pc }) ∨
 |              (dpred(mdata) = pcfalse ∧
 |              waiting_precond'
 |                      = waiting_precond \ { pc } ∧
 |              false_preconds'
 |                      = false_preconds ∪ { pc }) ∨
 |              (dpred(mdata) = pcnoval
 |              ∧ waiting_precond' = waiting_precond ∧
 |                  false_preconds' = false_preconds)) ∧
 |          ksar' ∈ waiting'
 |_____
```

We can prove by induction that the precondition will decrease in length each time there is a message such that *dpred* returns *pctrue*.

We can also prove that for any message, and for any KSAR in the waiting list that:

$$\lim \# waiting\_preconds = 0$$

and that

$$\lim \# false\_preconds = 0 \text{ or } + \infty$$

We can define the schema which will tell us whether a KSAR is to be made eligible. Such a KSAR has an empty *waiting_list*:

```
┌─ IsWaitingKSAREligible ─────────────────
│ ΞPCKSAR
├─────────────────────────────────────────
│ waiting_precond = ∅
│ false_preconds = ∅
└─────────────────────────────────────────
```

This schema *only* determines whether a KSAR can be executed: it does not say what to do when there are preconditions that are false. We can define an operation which, for example, gives schedulers access to the preconditions which are false:

```
┌─ FalsePreconds ──────────────────────────
│ ΞPCKSAR
│ untrue_preconds : KSPRECOND
├─────────────────────────────────────────
│ untrue_preconds = false_preconds
└─────────────────────────────────────────
```

FalsePreconds allows other level manager components access to those preconditions which are false, and so actions such as returning the KSAR to the triggered list, or resending the requests is possible. To perform the latter, we need the following:

```
┌─ ReturnFalsePreconds ────────────────────
│ ΔPCKSAR
├─────────────────────────────────────────
│ waiting_precond' = waiting_precond ∪ false_preconds
│ false_preconds' = ∅
└─────────────────────────────────────────
```

Our next task is to connect the various components that we have given here and in the last section so that we have a specification of the precondition evaluation process, together with the required operations on KSARs. This entails that we specify how preconditions send messages and how messages are returned to them. We will also need the triggered and eligible lists so that we can specify KSAR movement.

To do this, we begin by assembling the output message that is to form the request. If we compare the definition of $OMSG$ with that of $PRECOND$, we find that the port identifier is missing. We therefore need to find the relevant port:

$$
\begin{array}{|l}
\hline
\quad FindOutPort \underline{\hspace{6cm}} \\
\quad LMPorts \\
\quad to\_whom? : LMID \\
\quad portid! : PORTID \\
\hline
\quad \exists\, p : PORT \mid p \in ports \bullet \\
\qquad to\_whom? = port\_lm(p) \land \\
\qquad port\_type(p) = output \land \\
\qquad portid! = portid(p) \\
\hline
\end{array}
$$

To send the enquiry messages, we need to construct a message from the precondition and send it. First, we need to extract the destination level manager identifier and message data from the precondition and construct an output message. This is represented by the following schema:

$$
\begin{array}{|l}
\hline
\quad SendPCMessage \underline{\hspace{5cm}} \\
\quad my\_ksarid? : KSARID \\
\quad pc? : PRECOND \\
\quad me? : LMID \\
\quad portid? : PORTID \\
\quad omsg! : OMSG \\
\quad to\_whom! : LMID \\
\hline
\quad \exists\, mdata : DATA \mid mdata \\
\qquad = precond\_enq\_msg(precond\_enquiry(pc?)) \bullet \\
\quad to\_whom! = \\
\qquad precond\_enq\_dest(precond\_enquiry(pc?)) \land \\
\quad omsg! = \\
\qquad (portid?, output, to\_whom!, \\
\qquad\quad me?, mdata, my\_ksarid?) \\
\hline
\end{array}
$$

Where $to\_whom!$ is the identifier of the level manager to which the message is to be sent. The message that is constructed for sending is *omsg?*. The input variable *me?* is the identifier of the level manager within which the KSAR resides: the KSAR has identifier *my_ksarid?*.

We can define the complete message-sending operation for each precondition as:

$$
\begin{aligned}
PCSend \;\widehat{=}\; & \\
\exists\, & to\_whom?, to\_whom! : LMID; \\
& portid?, portid! : PORTID; \\
& omsg?, omsg! : OMSG \mid \\
& to\_whom? = to\_whom! \land \\
& portid? = portid! \land omsg? = omsg! \bullet \\
& FindOutPort \land SendPCMessage \\
& \land CorrectSend \land sendPort
\end{aligned}
$$

We expand this schema to derive:

$$
\begin{array}{|l}
\hline
\_\_PCSend _____ \\
\Xi LMPorts \\
my\_ksarid? : KSARID \\
pc? : PRECOND \\
me? : LMID \\
\hline
\end{array}
$$

$\exists\, to\_whom?, to\_whom! : LMID;$
          $portid?, portid! : PORTID;$
          $omsg?, omsg! : OMSG \mid$
          $to\_whom? = to\_whom! \wedge$
          $portid? = portid! \wedge omsg? = omsg! \bullet$
  $(\exists\, p : PORT \mid p \in ports \bullet$
     $to\_whom? = port\_lm(p) \wedge$
     $output = port\_type(p) \wedge$
     $portid! = portid(p)) \wedge$
  $(\exists\, mdata : DATA \mid$
     $mdata =$
          $precond\_enq\_msg(precond\_enquiry(pc?)) \bullet$
     $to\_whom! =$
          $precond\_enq\_dest(precond\_enquiry(pc?))$
     $\wedge$
     $omsg! =$
          $(portid?, output, to\_whom!, me?,$
              $mdata, my\_ksarid?)) \wedge$
  $(\exists\, portid : PORTID;\ porttyp : PORT\_TYPE;$
          $portlm : LMID \bullet$
     $portid = omsg\_portid(omsg?) \wedge$
     $porttyp = omsg\_porttype(omsg?) \wedge$
     $portlm = omsg\_portlm(omsg?) \wedge$
     $(\exists\, p : PORT \mid p \in ports \bullet$
          $portid(p) = portid \wedge$
          $port\_type(p) = porttype \wedge$
          $port\_lm(p) = portlm))$
  $\wedge\, comms\_send(omsg\_portid(omsg?), omsg?)$

We can simplify the definition of *PCSend* somewhat by a number of applications of bound-variable substitution. The most sensible form

that such a substitution can take is to identify all of the input variables
which are bound by the outermost quantifier with their corresponding
output variable (for example, we identify *to_whom?* with *to_whom!*).
In addition, we can make further simplifications by means of predicate
calculus theorems.

Our next task is to send all the messages that a Knowledge Source
precondition needs to send. We define it as follows:

```
┌─ SendKSARPrecondMessages ─────────────────────────────
│ Ξ WKSARS
│ my_ksarid? : KSARID
│ me? : LMID
├───────────────────────────────────────────────────────
│ ∃ wksar : PCKSAR | wksar = waiting(my_ksarid?) •
│     ∀ pc? : PRECOND | pc ∈ wksar.waiting_precond •
│         PCSend
└───────────────────────────────────────────────────────
```

(once again, we can use bound-variable substitution to remove the
decoration on *pc* and to simplify the resulting schema). Notice that
this schema allows us to alter the contents of *waiting_precond* as we
suggested above in connection with preconditions that evaluate to false.
The reader should notice that we have used schema selection in the
universal quantifier to access the *waiting_precond* component of *wksar*.

In a manner directly analogous to the above, we can define the evaluation schema for *all* preconditions in a waiting KSAR. To do this, we
need to access the contents of an input message and determine that it is
for a KSAR. This requires that we give an account of message routing
within a level manager. We will assume that all incoming messages are
stored in a message queue of type *MSG_QUEUE*. Each message is of
type *IMSG*. Within each message, there is a component of type *DES-
TINID*: this type, as we have already seen, includes system components
*as well as KSARID*s. We will assume a function:

$$destination\_ksar : DESTINID \rightarrow KSARID$$

which converts destination identifiers into KSAR identifiers. Precisely
how this function is defined will not concern us here, for it is of no
consequence. We will call the precondition evaluation function which

examines an input message and executes the evaluation function represented by the *EvalPrecondFromMsg* schema:

$$
\begin{aligned}
&EvalPrecondFromMsg \triangleq \\
&\quad \neg\ EmptyQueue \land \\
&\quad (\forall\ imsg? : IMSG \\
&\qquad imsg? \in iqueue \land \\
&\qquad (\exists\ destination\_ksar? : KSARID\ | \\
&\qquad\qquad destination\_ksar? = \\
&\qquad\qquad destination\_ksar(imsg\_destination(imsg?)) \\
&\qquad\qquad \land\ destination\_ksar? \in \text{dom } waiting\ \bullet \\
&\qquad EvalPrecond)) \\
&\qquad \Rightarrow Deqeue
\end{aligned}
$$

We can prove by induction that if all messages in the queue are such that there is a precondition which is satisfied, then the queue becomes empty. What we *cannot* prove, however, is that, for any message queue, all preconditions are satisfied.

We can also prove that for any message in the waiting list, we have either:

$$\# waiting\_precond' < \# waiting\_precond$$

or

$$\# false\_preconds' > \# false\_preconds$$

or

$$
\begin{aligned}
&\# waiting\_precond' = \# waiting\_precond\ \land \\
&\quad \# false\_preconds' = \# false\_preconds
\end{aligned}
$$

We are now in a position to define the schema which will remove all those preconditions whose waiting preconditions are empty and return them as a set to be added to the eligible list:

```
┌─ FindEligiblePreconditions ──────────────────────────
│ Δ WKSARS
│ ksars! : ℙ KSARID
├──────────────────────────────────────────────────────
│ ∀ k : KSARID •
│     k ∈ dom waiting ∧
│     (∃ PCKSAR • IsWaitingKSAREligible) ⇒
│                 k ∈ ksars!
└──────────────────────────────────────────────────────
```

Theorem 18

$$\text{dom } waiting = \varnothing \land FindEligiblePreconditions$$
$$\land \ ksars! = \varnothing$$

We next define how the waiting KSAR database is altered when the eligible KSARs have been determined:

```
┌─ RemoveEligibleKSARsFromWaiting ─────────────────────
│ Δ WKSARS
│ ksars? : ℙ KSARID
│ ksarset! : KSARSet
├──────────────────────────────────────────────────────
│ ∀ k ∈ ksars? •
│     (∃ PCKSAR •
│         waiting_ksar ∈ ksarset!) ⇒
│     waiting' = waiting ◁ (waiting \ ksars?)
└──────────────────────────────────────────────────────
```

where ◁ is the *domain restriction*, or *domain subtraction* operator. This schema outputs a set of KSARs: these are the KSARs whose waiting and preconditions are empty sets. The schema can be thought of working by making the waiting KSAR inaccessible to all future operations. In fact, we can prove that if *ksars?* is not empty, that *waiting* will decrease in length.

Theorem 19

$$RemoveEligibleKSARsFromWaiting \vdash \#waiting' < \#waiting$$

We can compose the two last schemata and hide the sets of KSAR identifiers in the obvious fashion to derive the interface schema that we require.

6.4   Knowledge Sources and Actions

The actions that we require Knowledge Sources to have in CASSANDRA systems are very similar to those we defined for the blackboard system in Chapter 4. In both systems, actions are composed of a set of production rules. The difference comes in the fact that, in CASSANDRA systems, Knowledge Source actions are permitted to send messages to other level managers. This implies that there is an action in addition to the three event-causing actions we defined for the blackboard system. This action consists of sending a message: it does not cause any events. The reason for this is that if we allowed Knowledge Sources to trigger on the basis of message-sending, we would be coupling triggers to communications, and we have resisted this (see Craig, 1988a).

The three event-causing actions have already been defined in Chapter 4, and we will use them intact in this Chapter. We will concentrate our attention on the message-sending action and on the schema which models action execution.

The message-sending action, which we will call *ActionSend* sends a message to another level manager. In order to execute the action, we require an object of type *DATA* (i.e., the data to be sent) and the identifier of the level manager. In addition, as we have seen with preconditions, we need a port identifier and the identifier of the level manager within which the action is executed. We can define the operations we need with reference to those that we defined for preconditions. Immediately, we require a schema which will create an object of type *OMSG* for the message-sending action:

MkActionMessage _____
$my\_ksar?$: $KSARID$
$to\_whom?$: $LMID$
$me?$: $LMID$
$msgdata?$: $DATA$
$portid?$: $PORTID$
$omsg!$: $OMSG$

$omsg! = (portid!, output, to\_whom?, me?, msgdata?)$

We define the action, which we call *LDBSend*, as:

$$LDBSend \;\hat{=}$$
$$\exists \, to\_whom! : LMID; \; portid?, portid! : PORTID;$$
$$omsg?, omsg! : OMSG \mid$$
$$portid? = portid! \land omsg? = omsg! \bullet$$
$$FindOutPort \land MkActionMessage \land$$
$$CorrectSend \land sendPort$$

By analogy with Knowledge Source actions in the blackboard system, we define an action type:

$$ACT\_TYPE ::= new \mid add \mid mod \mid send$$

We can now define the schema type for production rule atomic actions:

```
┌─ RuleAction ──────────────────────────────
│  acttype? : ACT_TYPE
│ ──────────────────────────────────────────
│  (acttype? = new ⇒ LDBCreate) ∨
│  (acttype? = add ⇒ LDBAdd) ∨
│  (acttype? = mod ⇒ LDBMod) ∨
│  (acttype? = send ⇒ LDBSend)
└────────────────────────────────────────────
```

Since the behaviour of rule actions is identical to the behaviour we specified in Chapter 4, with the exception that rule actions can now send messages, we will assume that they can be interpreted in exactly the same way. Similarly, with a few suitable modifications, in particular those that take into account the fact that there is no blackboard hierarchy, only one single local database that is not partitioned in any way, we can assume that rule condition evaluation is the same for CASSANDRA systems as it is for the blackboard system. We will also assume that Knowledge Source triggering operates in a way similar to its operation in the blackboard system: changes of a relatively minor nature must, again be made. In all these cases, the necessary modifications are left as exercises for the reader.

We will exploit the similarities between Knowledge Sources in blackboard and CASSANDRA systems and assume that they are evaluated in similar ways. Of course, in a CASSANDRA system, there is the added complication that preconditions can be present in Knowledge Sources. We will now define the Knowledge Source structure and the access functions that we require:

$$KS ==$$
$$(TRIGGER \times$$
$$(KS\_PRECOND \times$$
$$(LVARDECS \times ACTION)))$$

We can assume that the following projection functions are defined in the obvious way: *ks_trigger, ks_precondition, ks_localvars, ks_action*. The projection functions enable us to access Knowledge Source components in the usual way.

It should be noted that the component of type *LVARDECS* will be ignored throughout this Chapter. This is because we are not providing a specification of how local variables are treated. We gave the reasons for this when we specified the blackboard system and do not repeat them here.

One significant difference between the blackboard and CASSANDRA systems is that, in the latter, we cannot allow Knowledge Sources to be visible outside of their level manager. This requires us to define a schema which will represent the database in which a level manager's Knowledge Sources are stored:

```
┌─ LevelManagerKSs ────────────────────────────
│  kss : KSID → KS
```

and we define the initialisation schema:

```
┌─ InitLevelManagerKSs ─────────────────────────
│  LevelManagerKSs
│  ksset? : KSID → KS
│ ┌─────────────────────────────────────────────
│ │ ksset? ≠ ∅
│ │ kss' = ksset?
```

For Knowledge Sources, we do not define a Δ schema: once the Knowledge Sources have been initialised, they cannot be altered. We assume that there is a Ξ schema which is defined in the usual manner.

We must define a schema which will give us access to the Knowledge Sources in a level manager: this is required to gain access to triggers, preconditions and actions. KSARs, it will be remembered, need this facility.

```
┌─ GetKS ──────────────────────────────────────
│ ΞLevelManagerKSs
│ ksid? : KSID
│ ks! : KS
├──────────────────────────────────────────────
│ ksid? ∈ dom kss
│ ks! = kss(ksid?)
└──────────────────────────────────────────────
```

The way that KSARs gain access to Knowledge Sources is via the standard attribute that contains the Knowledge Source identifier. We leave the specification of the interface as an exercise (it is relatively straightforward and adds nothing to our investigation of the differences between blackboard and CASSANDRA systems).

6.5   The Level Manager Construct

In this section, we specify the Level Manager construct which is at the centre of the CASSANDRA architecture. This aspect of our specification will link everything together into a whole. In addition to defining the Level Manager, we need to specify its operating cycle and we need to show that Level Managers are modular in the sense that their internals are invisible to other Level Managers. As with Knowledge Sources and their actions and triggers, we will rely on our earlier blackboard specification to give us a number of schemata which we will include in the specification of the Level Manager construct. Typically, we will be assuming obvious modifications to these earlier schemata; where the modifications are not obvious, we will either present the schema intact, or else we will give an informal (i.e., English) explanation of the differences.

To begin the specification, let us once again list the components of a Level Manager. This list will be a little more full than others that we have given: the reasons for this additional detail should be clear.

- a local database;

- a local scheduler;

- a set of Knowledge Sources;

- a local cycle counter;

- a local event counter;

- a triggered list;

- a list of waiting KSARs;

- an eligible list;

- a set of ports;

- an input queue

We will define a schema to represent the level manager construct, but before we are able to specify the level manager schema, we will need to define some additional schemata. These additional schemata have to do with cycle and event counters, and with the *eligible list*. We will begin this definition task and aim, at the end of this section, to integrate all of the specification in a set of schemata that represent the level manager construct.

6.5.1   Level Manager Counters and Flags

We begin with the counters and flags that we need. In CASSANDRA systems, cycles and events are counted in a fashion directly analogous to blackboard systems. Also, we define termination to be controlled by a flag which can be set by Knowledge Sources, or by the level manager (in response, for example, to a special termination message or when it recognises that its goal has been satisfied or when an unrecoverable error occurs).

The schemata for the counters are as one would expect:

```
┌─ CycCount ──────────────────────────────────
│ cycno : N
│
```

This schema defines a state space which is composed of one variable of type natural. We assume that the Δ and Ξ forms of the schema are given by convention. The operations that must be defined over this space are: increment the value of *cycno*, examine its value, and, of course, initialize it (to zero). The schemata are immediate:

```
┌─ InitCycCount ──────────────────────────────
│ CycCount
├─────────────────────────────────────────────
│ cycno = 0
│
```

This schema initializes the contents of *cycno* to zero. We assume that the level manager always starts on cycle zero.

The increment operation is performed after all the actions of the chosen Knowledge Source have been executed. We define the schema for the increment operation as:

```
┌─ IncCycCount ───────────────────────────────
│ ΔCycCount
├─────────────────────────────────────────────
│ cycno' = cycno + 1
│
```

The current contents of the cycle counter are given by the *Current-Cycle* schema. This name is derived from the fact that the contents of the cycle counter represent the number of the interpreter cycle at the time of inspection. The schema is obvious:

```
┌─ CurrentCycle ──────────────────────────────
│ ΞCycCount
│ cyc! : N
├─────────────────────────────────────────────
│ cyc! = cycno
│
```

The schemata for the event counter are similar to those just presented for the cycle counter (and similar to those we gave in the blackboard specification). We give the schemata without comment.

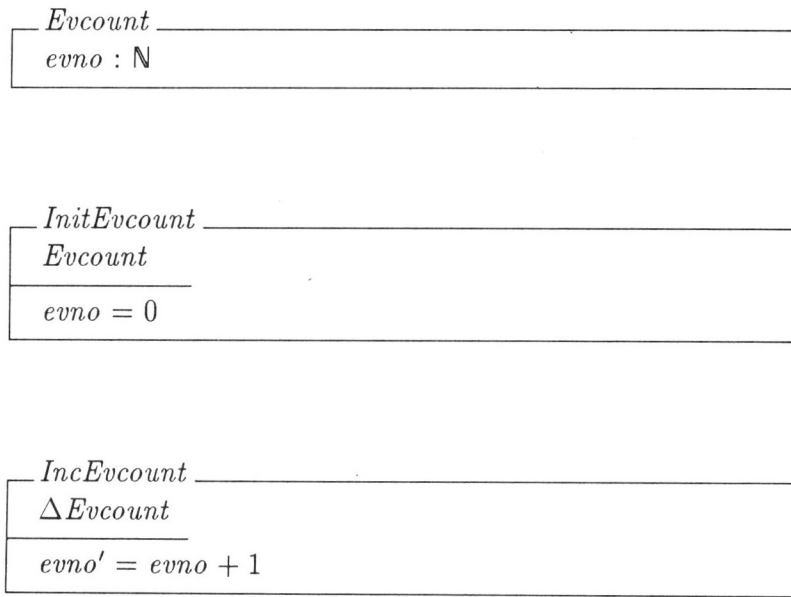

$\rule{0pt}{0pt}$ _Evcount_

$evno : \mathbb{N}$

$\rule{0pt}{0pt}$ _InitEvcount_

Evcount

$evno = 0$

$\rule{0pt}{0pt}$ _IncEvcount_

$\Delta Evcount$

$evno' = evno + 1$

We need an operation to reset the event counter to zero at the end of each interpreter cycle. This is needed because we assign events to numbers only *within* a cycle (we define the unique name of an event to be a pair which consists of a cycle and an event number). The reset schema is:

$\rule{0pt}{0pt}$ _ResetEvcount_

$\Delta Evcount$

$evno' = 0$

(Note that we could just allow events to be numbered sequentially from zero, without bothering to reset the counter at the end of each cycle. This would give a totally unique name for each event, and we would not need to consider event names as pairs. We adopt the present convention because it was the one we chose for the blackboard system, and we would like some conformity just so that we can make use of more familiar concepts and ideas.)

Just as we need to know the current cycle number, we also need to know the current event (in the creation of KSARs, for example). We therefore define the schema:

$$
\begin{array}{l}
\_\_CurrentEvent_____ \\
\Xi Evcount \\
evnum! : \mathbb{N} \\
\hline
evnum! = evno
\end{array}
$$

Finally, we need to connect the counters. We are adopting the convention that cycle counters are incremented after all the actions in the selected KSAR have been executed, and, at the same time, we reset the event counter. The cycle counter continues to be incremented at the end of each interpreter cycle until the level manager terminates, but the event counter is always reset. We define the following schema to do this:

$$NextCycle \cong IncCycCount \wedge ResetEvcount$$

Expansion of the above gives us the schema we require:

$$
\begin{array}{l}
\Delta CycCount \\
\Delta Evcount \\
\hline
cycno' = cycno + 1 \ \wedge \\
evno' = 0
\end{array}
$$

We next need to specify the termination flag. When the termination flag is *false*, the level manager continues processing as normal, but when it becomes *true*, the level manager must halt (and perhaps perform some processing such as sending shut-down messages before terminating). As was the case in the blackboard interpreter, we will allow the termination flag to be set by a number of agencies: Knowledge Sources and the level manager are the two primary ones. In the case of Knowledge Sources, the flag is set when the current problem is solved (this use is of most importance when the CASSANDRA system is set up so that each level manager has one and only one problem which it is to solve—when that problem has been solved, the level manager can terminate for it has nothing else to do). The level manager might set the flag when it receives a shut-down message from another level manager (or from the user or some other, external agency), or when it detects a fatal error from which it cannot recover; alternatively, the level manager might set the termination flag when it has consumed its quota of resources. At the level of the definition which we give in this Chapter, it is impossible to legislate for all cases, so we merely provide the facilities we believe necessary.

In order to define the termination flag and its associated operations, we will first define a new type. This type represents values of the flag. We choose not to use *true* and *false* for reasons that we have already given. Instead, we use a type with more mnemonic values:

$$TERMVAL ::= yes \mid no$$

We define the termination flag schema as:

$$
\begin{array}{|l}
\hline
\_\,TerminateFlag \,\_\!\\
\quad terminate : TERMVAL \\
\hline
\end{array}
$$

We assume that the Δ and Ξ forms are defined by convention. To initialize the flag, we set it to *no*:

$$
\begin{array}{|l}
\hline
\_\,InitTerminateFlag \,\_\!\\
\quad TerminateFlag \\
\hline
\quad terminate = no \\
\hline
\end{array}
$$

The next schema sets the flag:

$$
\begin{array}{|l}
\hline
\_\,SetCanTerminate \,\_\!\\
\quad \Delta Terminate \\
\hline
\quad terminate' = yes \\
\hline
\end{array}
$$

Notice that we do not have to supply any value to this schema. This is because the only possibility is to set the flag to the value which means that termination should be effected (setting the flag to *no* is just a no-operation, in other words).

The last schema we need for the termination flag is the one which allows us to test the flag. The schema is:

$$
\begin{array}{l}
\_\mathit{CanTerminate}\_\rule{20em}{0pt} \\
\quad \Xi\mathit{Terminate} \\
\rule{8em}{0.4pt} \\
\quad terminate = yes
\end{array}
$$

Note that this schema is testing the value of *terminate*, so the predicate of the schema is a test on the current state (not an assertion about what the state will be).

We have now completed the schemas for the counters and flags that the level manager needs.

6.5.2 Control Databases

In this sub-section, we will give the specification of some of the components of the control database. In particular, we will be concerned with the triggered and eligible lists, and their interactions. In addition, we will be concerned with the waiting list (the list of those KSARs that are waiting for messages from other level managers) and its relationship to the other databases. The aim is to define a schema called *Schedule*, which represents the local scheduler. This schema will apply the value stored in the level manager's *local_scheduler* variable to the eligible list.

The control databases are a little more complex in CASSANDRA systems than they are in blackboard systems. This complexity derives from the fact that there must be a waiting list. The definitions of the triggered and eligible lists is, in fact, quite simple, but their interactions are complex.

We define the basic operations and types that we need. We can assume that the triggered and eligible lists are both specified in terms of sets of KSARs.

We begin with the triggered list.

```
┌─ TriggeredList ──────────────────────────────
│ triggered_list : ℙ KSAR
│
└──────────────────────────────────────────────
```

```
┌─ InitTriggeredList ──────────────────────────
│ TriggeredList
├──────────────────────────────────────────────
│ triggered_list = ∅
└──────────────────────────────────────────────
```

The *AddTriggeredKSAR* schema defines the operation of adding a KSAR to the triggered list. This schema is used in the definition of the Knowledge Source triggering operation (which we have not defined in this Chapter because it is only a modified version of the one we gave for blackboard systems).

```
┌─ AddTriggeredKSAR ───────────────────────────
│ Δ TriggeredList
│ ksar? : KSAR
├──────────────────────────────────────────────
│ triggered_list' = triggered_list ∪ { ksar? }
└──────────────────────────────────────────────
```

The schema *RemoveTriggeredKSAR* removes *one* KSAR from the triggered list:

```
┌─ RemoveTriggeredKSAR ────────────────────────
│ Δ TriggeredList
│ ksar? : KSAR
├──────────────────────────────────────────────
│ triggered_list ≠ ∅
│ ksar? ∈ triggered_list
│ triggered_list' = triggered_list\{ ksar? }
└──────────────────────────────────────────────
```

We can also define another deletion schema, one which removes *sets* of KSARs from the triggered list:

```
┌─ RemoveTriggeredKSARs ──────────────────────────────────
│ ΔTriggeredList
│ ksars? : ℙ KSAR
├──────────────────────────────────────────────────────────
│ triggered_list ≠ ∅
│ ksars? ≠ ∅
│ ksars? ⊆ triggered_list
│ triggered_list' = triggered_list \ ksars?
└──────────────────────────────────────────────────────────
```

We can define the schemata for the eligible list in exactly the same way. We present the schemata without comment.

```
┌─ EligibleList ──────────────────────────────────────────
│ eligible_list : ℙ KSAR
└──────────────────────────────────────────────────────────
```

```
┌─ InitEligibleList ──────────────────────────────────────
│ EligibleList
├──────────────────────────────────────────────────────────
│ eligible_list = ∅
└──────────────────────────────────────────────────────────
```

```
┌─ AddEligibleKSAR ───────────────────────────────────────
│ ΔEligibleList
│ ksar? : KSAR
├──────────────────────────────────────────────────────────
│ eligible_list' = eligible_list ∪ { ksar? }
└──────────────────────────────────────────────────────────
```

```
┌─ AddEligibleKSARs ──────────────────────────────────────
│ ΔEligibleList
│ ksars? : ℙ KSAR
├──────────────────────────────────────────────────────────
│ eligible_list' = eligible_list ∪ ksars?
└──────────────────────────────────────────────────────────
```

```
┌─ RemoveEligibleKSAR ──────────────────────────────────
│ Δ EligibleList
│ ksar? : KSAR
├────────────────────────────────────────────────────────
│ eligible_list ≠ ∅
│ ksar? ∈ eligible_list
│ eligible_list' = eligible_list\{ ksar? }
└────────────────────────────────────────────────────────
```

```
┌─ RemoveEligibleKSARs ─────────────────────────────────
│ Δ EligibleList
│ ksars? : ℙ KSAR
├────────────────────────────────────────────────────────
│ eligible_list ≠ ∅
│ ksars? ⊆ eligible_list
│ eligible_list' = eligible_list\ksars?
└────────────────────────────────────────────────────────
```

We now have to account for the interactions between the triggered, waiting and eligible lists. The interactions are as follows.

All KSARs are placed in the triggered list when they are created. KSARs are only created when a Knowledge Source triggers. Once a KSAR is in the triggered list, there are two things that can happen:

- The KSAR's precondition is empty, and so it passes directly to the eligible list.

- The precondition is not empty, so messages have to be sent and the KSAR placed in the waiting list.

All KSARs in the eligible list can be scheduled for execution. This entails that the scheduler operate on the eligible list in order to determine which KSAR to execute next.

We have schemata for testing the preconditions of KSARs in the triggered list, and for transferring them to the waiting list: these are *WillWait* and *SleepKSAR*. *SleepKSAR* relies upon the fact that a new

KSAR of type *PCKSAR* has been created. The *WillWait* schema accesses KSARs by name, so we assume that there is some way of obtaining the name of each KSAR. In the blackboard specification, we defined a function to do this, and we will assume that it is available to us: we will assume that the function is called *ksar_id*. We can define the schema which transfers KSARs from the triggered list to the waiting list as follows:

```
┌─ TransferWaitingKSARs ──────────────────────────────
│ Δ TriggeredList
│ ksarids : ℙ KSARID
│ ksars : ℙ KSAR
│ ksars! : ℙ KSAR
├──────────────────────────────────────────────────────
│ ∀ ksar : KSAR | ksar ∈ triggered_list •
│     ksar_id(ksar) ∈ ksarids
│ ∀ ksarid? : KSARID | ksarid?inksarids •
│     WillWait ⇒
│         (∃ ksar : KSAR | ksar ∈ triggered_list •
│             ksar_id(ksar) = ksarid? ∧
│             ksar ∈ ksars ∧
│             RemoveTriggeredKSARs ∧
│             ksars! = ksars)
└──────────────────────────────────────────────────────
```

The next schema constructs waiting KSARs and adds them to the waiting list.

```
┌─ AddWaitingKSARs ───────────────────────────────────
│ ksars? : ℙ KSAR
├──────────────────────────────────────────────────────
│ ∀ ksar : KSAR | ksar ∈ ksars? •
│     (∃ ksarstruc : PCKSAR; ksarid : KSARID |
│             ksarid = ksar_id(ksar) ∧ InitPCKSAR •
│         SleepKSAR)
└──────────────────────────────────────────────────────
```

We combine these two schema to extract those KSARs that must wait and add them to the waiting list.

$$
\begin{aligned}
MakeWaitingKSARs \; \widehat{=} \; & \\
& TransferWaitingKSARs \; \wedge \\
& AddWaitingKSARs
\end{aligned}
$$

Note that $MakeWaitingKSARs$ removes the KSARs from the triggered list.

In order to transfer waiting KSARs to the eligible list, we need, essentially, to combine $FindEligiblePreconditions$ and $RemoveEligibleKSARsFromWaiting$. We call this schema $MakeWaitingKSARsEligible$:

```
┌─ MakeWaitingKSARsEligible ─────────────────────
│ Δ WKSARS
│ ksarset! : ℙ KSAR
├────────────────────────────────────────────────
│ `FindEligiblePreconditions
│ RemoveEligibleKSARsFromWaiting
└────────────────────────────────────────────────
```

At this point, we have the basic schemata we require for the specification of the scheduler schema. What we need to do now is to decide when we want to transfer KSARs from the triggered to the eligible lists. This can be done when all of the KSARs that will receive messages are removed, or it can be done when the waiting KSARs are added to the eligible list. For ease of presentation, we choose the latter. We define the schema $MakeSchedulerList$ to do this.

```
┌─ MakeSchedulerList ─────────────────────────────
│ Δ TriggeredList
│ Δ EligibleList
│ ksarset? : ℙ KSAR
├────────────────────────────────────────────────
│ ∃ ksars : ℙ KSAR |
│         ksars = ksarset? ∪ triggered_list •
│     triggered_list' = ∅ ∧
│     AddEligibleKSARs
└────────────────────────────────────────────────
```

We now combine *MakeSchedulerList* with *MakeWaitingKSARsEligible* to define the complete operation:

$$MakeSchedulerDB \; \hat{=}$$
$$MakeWaitingKSARsEligible \; \wedge$$
$$MakeSchedulerList$$

Notice that one consequence of this schema is that the triggered list is completely empty.

We can now define the type for the scheduler function:

$$SCHEDULER : \mathbb{P} \; KSAR \rightarrow KSAR$$

We can now define the schema that calls the scheduler as:

```
┌─ DoSchedule ─────────────────────────────────────
│ Δ EligibleList
│ ksar! : KSAR
├──────────────────────────────────────────────────
│ local_scheduler(eligible_list) = ksar!
│ RemoveEligibleKSAR
└──────────────────────────────────────────────────
```

This schema removes the chosen KSAR from the eligible list.

To define the *Schedule* schema, we need to combine all the schemata that manipulate the control database:

$$Schedule \; \hat{=}$$
$$MakeSchedulerDB \; \wedge$$
$$DoSchedule$$

The schema outputs a value of type *KSAR*, which is the KSAR that has been chosen for execution. The action execution schema is then applied to send messages and cause local events. We assume that action execution is specified by schemata that are directly analogous to those we defined for the blackboard architecture in Chapter 4.

6.5.3   The Level Manager Schemata

In this sub-section, we define the schemata for the level manager and also define the main interpreter loop: each level manager implements this as its main control loop. Once we have defined these structures, we will engage in some hiding in order to preserve the modularity of level managers.

We begin with the level manager schema, *LevelManager*:

LevelManager _____

    Evcount
    CycCount
    MSG_QUEUE
    LocalDB
    LMPorts
    WKSARS
    LevelManagerKSs
    me : *LMID*
    local_scheduler : *SCHEDULER*
    TriggeredList
    EligibleList

With the exception of *me* and *local_scheduler*, the schema is defined as a collection of all the main schemata that we defined above. In other words, the state space represented by the level manager schema is composed of the state spaces of its components. The variables *me* and *local_scheduler* are included so that the level manager's identifier (which must be unique within the system) is made available to it, and so that the level manager has a scheduling function to be used when selecting KSARs for execution. Values for both of these variables must be supplied when creating a new level manager.

The initialization schema for level managers is as follows:

```
┌─ InitLevelManager ─────────────────────────────────
│ LevelManager
│ InitEvcount
│ InitCycCount
│ InitMSG_QUEUE
│ InitTerminateFlag
│ InitLocalDB
│ InitLMPorts
│ InitWKSARS
│ InitTriggeredList
│ InitEligibleList
│ InitLevelManagerKSs
│ lmid? : LMID
│ sched? : SCHEDULER
├────────────────────────────────────────────────────
│ me' = lmid?
│ local_scheduler' = sched?
└────────────────────────────────────────────────────
```

The schema expands to the conjunction of the predicates of all the initialization schemata (those with the prefix *Init*, in other words). We do not expand the schema here, because it is somewhat long. The reader should note that some of the schemata that are included in the above have input variables for which values have to be supplied at initialization time (this affects the initialization of Knowledge Sources and ports, in particular).

There is an important condition on initialization schemata that needs to be mentioned: it is the implementability criterion. This criterion requires that there must always be a value which can reasonably be expected to initialize a variable in a specification. In other words, it requires that there be some value which will satisfy the initialization schema's predicate. For example, in the case of the two counters we defined earlier in this Chapter, the implementability criterion is satisfied by the initializing value of zero: the criterion requires that there be a proof that such values exist for the types of the variables mentioned in a schema. In the case of *Evcount*, we can state the condition as:

$$\exists\, v : \mathbb{N} \bullet InitEvcount$$

Since zero is a valid element of the naturals, the proof of the existence of this value establishes that the initialization can proceed. The implementability criterion for the level manager initialization schema is just the conjunction of those for the components, together with an additional constraint on the level manager identifier and the scheduler.

When we have defined the main loop for the level manager construct, we will have a complete specification. However, before defining the loop, we need to ensure that everything a level manager contains is invisible to every other level manager in a CASSANDRA system. In other words, we want to hide all the variables that appear in the level manager schema: this entails hiding all the variables that appear in the schemata named in the signature of *LevelManager*.

We define the schema *CassandraLevelManager* to be the version of *LevelManager* which has all of its signature variables hidden. This new schema will be the one that is used when constructing CASSANDRA systems. The definition is:

$$
\begin{aligned}
CassandraLevelManager \;\widehat{=}\; & \\
LevelManager\backslash & \\
(& evno, cycno, me, local\_scheduler, \\
& terminate, db, ports, iqueue, \\
& waiting, kss, triggered\_list, \\
& eligible\_list)
\end{aligned}
$$

Nothing inside an instance of *CassandraLevelManager* is visible to other software components, and, in particular, is invisible to all other level managers in a CASSANDRA system.

The reader might be puzzled about this because there appears to be no way in which level managers can communicate with anything: even the level manager's ports are hidden. (On this point, it should be remembered that ports are, in any case, names for channels which are private to the level manager in which they reside.) The reply is that, as part of the initialization code, it is necessary to connect each level manager to the communications system services so that messages can be sent and received. Since we have chosen to give only a minimal specification of the interface between level managers and the communications system, we are unable to go into details (this is another example of where we are in ignorance—we simply cannot make any assumptions about what the interface should look like, nor can we make any stipulations because we want CASSANDRA systems to be implementable using a wide variety of different communications systems and not just, say, the one provided by Sun Microsystems).

Finally, then, we can move on to the definition of the main control loop. We want the loop to iterate until the termination flag is set. We use the cycle counter as a control on the loop, in effect using it to identify each iteration. This gives:

$$LMMainCycle \; \hat{=}$$
$$\forall \: CycCount \; \bullet \; \neg \; CanTerminate \; \Rightarrow \; InnerLoop$$

The schema refers to $InnerLoop$: this is a schema which defines the details of the main cycle. The definition of $InnerLoop$ is rather more complex than might be expected: this is because there are choices that can be made. We will give one version of the inner loop and then discuss the alternatives.

$$InnerLoop \; \hat{=}$$
$$InputMessages \; \wedge$$
$$EvaluatePreconds \; \wedge$$
$$Schedule \; \wedge$$
$$ExecuteRules \; \wedge$$
$$NextCycle$$

where $ExecuteRules$ is a schema that we have not defined, and is one that specifies how the actions of Knowledge Sources are executed: it is directly analogous to the one we defined for blackboard systems. $ExecuteRules$ is the schema which causes Knoweldge Sources to trigger, and it also, therefore, causes local events (it also sends messages to other level managers). The other component of this schema worthy of note is the $Schedule$ schema: this appears as an explicit component in CASSANDRA systems because of the separation of the triggered and eligible lists (see the discussion in the previous sub-section).

Now, the problem that we face in defining $InnerLoop$ is that there are different orderings that are possible. We have defined the schema in terms of a conjunction of schemata, and have, therefore, avoided imposing any order upon the component schemata (since $p \wedge q$ is the same as $q \wedge p$). We would prefer to define *InnerLoop* in terms of schema composition, because there is, at least on one account of the loop, a strict order in which the component operations should be performed. For example, we want to receive all incoming messages before evaluating preconditions; we want to evaluate preconditions before scheduling action executions. Although we *could* specify an ordering, there is a problem connected with message-passing: does the communications architecture interrupt level manager processing in order to pass it messages, or does the level manager poll the input ports (and if so, when)? If the communications architecture causes interrupts, the queue handling code can be executed at any time during the loop; if the level manager polls the ports, what is the best point for it to do so? The answer to the latter question may be crucially dependent upon the application and upon the details of the implementation (for there may be time-critical code that needs to be executed by the application at some point in the loop, for example).

We have chosen to define the loop in what amounts to a nondeterministic fashion so that proofs can be given and so the decision as to the ordering of the component operations can be deferred until later in the specification process. There is nothing at all wrong with this: we have accounted for everything that needs to be included in the schema and we can rely upon the laws of propositional calculus to give us proofs of those properties that we require *at this level of specification*—for example, in an actual implementation, some of the operations might be performed in parallel, and we cannot know this at the level at which we are doing things.

With the definition of the control loops, we have completed the definition of the CASSANDRA architecture. The last task is to define the schema for the functioning of a level manager. This schema again poses problems. We will give the schema and then discuss it.

$$CassandraLevelManagerCode \;\widehat{=}$$
$$InitLevelManager \;\mathring{,}\; MainCycle\mathring{,}$$
$$LevelManagerTermination$$

(note that we are using the version of the initialization schema that has not had its variables subjected to hiding—this is for convenience).

The final schema performs the relevant initialization and then executes the main loop. These two components are (relatively) uncontroversial. The controversial component is the last one: *LevelManagerTermination*. We do not specify this operation any further. The reason for this is that, for some applications, it will be necessary to engage in some kind of post-processing once all the problem-solving activities within a level manager have ceased. One example of such processing is the sending of messages to announce the fact that the level manager is about to terminate. We cannot know in advance of an application what such activity should consist of. What we do, therefore, is to leave the possibilities open. We even allow (informally) for the fact that *LevelManagerTermination* should be the null schema (the one which represents the no-operation).

With this schema, the definition of the CASSANDRA architecture is now complete.

7

Conclusions

In this book, we have presented the top-level specifications of the black-board and CASSANDRA architectures. The specifications have been given in some detail, although we have not covered every conceivable angle: indeed, some aspects of the blackboard architecture have had to be omitted for reasons of space (but these aspects deal only with more superficial topics such as variable-binding). In the case of the blackboard specification, with one or two minor alterations (principally, those connected with Knowledge Source preconditions), the formal specification accurately reflects the informal specification that we gave in Chapter 3.

The CASSANDRA specification, as was to be expected since it is derived from the blackboard architecture, relies heavily on the blackboard specification for the majority of its constructs. There are some cases in which the schemata that we actually gave in the last Chapter require some modification in order to fit the reduced context of the second architecture (we have left these modifications as exercises for the reader, because they amount to very little more than the deletion of variables from signatures and from predicates). The CASSANDRA specification is complete in that it defines the possible behaviours of Knowledge Source triggers, preconditions and actions. It also defines the possible behaviours of level managers.

In addition, the specification is complete as far as the communications-related aspects of level managers are concerned: in particular, it stipulates the behaviours of ports and channels. As we emphasised in the last Chapter, the CASSANDRA specification does not attempt to integrate the level manager construct with the communications architecture provided by any particular communications system (such as that provided by, for example, ETHERNET with TCP/IP, or by a Cambridge Ring): in a sense, the communications architecture and the facilities it provides are in an indentical position with respect to the CASSANDRA architecture as are external databases for the blackboard architecture—we cannot know what will be necessary in order to integrate the problem-solver with this external software, so we have not even tried to perform this task.

The CASSANDRA specification is intended to be a *standard* for the architecture, even though we have ignored all issues relating to parallelism. The Z language does not, at the moment, provide any constructs for the specification of parallel programs, and we would have had to have used another Formalism in addition to Z if we had engaged in this second level of specification: an extra notation, together with a more complex semantics, was considered to be too of a complication at this stage—perhaps we will undertake this exercise at some time in the future. Given that caveat, what we intend, here, is that anyone wishing to implement a CASSANDRA system should follow the specification that we gave in the last Chapter. With the blackboard architecture, we must content ourselves with the fact that we have presented our interpretation (or a logical variation on it). We believe that the exercises have both been moderately successful.

It should, of course, be remembered that the specifications presented above are concerned with the top-level of the systems in question. We have not undertaken a complete refinement exercise and presented the code that would be generated thereby. There are some examples presented in the Appendix, but they do not go all the way to code, and they are not complete: we only deal with a couple of schemata. This does not mean that the specifications we have actually presented are useless: on the contrary, they form the basis for the refinement process, and, as such, they are indispensible. In addition, we have been able to use the specifications to indicate and sometimes prove properties of the two architectures. In fact, the proofs that we have given in the two formal specification Chapters (Chapters 4 and 6) serve to define properties of the systems (and also prove properties about the specifications themselves): the fact that we can derive these results (which represent properties that we consider intuitive about the architecture) indicates that the specifications are essentially sound, and that they can form the basis of an implementation.

Furthermore, the specifications as given form relatively complete contexts within which to investigate the properties of the two architectures at a theoretical level: the fact that we do not have to resort to building the systems appears, to us, to be a benefit of this exercise. The reason for including proofs in the two formal specification Chapters was so that properties of the two architectures could be presented: these properties should be as much a part of the understanding of the architectures as the simple statement of the components and their intended roles and behaviours. This explains why the descriptive flow of the Chapters has been interrupted in order to present formally defined properties. The reader should note that not all properties that are provable have been proved: there are many results that relate to scheduling and to events that *ought* to be proved, but, without more concrete examples, we are unable to prove them.

This last point is an important one. What we have done is to give a specification of all those components of the two architectures which are *problem-independent*. We have not attempted to examine those issues which are raised when using either a blackboard or a CASSANDRA system to solve a problem. In this sense, we have concentrated on the domain-independent aspects of the architecture, and this is most in evidence when scheduling is concerned. In the two specifications, we have assumed that the scheduler is a function which selects *one* KSAR to be executed: we make no other assumptions about it. It turns out, of course, that scheduling is one of the most critical aspects of the construction of advanced problem-solving systems. If a scheduler does not perform adequately, the wrong Knowledge Sources are executed, and problem-solving is hindered. Unfortunately, scheduling is task-specific: generic schedulers are possible (and some generic strategies have been discovered by, for example, Hayes-Roth et al. (1986)), but we have chosen not to specify them. What this boils down to is the fact that the various sets of strategies that have been identified require additional assumptions to be made about the structure and function of the blackboard system interpreter. We were unwilling to make these assumptions in our specification because we wanted to present a specification that made our interpretation of the architecture as explicit as possible. Therefore, we have relegated scheduling to the role of a function that is not further specified.

The principal lesson of the two specifications is that the formal specification of problem-solving architectures for knowledge based systems is a feasible exercise (some might argue that it is *desirable*). Although AI software tends to be radically different in nature and sometimes in form from conventional software, it is amenable to formal specification. This does not mean that AI software is particularly easy to specify formally: the search for the schema defining rule condition-elements was long, and we are still not completely satisfied with it. There are other aspects of the specification that required considerable amounts of work (indeed, the entire blackboard specification was re-worked from scratch three times before it seemed to be in a form suitable for use). During a refinement of the specifications given in this book, we expect to find areas that will require further revision: this accords with Jones' remarks (1980). This is not particularly a matter for concern because specifications for conventional software are frequently revised. What is probably an issue for AI software is that the kind of revisions may be different and more radical, and they may be required more frequently. In addition, one might add that the existence of a formal specification, at least for some AI systems, can obviate the need for large amounts of implementation.

The aspect of the specification process that has not been covered in this book is the opportunity for parallelism as we noted above in the case of CASSANDRA. At various points, we have noted that there is opportunity for parallel execution: in some cases, these points were novel to us. We have not been able to treat parallelism for two reasons:

1. The area is large and complex and would require a separate volume in its own right. The parallelization of problem-solving architectures as complex as the blackboard and CASSANDRA architectures is a non-trivial exercise and requires that the fundamental concepts be re-thought. We did not have the scope to examine this interesting possibility.

2. We believe that the currently available specification languages which deal with parallelism are not yet as developed as, for example, Z. In addition, they have not attracted the kind of background literature that can be usefully employed to provide the foundations for a book such as the present one.

At some stage, we intend examining parallelism in problem-solving architectures from a formal viewpoint.

As parallelism is an interesting area for further study, so too is knowledge representation. We have been concerned exclusively with an attribute-value scheme, yet we have said nothing about what attributes and values represent. We feel that this is an important area, and one that has not attracted sufficient attention. It should be noted that we do not mean the formal specification of knowledge representation systems, just as we do not mean the use of logic as a knowledge representation: what we intend is a thorough investigation, using formal techniques, of the semantics of knowledge representations sytems and languages.

Appendix A

Example Refinement

A.1 Introduction

In this Appendix, we will outline the refinement process that must take place when deriving an implementation from the top-level specification that has already been presented. For the purposes of the Appendix, we will concentrate on the blackboard system specification from Chapter 4. Given space limitations, we cannot hope to cover all of the refinement process: instead, we will show how to refine one aspect of the specification. The refinement will also be incomplete (again for reasons of space), and we will not, in fact, reach the level at which programming language code can be generated from the refined specification.

We begin with a short introduction to the refinement process, and then move on to the example upon which we will concentrate. We have chosen the example with some care, and the structures that we employ in the refinement process have also been chosen for good reasons: these reasons will be explained in full below.

A.2   The Refinement Process

In this section, we briefly explain the refinement process. A more complete account can be found in, for example, the books by Jones (1980, 1986) and by Morgan (1990).

Refinement can be described as the process of converting an abstract specification into code. This task is undertaken in a number of steps, each of which requires the development of an intermediate representation of the original specification. On each step, the goal is to refine an abstract structure (the specification that was developed on the previous step) into a more concrete one. Once this has been done, the more concrete specification becomes the abstract specification and is subjected to refinement into a yet more concrete one. The process involves the successive transformation of the formal specification: when a specification that is executable is arrived at, the process terminates (see Morgan (1990) for a more extended account of the process). In an ideal world, the conversion into program code is achieved using a formal specification of the constructs of the programming language (cf. Jones, 1980), but it is more usual for the step into code to rely upon "obvious" properties of the programming language (for example, the property that arrays can be represented as finite sequences).

In summary, the refinement process entails the conversion of one specification (the *abstract* specification) into another (the *concrete* one). The concrete specification is closer to the implementation in the sense that it is more detailed: note that concrete specifications can still be relatively abstract (for example, they may still contain specifications in terms of structures that are not supported by the programming language which will eventually be used). What matters is the fact that the operations and data structures are more detailed in their presentation than they are in the abstract specification. Furthermore, during the refinement process, only some parts of the specification will be refined to a more concrete level, the remainder being kept at a more abstract one (that is, they are left to be refined later): the current state of the specification, in other words, will be a combination of more and less abstract parts. The refinement process has the property that it is *monotonic*: that is, the refinement of some parts of the specification by one or more levels does not have any effects upon the rest of it (i.e., those parts which are not being refined). In other words, the refinement of one part of a specification does not change those parts which have not been refined.

A specification in Z is composed, in the simplest case, of a collection of schemata. The schemata represent data types and the operations that are defined over them. An abstract specification in Z will consist of exactly the schemata that we discussed above. A concrete specification will also be composed of a set of schemata, but these schemata will represent the program or system at a level of greater detail than the abstract one. Part of the refinement process will consist, then, of mapping the schemata of the abstract specification to the schemata of the concrete one: this involves relating the sets of schemata in various ways. This is necessary in order to show that the concrete schemata really do capture the model that is described by the abstract specification.

A specification is fundamentally composed of two kinds of structures: those representing data types and structures, and those representing operations. In the refinement process, an abstract specification must be converted into a more concrete one. In the case of data types and structures, this involves finding a representation of the original, abstract specification which is more concrete. It also involves showing properties of the new, concrete representation: in particular, it is necessary to show that the concrete representation is *adequate* as a model of the abstract structure. Part of the adequacy condition is that it must be shown that the concrete representation can genuinely serve as an implementation of the abstract one. This involves relating concrete states to abstract ones: there must be an *explicit* relation between the two sets of states. This is achieved, in Z, using an *abstraction* schema.

By convention, if we have a data type specification D, we will call the abstraction schema *AbsD*. The role of the abstraction schema is to define the relationships which exist between abstract states (the states defined by the abstract representation) and concrete states.

Following Spivey (1989), let us call the abstract state of a data type *Astate*, and let the concrete state be *Cstate*. The signature of the abstraction schema, *Abs*, is *Astate* ∧ *Cstate*. It is quite usual for one abstract state to be represented by more than one concrete state. Conversely, more than one abstract state can be represented by the same concrete state—this can happen when the abstract state contains information that cannot be extracted by any of the operations defined over its abstract data type.

Given the rather complex relation between abstract and concrete representations, there are three conditions that must be shown to be satisfied by a refinement step. The first condition ensures that the concrete operation terminates whenever the abstract one is guaranteed to terminate. If the abstract and concrete states are related by the schema *Abs*, and if the abstract state satisfies the precondition of the abstract operation, the concrete state must satisfy the precondition of the concrete operation. This can be written as:

$$\forall Astate;\ Cstate;\ x? : X \bullet$$
$$\text{pre } Aop \land Abs \Rightarrow \text{pre } Cop$$

where *Aop* is the abstract operation and *Cop* is the concrete one.

The second condition ensures that the state after the concrete operation represents one of those abstract states in which the abstract operation *could* terminate. If both abstract and concrete operations are guaranteed to terminate, then every possible state after the concrete operation must be related by *Abs′* to a possible state after the abstract operation. We can write this condition as:

$$\forall Astate;\ Cstate;\ Cstate';\ x? : X;\ y! : Y \bullet$$
$$\text{pre } Aop \land Abs \land Cop \Rightarrow$$
$$(\exists Astate' \bullet Abs' \land Aop)$$

Both of the above conditions should be proved for each operation on the data types.

The third condition relates the initial states of the abstract and concrete types. Each initial state of the concrete type that is possible must represent a possible initial state of the abstract type:

$$\forall\, Cstate \bullet$$
$$\qquad Cinit \Rightarrow (\exists\, Astate \bullet Ainit \wedge Abs)$$

where $Cinit$ is the concrete initialization schema, and $Ainit$ is the corresponding abstract initialization schema.

We have presented the conditions for data types because we believe quite strongly that, once an adequate representation for data has been chosen, other choices and operations become easier.

The second major component of a specification concerns the operations that are defined over data types. In terms of refinement, it is necessary to engage in *operation refinement*. This is similar to data type refinement, but concerns the development of concrete operations and not concrete data types.

If a concrete operation Cop is an operation refinement of an abstract operation Aop, there are two ways in which these two operations can differ. The precondition of Cop can be more liberal than the precondition of Aop (in the sense that the precondition of Cop is true in more situations than that of Aop): this entails that Cop is guaranteed to terminate for more states than Aop. In addition, Cop can be more deterministic than Aop: in other words, for some states before the operation, the range of possible after states for Cop may be smaller than for Aop. If Aop is guaranteed to terminate and if Cop is also guaranteed to terminate, every state which Cop might produce must be one of those which Aop might produce. We can express this symbolically as:

$$\forall\, State;\ x? : X \bullet \operatorname{pre} Aop \Rightarrow \operatorname{pre} Cop$$

where Aop is the abstract operation and where Cop is the concrete one.

If the precondition of Aop is satisfied, every result which Cop might produce must be a possible result of Aop. We can write this as:

$$\forall\, State;\ State';\ x? : X;\ y! : Y \bullet$$
$$\qquad \operatorname{pre} Aop \wedge Cop \Rightarrow Aop$$

If both of these conditions is satisfied, the concrete operation is suitable for all purposes for which the abstract one was suitable. If the abstract operation reliably terminates, so too can the concrete one. Also, if the abstract operation reliably terminates, and thereby produces a state which has a certain property, the second condition ensures that all states which might be reached by the concrete operation can also be reached by the abstract one: this ensures that the concrete operation will also produce a state which satisfies the property.

We have now defined the relationship between the abstract and concrete specifications that are derived by the refinement process. In addition to data type and operation refinement, there is function refinement: this obeys similar, but simpler, conditions, and the reader is referred to (Spivey, 1989, Chapter 5) for more details.

The establishment of the conditions listed above is an important part of the refinement process. For each pair of abstract and concrete specifications, the relevant conditions should be shown to obtain. Unless they do obtain, there is no guarantee that the refinement process is correct: correctness of the eventual program depends as much (if not more) on the correctness of refinement as on the choice of representation. With these remarks in mind, we will now present the example refinement. This example concentrates on aspects of the blackboard system whose top-level, that is abstract, specification we gave in Chapter 4.

A.3   Data Refinement

In this section, we consider the issue of data refinement in a specification. We have already seen how the abstract operations defined in a specification are gradually refined into executable code by the definition of intermediate specifications, each of which is of a more concrete nature than the previous one. In a similar way, the data types that are defined as part of the original, abstract specification must be subjected to a refinement process: this process is called *data refinement*.

The aim of the data refinement process is identical to that for operations. The original specification is too abstract to implement directly.

The specification must be gradually made more concrete until it contains constructs that correspond directly to the types that are directly representable in the programming language being used. The process typically takes a number of stages, and on each stage the data type specification becomes more concrete in the sense that it becomes closer to what can be directly implemented. Sometimes, it must be noted, the refinement process can be performed in one step: in other words, the original specification may be written in such a way that it may be mapped directly onto the implementation language, but this is rare. In any case, the advantages to be obtained from being as abstract as possible are lost when this one-step specification process is assumed to be the norm: even when aiming for an implementation in a very high-level language such as **ML** or **LISP**, it is still worth being as abstract as possible, and then engaging in a number of refinement steps.

There are constraints on the refinement process for data types, just as there are for operations. In particular, it is necessary to ensure that the more concrete specification is a faithful representation of the abstract one. This relationship should be shown using mathematical proofs. In this section, we will discuss the proofs that are necessary in data refinement.

The first step in refining an abstract data type is to define a more concrete version. The schema which defines the concrete type *must not* have any variable names in common with the abstract type's schema. Now, since each of these types has a state, we will refer (following Spivey (1989, Chapter 5)) to the state of the abstract type as *Astate*, and to that of the more concrete version as *Cstate*. The concrete type can be thought of as implementing the abstract type, so we want to prove that the implementation captures all the important features of the abstract type.

In order to relate the concrete and abstract types, we need to define a schema which relates the abstract and concrete types. This schema will be called the *Abs*, or *abstraction* schema. The signature of *Abs* is the same as that of *Astate* $\land$ *Cstate*. The predicate of this schema holds (is true) if the concrete state is one of those which represent the abstract state. It should be noted that one abstract state can be represented by more than one concrete state (indeed, this is quite usual—see Spivey, 1989, Chapter 5, p. 139). On the other hand, many abstract states can be represented by one concrete state: this happens, for example, whenever the abstract state contains information that cannot be extracted by any of the operations defined over it.

When each concrete state represents a unique abstract state, matters become simpler. Following Spivey (1989), we only consider this case here. If the concrete state represents a unique abstract state, it becomes unnecessary for every abstract state to be represented. In fact, it is necessary only for enough abstract states to be accounted for so that the result of each operation is can be represented. In other words, for each execution of an operation defined over the abstract type, the state of that type after the execution of the operation should be representable in the concrete type. The obvious consequence of this is that, if the abstract type has states that cannot be reached or obtained by the execution of the operations defined over it, that state need not be represented by the concrete type.

There are two conditions which must be satisfied before a data refinement is correct. These conditions are analogues of those we met when describing operation refinement. The first condition ensures that a concrete operation terminates whenever the corresponding abstract is guaranteed to terminate. If an abstract and a concrete state are related by the abstraction schema Abs, and the abstract state satisfies the precondition of the abstract operation, the concrete state must satisfy the precondition of the concrete operation. This can be written as:

$$\forall Astate;\ Cstate;\ x? : X \bullet$$
$$\text{pre } Aop \wedge Abs \Rightarrow \text{pre } Cop$$

where Aop is the abstract operation, Cop is the concrete operation, and $x?$ is the input variable of type X of (both of) the operations. The symbol pre denotes the precondition, so pre Aop is the schema which represents the precondition of Aop. A precondition schema is derived from the operation schema by hiding the after state and output variables using existential quantification. Thus, if a schema is defined as:

```
┌─ Op ──────────────────────────────────────────
│ State
│ State'
│ x? : X
│ y! : Y
├──────────────
│ S
│
└───────────────────────────────────────────────
```

the precondition, pre Op is the schema:

```
┌─ pre Op ──────────────────────────────────────
│ State
│ x? : X
├──────────────
│ ∃ State'; y! : Y •
│     S
│
└───────────────────────────────────────────────
```

The second condition ensures that the state after a concrete opera-tion has been executed represents one of those abstract states in which the corresponding abstract operation could terminate. In other words, the state after the execution of a concrete operation must be one of the abstract states which results from the execution of the correspond-ing abstract operation. If the abstract and concrete states are related by Abs, and both abstract and concrete operations are guaranteed to terminate, every possible state after the concrete operation must be related by Abs' to a possible state after the execution of the abstract operation. In other words, the after states of the two operations (the abstract and concrete ones) must be related by the after state repre-sented by Abs' for the concrete operation to be a possible representation of the abstract one. This can be written as:

$$\forall Astate; \ Cstate; \ Cstate'; \ x? : X; \ y! : Y \ \bullet$$
$$\text{pre } Aop \land Abs \land Cop \Rightarrow$$
$$(\exists Astate' \bullet Abs' \land Aop)$$

Both of these conditions should be proved for each operation on the data type.

There is a third condition which can (and should be proved). This condition pertains to the initial states of data types. We state it in symbols before explaining it:

$$\forall\, Cstate \bullet$$
$$Cinit \Rightarrow (\exists\, Astate \bullet Ainit \wedge Abs)$$

This states that every possible initial state of the concrete type must represent a possible initial state of the abstract type. This condition guarantees that the initialisation of the concrete type cannot yield an illegal (or unwanted, or unreachable) initial state of the abstract type.

A.4   Function Refinement

We conclude this overview of the refinement process with the case of a functional relation between concrete and abstract types. This case is simpler than that of operation refinement, and obtains whenever the abstraction schema, when viewed as a relation between concrete and abstract types, is a *total* function. This property of the *Abs* schema is expressed by:

$$\forall\, Cstate \bullet$$
$$\exists_1 Astate \bullet Abs$$

In words, this states that each concrete state represents a unique abstract state, and that each possible pair of states is related by the *Abs* schema. Furthermore, if one concrete state is mapped by *Abs* to two abstract states, then those abstract states must be identical.

The first condition is the same as before, namely:

$$\forall\, Astate;\ Cstate;\ x? : X \bullet$$
$$\text{pre}\ Aop \wedge Abs \Rightarrow \text{pre}\ Cop$$

Because of the total functional relationship, the existential quantifier in the second condition can be omitted. The condition, when simplified, becomes:

$$\forall\, Astate;\ Astate';\ Cstate;\ Cstate';\ x? : X;\ y! : Y \bullet$$
$$\text{pre}\ Aop \wedge Abs \wedge Cop \wedge Abs' \Rightarrow Aop$$

In a similar fashion, the third condition can be simplified and the existential quantifier omitted:

$$\forall \, Astate; \; Cstate \bullet Cinit \wedge Abs \Rightarrow Ainit$$

These simplified conditions are equivalent to the ones given in the last section, provided that the *Abs* schema is a total function. The advantage of these schemata is that the proof that the *Abs* schema is total need only be undertaken once for the whole data type: this work does not have to be repeated for each operation because the initial proof covers *all* possible states.

A.5   Example Refinement

In this section, we will present an example of the refinement process. The example concerns the refinement of the blackboard database and the entries it contains. We will concentrate on the refinement of entries, although we will show how to refine the abstraction level and blackboard types. We give proofs of correctness of the refinement steps for the entry type, but we only indicate them for the others. As will be seen, refinement actually involves a fair amount of work because it requires the definition of new types and operations defined over them, and it also involves the definition of an abstraction relation to link the abstract and concrete types; in addition, refinement requires the proof of a number of results. There is, naturally, a resistence to all this work: we have found it beneficial (as well as interesting).

It is often the case that refinement causes the original specification to change. A change might occur because the concrete representation does not relate to the abstract one in a convenient way; it might occur because the abstract type blocks certain operations on the concrete representation. We found that the specification of entries and the blackboard that we originally intended for Chapter 4 was difficult to work with when we came to the refinement stage: what we found was that the states with which we had to deal were too complex to be managed easily as part of the proof process. We were led to the re-specification of the blackboard: this is the version that is now to be found in Chapter 4 and we believe that it is an adequate representation (and a better one

than the previous version). There is nothing wrong with revising specifications that are higher in the refinement hierarchy (i.e., specifications
that are more abstract) in the light of refinement and the definition of
concrete types: indeed, in our experience, this is common and leads to
better overall specifications. A similar opinion is held by Jones (1986).

In the current section, we cannot hope to give a refinement into
code: this is a comparatively lengthy process. Instead, the refinement
that we present takes the specification of Chapter 4, section 2, in its
entirety and descends one level: in other words, the refinement that we
present is the *immediate* refinement of the blackboard, abstraction levels and entries. We would expect there to be *at least* one more level of
refinement because the types that we define below are not supported by
many programming languages (although **LISP** is an exception). The
full specification of the blackboard system is intended by us to be implemented in a conventional programming language such as **Ada** or **C**,
and the constructs that we use in the refinement do not correspond to
types provided as basic in these languages: this fact suggests that there
must be another level of refinement which will produce a specification
that maps onto the types provided by the implementation language.

As the reader will see, the refinement presented below relies heavily
upon the use of sequences. Sequences are *similar* to one-dimensional
arrays, and their elements are of uniform type. The difference between
a sequence and an array is that the former's size need not be stated:
in other words, there need not be an upper limit on the number of
elements in a sequence. In a sense, sequences are similar to lists (but
not **LISP** lists which are truly polymorphic in the sense that a given
list can contain elements of different types—for example, a **LISP** list
can hold numbers, atoms, lists and functional objects all at the same
time) because insertions and deletions at any point are possible. Given
the nature of the objects we are specifying, we cannot always put an
upper limit on the number of elements (although we can for objects
of type *Blackboard*), so an array representation is not suitable. All of
these arguments lead to the conclusion that the refinement that we give
is still a little too abstract and that it needs further refinement before
implementation is possible.

Initially, we wanted to refine entries and abstraction levels in one
step into hash tables, and we started developing a hash table specifi-

cation. This is a possible implementation for the structures that we define, but we found that the specification of the relationships between the schemata we defined in Chapter 4 and the hash table were rather too complex. We therefore adopted an alternative approach which might, at first sight, seem redundant: we aimed to separate the domain and range of each type. The rationale for this was that we knew that we needed domain elements as keys and range elements as data values. One way in which the domain can be separated from the range of a function or relation is to take the graph: this is what we have done. In addition, we have defined the graph elements as forming sequences. We do not particularly care about the ordering on the elements (indeed, we typically forget the ordering), but the properties of sequences make them attractive. We could, of course, have represented the graph just as a set, but this would have involved explicit set construction or quantification: the use of sequences just makes the specification easier. Apart from the convenient mathematical properties of sequences, we also have in mind an implementation for most of the types in terms of array-like objects, and so sequences serve to remind us that this will be the end result.

We are going to re-write the relevant definitions from Chapter 4 in their *entirety*. This involves the definition of a new set of schemata. In addition, we will have to define abstraction schemata to relate the concrete (refined) specification to the abstract one (the one we gave in Chapter 4). Finally, we need to prove that we have a correct refinement, and this involves the definition of precondition schemata. At various points in the refinement, we will repeat schemata that appeared in Chapter 4: this should help the reader avoid having to refer back and forth, even though it lengthens the text. Because the correctness of a refinement step is so important, we would like the reader to have a relatively easy time, and we would like to avoid the curses that would be inevitable if we did not include previous material!

The emphasis will be on the refinement of the *ENTRY* type. This type is of particular importance because the whole blackboard specification rests upon its correctness. We will go into details on the refinement in this case, but we will not prove *all* the necessary results (some of them are rather tedious), although we do state them. If we were producing the specification in order to produce real software (or if we were reproducing the specification documents of the blackboard system), we would give proofs of all results: here, space is limited and we cannot give all the details.

Once we have completed the refinement of *ENTRY*, we will proceed to the refinement of *ABSLEV*, and then to that of *Blackboard*. In the case of the last two types, we will only talk about the results, even though we produce all the relevant schemata.

Before moving on, we need to say a word or two about terminology. In each case, we refine an abstract type T into a concrete type $T1$. We add a suffix *1* to the name of the abstract type in order to derive the name of the concrete one. Thus, the refinement of *ENTRY* is *ENTRY1*; the refinement of *ABSLEV* is *ABSLEV1*, and the refinement of *Blackboard* is *Blackboard1*. The name of the *Abs* schema—the schema which relates abstract and concrete representations—for type T will be *AbsT*. The abstraction schema which relates *ENTRY* and *ENTRY1* is therefore called *AbsENTRY*. We will assume that all types defined in Chapter 4 are still in scope and can be referenced without redefinition.

A.5.1   Entry Refinement

In this subsection, we present the first refinement of the *ENTRY* type. This type represents the entries on the blackboard, and was specified in Section 4.2. We will assume that we do not need to refine the types *ATTR* and *VAL* at this stage: we do not, as yet, need to go into the details of their representation—refinement of these types can occur on a subsequent iteration. We are free, therefore, to concentrate on the refinement of the *ENTRY* type and of the operations that are defined over it. The refinement that we present uses an auxilliary type that we defined in Chapter 4:

$$AVL == ATTR \times VAL$$

We noted there that the *AVL* type would be used later. In this subsection, we will make extensive use of it.

The type *AVL* represents the graph of the mapping from attributes to values that we use as the basis of the *ENTRY* type. We will define the concrete representation of the mapping as a sequence of *AVL*. This might appear to introduce additional structure into the concrete representation, but we want, eventually, to refine the entry type into something that is relatively efficient at runtime, and the additional structure can serve as a reminder of this. In addition, sequences can be, in some cases, easier to manipulate than sets, so we chose them as the intermediate representation.

To begin the refinement step, recall that the schema for *ENTRY* is:

$$
\begin{array}{|l}
\_\,ENTRY \,_____ \\
\hline
slots : ATTR \nrightarrow VAL \\
knownslots : \mathbb{P}\, ATTR \\
\hline
knownslots = \mathrm{dom}\, ATTR \\
\hline
\end{array}
$$

We refine the *ENTRY* schema by defining a new representation which we call *ENTRY1*:

$$
\begin{array}{|l}
\_\,ENTRY1 \,_____ \\
\hline
eslots : \mathrm{seq}\, AVL \\
numslots : \mathbb{N} \\
\hline
numslots = \#eslots \\
\hline
\end{array}
$$

We have represented the mapping $ATTR \nrightarrow VAL$ as a sequence:

$$\mathrm{seq}(ATTR \times VAL)$$

The variable *numslots* is used to keep track of how many attribute-value pairs are in *eslots*, and to make indexing easier.

We need to relate *ENTRY* and *ENTRY1* in order to show that the latter is an adequate representation of the former. We do this by defining a schema called *AbsENTRY*:

AbsENTRY _____

ENTRY
ENTRY1

$numslots = \#knownslots$

$knownslots = \{\ i : 1 .. numslots \bullet first(eslots(i))\ \}$

$(\forall i : 1 .. numslots;\ a : ATTR\ |$
$\qquad\qquad a \in knownslots \wedge a = first(eslots(i)) \bullet$
$\qquad slots(a) = second(eslots(i)))$

The schema does its job as follows. The role of the *Abs* schema is
to relate the concrete and abstract states. In this case, it must relate
numslots and *knownslots*. It does this on the first two lines of the predicate. First, the predicate asserts that there are as many elements of the
sequence as there are elements in the domain of *slots*: by definition, this
is the same as the number of elements of *knownslots*. Secondly, every
element of *knownslots* must be the first component of a pair in *eslots*:
this is the second line. The universally quantified formula that is the
third element of the predicate relates *slots* and *eslots*. It does so by
stating that the application of *slots* to every element of *knownslots* is
the same as extracting the second component of the pair of which the
attribute is the first component—this requires that the index into the
sequence *eslots* must be the same in each case. The schema that we
have defined to relate *ENTRY* to *ENTRY1* is adequate to do the job
required of it: in particular, the seemingly redundant second line of the
predicate will serve us well.

We must define an initialization operation for *ENTRY1*. It is:

InitENTRY1 _____

ENTRY1

$eslots = \langle\rangle$

As was to be expected, all the initialization schema does is to assert that the sequence *eslots* is empty. We can compare this with the
InitENTRY schema which initializes the *ENTRY* type:

$$\boxed{\begin{array}{l} \underline{\mathit{InitENTRY}} \\ \mathit{ENTRY} \\ \hline knownslots = \varnothing \end{array}}$$

The relationship between the two is clear, but we need to prove that the initialization schema for $\mathit{ENTRY1}$ can serve to initialize objects of ENTRY when reflected upward. In other words, we need to prove the following result.

Theorem 1

$$\forall \mathit{ENTRY}1 \bullet \mathit{InitENTRY}1 \Rightarrow$$
$$(\exists \mathit{ENTRY} \bullet \mathit{InitENTRY} \wedge \mathit{AbsENTRY})$$

PROOF   We begin by rewriting the statement to give:

$$\forall \mathit{ENTRY}1 \bullet eslots = \langle \rangle \Rightarrow$$
$$(\exists \mathit{ENTRY} \bullet$$
$$knownslots = \varnothing \wedge numslots = \#knownslots \wedge$$
$$knownslots = \{\ i : 1 .. numslots \bullet first(eslots(i))\ \} \wedge$$
$$(\forall i : 1 .. numslots;\ a : ATTR\ |$$
$$a \in knownslots \wedge a = first(eslots(i)) \bullet$$
$$slots(a) = second(eslots(i))))$$

Clearly, $eslots = \langle \rangle$ implies that $numslots = 0$, which implies that $knownslots = \varnothing$. Also, we have:

$$knownslots$$
$$= \{\ i : 1 .. numslots \bullet first(eslots(i))\ \}$$
$$= \{\ i : 1 .. 0 \bullet first(eslots(i))\ \}$$
$$= \varnothing$$

since $0 < 1$.

Because $knownslots = \varnothing$, for all $a\text{: } ATTR$, $a \notin knownslots$, so the antecedent of the universal is false, and the implication is trivially true. Therefore, dom $slots = \varnothing$. $\square$

This result establishes the fact that the initialization schema for $\mathit{ENTRY1}$ is an adequate representation of the initialization schema for

ENTRY. It has relied upon the *AbsENTRY* schema to relate the two schemata and the types upon which they rest.

With this result behind us, we can move on to the consideration of the operations that are defined over *ENTRY1*, and we can relate them to the corresponding ones for *ENTRY*.

The first operation that we define is called *GetAttr1*: this operation corresponds to *GetAttr*. The schema for *GetAttr1* is:

```
┌─ GetAttr1 ────────────────────────────────
│ ΞENTRY1
│ a? : ATTR
│ v! : VAL
├──────────────────────────────────────────
│ ∃₁ i : 1 .. numslots •
│     a? = first(eslots(i)) ∧
│           v! = second(eslots(i))
└──────────────────────────────────────────
```

(Note that assume that the Ξ and Δ schemata for *ENTRY1* are defined by convention.)

The schema for *GetAttr* is:

```
┌─ GetAttr ─────────────────────────────────
│ ΞENTRY
│ a? : ATTR
│ v! : VAL
├──────────────────────────────────────────
│ a? ∈ knownslots
│ v! = slots(a?)
└──────────────────────────────────────────
```

Again, we have to relate the two schemata by a proof. The result that we prove immediately below is concerned with the preconditions of the two operations:

Theorem 2

$$\forall ENTRY;\ ENTRY1;\ a? : ATTR \bullet$$
$$\text{pre } GetAttr \land AbsENTRY \Rightarrow \text{pre } GetAttr1$$

PROOF   In order to prove this result (and we will prove a similar result for the other operations), we need to find the preconditions of *GetAttr* and *GetAttr1*. The precondition of a schema is derived by existentially quantifying over the after state and output variables of the schema. We aim to derive the following existentially quantified formula:

$$\exists \, ENTRY1' \bullet$$
$$(\exists \, i : 1 \, .. \, numslots; \; v! : VAL \bullet$$
$$a? = first(eslots(i)) \wedge$$
$$v! = second(eslots(i)))$$

To do this we need to derive each conjunct separately from:

$$\text{pre } GetAttr \wedge AbsENTRY$$

The proof reduces to showing that there is an index i such that it indexes the input attribute, and to showing that the ouput is correct.

By assumption, $a? \in knownslots$, so:

$$a? \in \{ \; i : 1 \, .. \, numslots \bullet first(eslots(i)) \; \}$$

which certainly entails that there is a value of i such as we desire. Thus:

$$\exists \, i : 1 \, .. \, numslots \bullet a? = first(eslots(i))$$

Under the assumption of this value of i, we need to prove that the outputs of the two schemata are related. This is simple:

$$v! = second(eslots(i)) \qquad\qquad\qquad \text{[Def } GetAttr1]$$
$$= slots(first(eslots(i))) \qquad\qquad \text{[Def } AbsENTRY]$$
$$= slots(a) \qquad\qquad\qquad\qquad\quad \text{[Def } GetAttr]$$

This clearly allows us to derive the desired result. $\square$

The next operation is the addition operation for attribute-value pairs. We define *AddAttr1* as:

$\_AddAttr1_____$
$\Delta ENTRY1$
$a? : ATTR$
$v? : VAL$

$(\forall i : 1 .. numslots \bullet$
$\qquad a? \neq first(eslots(i)))$
$eslots' = eslots \,^\frown \langle(a?, v?)\rangle$

This schema's predicate first establishes that $a?$ is not in any element of the sequence *eslots*. The quantified formula is equivalent to:

$\neg\,(\exists i : 1 .. numslots \bullet$
$\qquad a? = first(eslots(i)))$

The second part of the predicate merely adds a new pair to the end of *eslots*.

The corresponding abstract schema is:

$\_AddAttr_____$
$\Delta ENTRY$
$a? : ATTR$
$v? : VAL$

$a? \notin knownslots$
$slots' = slots \cup \{a? \mapsto v?\}$

We can now prove a result similar to the previous one: this result shows the correctness of the preconditions.

Theorem 3

$\forall ENTRY;\ ENTRY1;\ a? : ATTR;\ v? : VAL \bullet$
$\qquad$ pre $AddAttr \wedge AbsENTRY \Rightarrow$ pre $AddAttr1$

PROOF   We begin by writing the statement in full, retaining the quantifiers. Then we will apply the quantifier elimination rules, stating which constants we are substituting for which quantified variable.

The full statement is:

$$\forall ENTRY;\ ENTRY1;\ a?: ATTR;\ v?: VAL \bullet$$
$$(\exists\, ENTRY' \bullet$$
$$\quad a? \notin knownslots\ \wedge$$
$$\quad slots' = slots \cup \{a? \mapsto v?\}) \wedge$$
$$numslots = \#knownslots\ \wedge$$
$$knownslots = \{i : 1\,..\,numslots \bullet first(eslots(i))\} \wedge$$
$$(\forall\, i : 1\,..\,numslots;\ a : ATTR\ |$$
$$\qquad a \in knownslots \wedge a = first(eslots(i)) \bullet$$
$$\quad slots(a) = second(eslots(i)))$$
$$\Rightarrow$$
$$(\exists\, ENTRY' \bullet$$
$$\quad (\forall\, i : 1\,..\,numslots \bullet$$
$$\qquad a? \neq first(eslots(i))) \wedge$$
$$\quad eslots' = eslots \,\frown\, \langle(a?, v?)\rangle)$$

By four steps of Universal Elimination, subsituting a_1 for $a?$, v_1 for $v?$, $numslots_1$ for $numslots$, $slots_1$ for $slots$, and $eslots_1$ for $eslots$, we have:

$$a_1 \notin knownslots_1\ \wedge$$
$$(\exists\, ENTRY \bullet slots' = slots_1 \cup \{a_1 \mapsto v_1\}) \wedge$$
$$numslots_1 = \#knownslots_1\ \wedge$$
$$knownslots_1 = \{i : 1\,..\,numslots_1 \bullet first(eslots_1(i))\} \wedge$$
$$(\forall\, i : 1\,..\,numslots_1;\ a : ATTR\ |$$
$$\qquad a \in knownslots_1 \wedge a = first(eslots_1(i)) \bullet$$
$$\quad slots_1(a_1) = second(eslots_1(i)))$$
$$\Rightarrow$$
$$(\exists\, ENTRY1' \bullet$$
$$\quad (\forall\, i : 1\,..\,numslots \bullet$$
$$\qquad a_1 \neq first(eslots_1(i))) \wedge$$
$$\quad eslots' = eslots_1 \,\frown\, \langle(a_1, v_1)\rangle)$$

Note that $a_1 \notin knownslots_1$ has been moved outside the existential quantifier because none of its variables depend on the variables bound by the quantifier.

By assumption, the consequent becomes:

$$(\forall\, i : 1 \,..\, numslots \,\bullet$$
$$\qquad a_1 \neq first(eslots_1(i))) \wedge$$
$$eslots_2 = eslots_1 \,\frown\, \langle (a_1, v_1) \rangle$$

By eliminating the remaining universal in the antecedent (substituting a new i for i, and a_1 for a), and by assumption that $slots_2$ is a suitable instantiation of $slots'$, we obtain the final form of the statement:

$$a_1 \notin knownslots_1 \wedge$$
$$slots_2 = slots_1 \cup \{a_1 \mapsto v_1\} \wedge$$
$$numslots_1 = \#knownslots_1 \wedge$$
$$knownslots_1 = \{i : 1 \,..\, numslots_1 \,\bullet\, first(eslots(i))\} \wedge$$
$$(a_1 \in knownslots_1 \wedge a_1 \neq first(eslots_1(i))$$
$$\qquad\qquad \Rightarrow slots_1(a_1) = second(eslots_1(i)))$$
$$\Rightarrow$$
$$\qquad (\forall\, i : 1 \,..\, numslots \,\bullet\, a_1 \neq first(eslots_1(i))) \wedge$$
$$\qquad eslots_2 = eslots_1 \,\frown\, \langle (a_1, v_1) \rangle$$

Note two things. Firstly, we retain the universal in the consequent (below we will show that it obtains). Second, the antecendent of the implication that appears in the antecedent is trivially true. That is, since:

$$a_1 \notin knownslots_1$$

it must be the case that:

$$slots_1(a_1) = second(eslots_1(i))$$

We can divide the proof into two parts (as we did before).
First, we derive the universally quantified formula in the consequent. We have that:

$$a_1 \notin knownslots_1$$

which implies that:

$$a_1 \notin \{\, i : 1 \,..\, numslots_1 \,\bullet\, first(eslots_1(i)) \,\}$$

So:

$$\forall\, i : 1 \mathinner{\ldotp\ldotp} numslots_1 \bullet a_1 \neq first(eslots_1(i))$$

The second part requires us to show that:

$$slots_2 = slots_1 \cup \{\, a_1 \mapsto v_1 \,\}$$
$$\Rightarrow eslots_2 = eslots_1 \mathbin{\frown} \langle (a_1, v_1) \rangle$$

We need to show that:

$$slots_1(a_1)$$
$$= second(eslots_2(i)) \qquad\qquad\qquad\qquad\qquad \text{[for some } i]$$
$$= second(eslots \mathbin{\frown} \langle (a_1, v_1) \rangle (i)) \qquad\qquad\qquad \text{[for some } i]$$
$$= v_1$$

Therefore, for some i, we have:

$$slots_2(a_1)$$
$$= slots_2(first(eslots_2(i))$$
$$= (slots_1 \cup \{\, a_1 \mapsto v_1 \,\})(first(eslots_2(i)))$$
$$= (slots_1 \cup \{\, a_1 \mapsto v_1 \,\})(first(eslots_1 \mathbin{\frown} \langle (a_1, v_1) \rangle (i))$$
$$= \{\, a_1 \mapsto v_1 \,\}(first(eslots_1 \mathbin{\frown} \langle (a_1, v_1) \rangle (i)))$$
$$\qquad\qquad\qquad\qquad\qquad\qquad \text{[Since } a_1 \notin \operatorname{dom} slots_1]$$
$$= \{\, a_1 \mapsto v_1 \,\}(first(a_1, v_1))$$
$$\qquad\qquad \text{[Since } a_1 \notin \{\, i : 1 \mathinner{\ldotp\ldotp} \#eslots_1 \bullet first(eslots_1(i)) \,\}]$$
$$= \{\, a_1 \mapsto v_1 \,\}(a_1)$$
$$= v_1$$

We have the desired conclusion. $\square$

Finally, we define $ModAttr1$:

```
┌─ ModAttr1 ──────────────────────────────────
│ ΔENTRY1
│ a? : ATTR
│ v? : VAL
├──────────────────────────────────────────────
│ ∃₁ i : 1 .. numslots •
│     a? = first(eslots(i)) ∧
│     second(eslots'(i)) = v?
└──────────────────────────────────────────────
```

Note that the predicate contains a quantifier which should correspond to the test in *ModAttr* for the presence of the attribute $a?$. Note also that the second conjunct of the quantified formula can be written as:

$$eslots'(i)$$
$$= (a?, v?)$$
$$= eslots \oplus \{i \mapsto (a?, v?)\}$$

The schema *ModAttr* is:

```
┌─ ModAttr ──────────────────────────
│  ΔENTRY
│  a? : ATTR
│  v? : VAL
├─────────────────────────────────────
│  a? ∈ knownslots
│  slots' = slots ⊕ {a? ↦ v?}
└─────────────────────────────────────
```

We now prove the precondition result for these two schemata:

Theorem 4

$$\forall ENTRY;\ ENTRY1;\ a? : ATTR;\ v? : VAL \bullet$$
$$\text{pre } ModAttr \land AbsENTRY \Rightarrow$$
$$\text{pre } ModAttr1$$

PROOF   Again, the proof rests on two parts.

First, we need to prove that there is the required attribute in *slots*. We have:

$$a? \in knownslots \Rightarrow$$
$$\exists i : 1 .. numslots \bullet first(eslots(i)) = a?$$

So there exists an element of *eslots* which is a known slot (element of *knownslots*.

For the value of i given by the above implication, we need to show that:

$$slots'(a?) = v? = second(eslots'(i))$$

We know that:

$$slots' = slots \oplus \{a? \mapsto v?\}$$

because $a? \in \text{dom} slots$, and $a? \in \text{dom } slots'$. And we know, by definition of *ModAttr*, that:

$$slots'(a?) = v?$$

Since

$$(eslots \oplus \{i \mapsto (a?, v?)\})(i) = (a?, v?)$$

for the value of i which was determined above, we have:

$$
\begin{aligned}
slots'(a?) \\
&= second(eslots'(i)) \\
&= second((eslots \oplus \{i \mapsto (a?, v?)\})(i)) \\
&= second((a?, v?)) \\
&= v?
\end{aligned}
$$

Since the desired value of i is unique, the result follows. $\square$

In the last section, we stated that there are a number of different theorems that ought to be proved in order to ensure that the refinement step is correct. So far, we have concentrated on one particular form of proof, and one that deals exclusively with the correctness of the data type refinement. Next, we will give a result which concerns operation refinement.

Theorem 5

$$
\begin{aligned}
\forall ENTRY; \ ENTRY1; \ ENTRY1'; \ a? : ATTR; \ v? : VAL \ \bullet \\
\text{pre } AddAttr \land AbsENTRY \land AddAttr1 \Rightarrow \\
(\exists ENTRY' \ \bullet \ AbsENTRY' \land AddAttr)
\end{aligned}
$$

The expansion of this schema is quite forbidding, but the proof is readily obtained, once the details have been waded through.

We will give no more theorems and proofs because we wish to give the refinement of the *ABSLEV* schema and its associated operations. We should stress the fact that all proofs *should* be undertaken just so as to be sure that the refinement is correct. The process is undoubtedly tedious, but it pays dividends.

A.5.2   Abstraction Level Refinement

In this subsection, we present the schemata which comprise the refinement of the *ABSLEV* type and its associated operations. We call the concrete type *ABSLEV1*, and we call the abstraction schema *AbsAB-SLEV*. Unlike the previous subsection, we present no proofs of correctness. This subsection continues the process of data refinement.

Before we start, we need to define a synonym type:

$$EPR == EID \times ENTRY1$$

This type is the graph of the mapping $EID \twoheadrightarrow ENTRY$ that is to be found in the definition of *ABSLEV*. We will use this new type extensively below.

We begin with the schema for the concrete data type:

$$
\begin{array}{|l}
\hline
\_ABSLEV1 \underline{\hspace{4cm}} \\
\quad ents : \mathrm{seq}\, EPR \\
\quad levents : \mathbb{N} \\
\hline
\quad levents = \#ents \\
\hline
\end{array}
$$

We represent the mapping in *ABSLEV* using another sequence. The remarks we made in connection with *ENTRY1* also apply to this case. We repeat the *ABSLEV* schema for comparison:

$$
\begin{array}{|l}
\hline
\_ABSLEV \underline{\hspace{4cm}} \\
\quad entries : EID \twoheadrightarrow ENTRY \\
\quad knownents : \mathbb{P}\, EID \\
\hline
\quad knownents = \mathrm{dom}\, entries \\
\hline
\end{array}
$$

The abstraction schema is given by:

```
┌─ AbsABSLEV ──────────────────────────────────
│ ABSLEV
│ ABSLEV1
├───────────────────────────────────────────────
│ levents = #knownents
│ knownents = { i : 1 .. levents • first(ents(i)) }
│ ∀ i : 1 .. levents; e : EID |
│         e ∈ knownents ∧ e = first(ents(i)) •
│     entries(e) = second(ents(i))
└───────────────────────────────────────────────
```

This schema is quite obviously related to the *AbsENTRY*. In fact, a point worth noting is that the structure of the types *ENTRY*, *ENTRY1*, *ABSLEV*, and *ABSLEV1* are very similar—this suggests that there is common structure which could be derived.

We initialize *ABSLEV1* in the obvious way:

```
┌─ InitABSLEV1 ───────────────────────────────────
│ ABSLEV1
├───────────────────────────────────────────────
│ ents = ⟨⟩
└───────────────────────────────────────────────
```

To obtain an entry from the concrete abstraction level, we use *GetEntry1*:

```
┌─ GetEntry1 ─────────────────────────────────────
│ ΞABSLEV1
│ enm? : EID
│ e! : ENTRY1
├───────────────────────────────────────────────
│ ∃ i : 1 .. levents |
│         enm? = first(ents(i)) •
│     e! = second(ents(i))
└───────────────────────────────────────────────
```

To add a new entry to the concrete abstraction level, we define *AddEntry1*:

AddEntry1 _____
$\Delta ABSLEV1$
$enm? : EID$
$e? : ENTRY1$

_____

$(\forall i : 1 \,..\, levents \, \bullet$
$\quad\quad first(ents(i)) \neq enm?)$

$ents' = ents \,\frown\, \langle (enm?, e?) \rangle$

The three schemata which operate on the entries in a concrete abstraction level are defined in a fashion directly analogous to the definitions in Chapter 4:

GetEntryVal1 _____
$\Xi ABSLEV1$
$enm? : EID$

_____

$\exists i : 1 \,..\, levents \mid$
$\quad\quad\quad\quad enm? = first(ents(i)) \, \bullet$
$\quad\quad (\exists \Xi ENTRY1 \mid ENTRY1 = second(ents(i)) \, \bullet$
$\quad\quad\quad GetAttr1)$

AddEntryVal1 _____
$\Xi ABSLEV1$
$enm? : EID$

_____

$\exists i : 1 \,..\, levents \mid$
$\quad\quad\quad\quad enm? = first(ents(i)) \, \bullet$
$\quad\quad (\exists \Delta ENTRY1 \mid$
$\quad\quad\quad\quad ENTRY1 = second(ents(i)) \, \bullet$
$\quad\quad\quad AddAttr1)$

Finally, we have:

```
┌─ ModEntryVal1 ──────────────────────────────
│ ΞABSLEV1
│ enm? : EID
├──────────────────────────────────────────────
│ ∃ i : 1 .. levents |
│          enm? = first(ents(i)) •
│     (∃ ΔENTRY1 |
│             ENTRY1 = second(ents(i)) •
│          ModAttr1)
└──────────────────────────────────────────────
```

It is interesting to observe that, with the exception of *AddEntry1*, all of the schemata that we have defined leave the before state of *ABSLEV1* invariant: that is, they do not alter the contents of the abstraction level. This property makes the proofs of correctness of the refinement particularly easy because the primed state (the after state) is identical to the unprimed state: thus, any existential formulae which quantify over the primed state will be satisfied by the unprimed state. Because of this property, the proofs are omitted: in addition, they rest upon the proofs involving *AbsENTRY* because of the property just mentioned.

A.5.3 Blackboard Refinement

Here, we will consider the refinement of the blackboard type, *Blackboard*. We modelled this type as:

```
┌─ Blackboard ────────────────────────────────
│ levels : seq ABSLEV
│ numlevels : ℕ
├──────────────────────────────────────────────
│ numlevels = #levels
└──────────────────────────────────────────────
```

The new schema that we define for the concrete representation is:

```
┌─ Blackboard1 ───────────────────────────────
│ blevels : seq ABSLEV1
│ nlevels : ℕ
├──────────────────────────────────────────────
│ nlevels = #blevels
└──────────────────────────────────────────────
```

These two schemata are very similar: they differ in the variable names they contain and in the type of the sequence (they are not merely alphabetic variants, in other words). Because of the similarity, we expect the definitions of all the schemata defined over *Blackboard1* to be very similar to those defined over *Blackboard.* This will turn out to be the case. The reason for this is that we do not need to refine the blackboard type very much at this stage: we want it to be at about the same level of abstraction as *ENTRY1* and *ABSLEV1*, and this is the case. We could introduce a limit variable into the *Blackboard1* schema with the intention of deriving an array implementation on the next refinement, or we could leave this until later (which is what we do here—we do intend to implement the blackboard as an array).

The similarities are further evidenced by the fact that we need to define a $\Delta Blackboard1$ schema:

$$
\begin{array}{|l}
\underline{\Delta Blackboard1}\underline{\hspace{7cm}} \\
Blackboard1 \\
Blackboard1' \\
\hline
nlevels' = nlevels \\
\end{array}
$$

Next, we define the abstraction schema:

$$
\begin{array}{|l}
\underline{AbsBlackboard}\underline{\hspace{6cm}} \\
Blackboard \\
Blackboard1 \\
\hline
nlevels = numlevels \\
\forall\, l : 1 .. nlevels; \\
\quad ABSLEV;\ ABSLEV1\ | \\
\qquad ABSLEV = levels(i)\ \wedge \\
\qquad\quad ABSLEV1 = blevels(i)\ \bullet \\
\quad AbsABSLEV \\
\end{array}
$$

This schema is interesting because it includes an instance of *AbsAB-SLEV.* This is warranted by the fact that the abstraction relation for the blackboard depends upon the abstraction relation defined for abstraction levels. The binding of *ABSLEV* and *ABSLEV1* in the quantifier is included just so that we are sure of where the abstraction levels come from and so that we know to which pairs of abstraction levels the instance of *AbsABSLEV* refers.

With the blackboard type, it is the case that the schemata $\Xi Blackboard$ and $\Xi Blackboard1$ are included more often than are $\Delta Blackboard$ and $\Delta Blackboard1$. This entails that proofs will be considerably simplified (for reasons we gave in the last subsection), and will rely upon proofs performed for *ABSLEV1*. However, as we noted above, the latter set of proofs are considerably simplified and rely upon those for *ENTRY1*. We do not include the relevant proofs for these reasons.

We define the initialization schema as:

$$
\begin{array}{|l}
\underline{\quad InitBlackboard1 } \\
Blackboard1 \\
\hline
\forall\, i : 1 \,..\, nlevels;\ ABSLEV1 \mid \\
\qquad\quad ABSLEV1 = blevels(i)\ \bullet \\
\quad InitABSLEV1 \\
\end{array}
$$

This corresponds very closely to the initialization schema for *Blackboard*.

We will define a schema to check the validity of an abstraction level identifier:

$$
\begin{array}{|l}
\underline{\quad KnownLevel1 } \\
\Xi Blackboard1 \\
l? : LEVID \\
\hline
1 \leq l? \leq nlevels \\
\end{array}
$$

We will use this schema in exactly the same way as we used *KnownLevel*.

We now define the operations on the blackboard, leaving the entry creation schemata until last.

We begin with *GetENTRYBB1*:

```
┌─ GetENTRYBB1 ─────────────────────────────────
│ ΞBlackboard1
│ l? : LEVID
├───────────────────────────────────────────────
│ ∃ΞABSLEV1 | ABSLEV1 = blevels(l?) •
│     GetEntry1
└───────────────────────────────────────────────
```

We define the full operation as:

$$GetBBEntry1 \mathrel{\widehat{=}} KnownLevel \land GetENTRYBB1$$

We can expand this schema to be sure that it is what we require:

```
┌───────────────────────────────────────────────
│ ΞBlackboard1
│ l? : LEVID
│ enm? : EID
│ a? : ATTR
│ v? : VAL
├───────────────────────────────────────────────
│ 1 ≤ l? ≤ nlevels
│ ∃ΞABSLEV1 | ABSLEV1 = blevels(l?) •
│     ∃ i : 1 .. levents | enm? = first(ents(i)) •
│         ∃ΔENTRY | ENTRY = second(ents(i)) •
│             ∃ j : 1 .. numslots •
│                 a? = first(eslots(i)) ∧
│                 eslots' = eslots ⊕ {i ↦ (a?, v?)}
└───────────────────────────────────────────────
```

Next, we define the three operations that access and alter the state of entries on the blackboard. We begin with *GetBBVAL1*:

```
┌─ GetBBVAL1 ───────────────────────────────────
│ ΞBlackboard1
│ l? : LEVID
├───────────────────────────────────────────────
│ ∃ΞABSLEV1 | ABSLEV1 = blevels(l?) •
│     GetEntryVal1
└───────────────────────────────────────────────
```

We compose this schema, as usual, to provide the complete version:

$$GetBBVal1 \mathrel{\widehat{=}} KnownLevel1 \land GetBBVAL1$$

Now, for the add, modify and create operations, we will give the schemata that actually cause blackboard events. We will simply import the event schemata into the refinement without change: this is because they already have a structure that is adequate for our needs, and, at this stage, there is nothing into which we could refine them. In any case, if we were aiming for an implementation in **Ada** or **C**, we could refine the *BBEVENT* type directly into enumeration type. We begin these schemata with the ADD-event causing operation:

$$
\begin{array}{|l}
\_AddBBVAL1 _____ \\
\Xi Blackboard1 \\
l? : LEVID \\
\hline
\exists \Xi ABSLEV1 \mid ABSLEV1 = blevels(l?) \bullet \\
\quad AddEntry1 \\
\end{array}
$$

The interface is:

$$BBAddEvent1 \mathrel{\hat{=}} KnownLevel1 \wedge AddBBVAL1 \wedge MkAddEvent$$

The modification operation is:

$$
\begin{array}{|l}
\_ModBBVAL1 _____ \\
\Xi Blackboard1 \\
l? : LEVID \\
\hline
\exists \Xi ABSLEV1 \mid ABSLEV1 = blevels(l?) \bullet \\
\quad ModEntryVal1 \\
\end{array}
$$

The interface schema is:

$$BBModEvent1 \mathrel{\hat{=}} KnownLevel1 \wedge ModBBVAL1 \wedge MkModEvent$$

In order to define the creation schema, we need an operation which will add a new entry structure, together with its identifier, to the named abstraction level—to the abstraction level on which it must reside, in other words. We therefore define the following schema:

$$
\begin{array}{|l}
\_\_AddBBEntry1 _____ \\
\Xi Blackboard \\
l? : LEVID \\
enm? : EID \\
e? : ENTRY1 \\
\hline
\exists\, \Delta ABSLEV1 \mid ABSLEV = blevels(l?)\ \bullet \\
\quad AddEntry1 \\
\end{array}
$$

In order to have entries to add to the blackboard, we need a mechanism for creating them. We have not defined the creation schema for *ENTRY1* upto this point: the reason for this is that we believe that it belongs here with the remainder of the creation schemata. We define the creation schema, *CreateENTRY1* as:

$$
\begin{array}{|l}
\_\_CreateENTRY1 _____ \\
ENTRY1 \\
avps? : \mathbb{P}\ AVL \\
\hline
\# avps? = numslots \\
avps? = \mathrm{ran}\ eslots \\
\forall\, av : AVL \mid av \in avps?\ \bullet \\
\quad (\exists\, i : 1 .. numslots\ \bullet \\
\qquad av = eslots'(i)) \\
\forall\, i, j : 1 .. numslots\ \bullet \\
\quad eslots(i) = eslots(j) \Rightarrow i = j \\
\end{array}
$$

The third quantified formula in the predicate asserts that each element of *avps?* appears exactly once in *eslots'*.

We use this schema and the last one to define the NEW event causing schema:

$$
\begin{aligned}
BBNewEvent1 \;&\widehat{=}\; \\
&CreateENTRY1\, \fatsemi \\
&\quad (NewEntryName\, \fatsemi \\
&\qquad (AddBBEntry1 \land KnownLevel1))
\end{aligned}
$$

Finally, we turn our attentions to the *Find* operation for the concrete blackboard: we call the refined version *Find1*. The operation relies upon a refined version of *BBContents*:

```
┌─ BBContents1 ──────────────────────────────────
│ ΞBlackboard1
│ conts! : ℙ(EID × LEVID)
├────────────────────────────────────────────────
│ ∀ l : 1 .. nlevelsABSLEV | ABSLEV = blevels(l) •
│         (∀ e : 1 .. levents; enm : EID | e = ents(e) •
│              (e, l) ∈ conts!)
└────────────────────────────────────────────────
```

The *Find1* operation is defined in a fashion directly analogous to the *Find* operation. We define a schema *BBFind1* which actually does the work and then we use composition to create the schema for *Find1*.

```
┌─ BBFind1 ──────────────────────────────────────
│ ΞBlackboard
│ conts? : ℙ(EID × LEVID)
│ ents! : ℙ EID
│ pred? : PGRAPH
├────────────────────────────────────────────────
│ ∀ ent : EID × LEVID;
│         e? : EID; l? : LEVID |
│              ent ∈ conts? ∧
│              e = first(ent) ∧
│              l = second(ent) •
│         (∀ pv : POSSVALS; ?a : ATTR; vs : ℙ VAL •
│              pv ∈ pred? ∧
│              a? = first(pv) ∧ vs = second(pv) ∧
│              GetBBVal1 ∧ v! ∈ vs ⇒
│              e ∈ ents!)
└────────────────────────────────────────────────
```

$Find1 \mathrel{\widehat{=}} BBContents1 \mathbin{\text{\fontsize{}{}$\S$}} BBFind1$

With this definition, our outline of the refinement process is at an end.

Appendix B

Alternative FIND Operation

B.1 Introduction

This Appendix was written during the final stages of production: it contains an alternative version of the *Find* operation defined in the Chapter on the blackboard specification (the operation is also used in CASSANDRA, so it has more than passing importance). In that Chapter, we went to considerable lengths to define a higher-order relation in terms of its graph. On reflection, there is an easier way of defining the operation: that definition is the subject of this short Appendix.

B.2   FIND

We begin by defining the types:

$$[EID, ATTR, VAL]$$

(these are entry identifiers, attribute names and values). These types, as will be remembered form the basis of the blackboard specification.

Next, we define the type for abstraction levels:

$$ABSLEV == EID \nrightarrow (ATTR \nrightarrow VAL)$$

and that for the blackboard:

$$BB == \text{seq } ABSLEV$$

These (new) definitions capture the essence of the ones given above. The main difference is that, for present purposes, we do not need the additional structure that was employed in the original definition of *ABSLEV*. The reader will see that, here, we define *ABSLEV* as a partial function from entry identifiers to attribute-value pairs; in the definition given in the main part of the text (in Chapter 4, that is), abstraction levels were of type:

$$EID \nrightarrow ENTRY$$

where *ENTRY* is a schema type. Because we are only interested in the values that are stored in attribute-value pairs, we can ignore the state information that each object of type *ENTRY* contains.

To ease the definitions that follow, we define the following functions:

$$
\begin{array}{|l}
attrs : (ATTR \nrightarrow VAL) \rightarrow \mathbb{P}\, ATTR \\
vals : (ATTR \nrightarrow VAL) \rightarrow \mathbb{P}\, VAL \\
\hline
\forall\, a : ATTR \nrightarrow VAL \bullet \\
\quad attrs(a) = \text{dom}\, a \\
\quad vals(a) = \text{ran}\, a
\end{array}
$$

Using these two defintions, we can now define a function $find_b$ which returns the set of entry identifiers. This set contains the identifiers of

those entries which are present on the blackboard (the first argument of
the function) which satisfy some relation between attributes and values
(the second argument). The relation is completely general, and there is,
thus, no need to define complex conjunctions, disjunctions or negations
of relations. The definition is:

$$
\begin{array}{l}
\mathit{find_b} : (BB \times (ATTR \leftrightarrow VAL)) \to \mathbb{P}\ EID \\
\hline
\forall\, b : BB;\ r : ATTR \leftrightarrow VAL\ \bullet \\
\quad \mathit{find_b}(b, r) = \\
\qquad \bigcup\{i : 1 .. \#b;\ e : EID| \\
\qquad\qquad e \in \operatorname{dom} b(i)\ \wedge \\
\qquad\qquad attrs(b(i)(e)) \neq \varnothing\ \wedge \\
\qquad\qquad attrs(b(i)(e)) \subseteq \operatorname{dom} r\ \wedge \\
\qquad\qquad vals(b(i)(e)) \subseteq \operatorname{ran} r\ \bullet \\
\qquad e\}
\end{array}
$$

In an entirely analogous fashion, we can define $\mathit{find_l}$, which searches
only one abstraction level:

$$
\begin{array}{l}
\mathit{find_l} : (ABSLEV \times (ATTR \leftrightarrow VAL)) \to \mathbb{P}\ EID \\
\hline
\forall\, al : ABSLEV;\ r : ATTR \leftrightarrow VAL\ \bullet \\
\quad \mathit{find_l}(al, r) = \\
\qquad \{e : EID| e \in \operatorname{dom} al\ \wedge\ attrs(al(e)) \subseteq \operatorname{dom} r\ \wedge \\
\qquad\qquad vals(al(e)) \subseteq \operatorname{ran} r\ \bullet \\
\qquad e\}
\end{array}
$$

We have the following proposition (which we do not prove):

$$
\vdash \mathit{find_b}(b, r) = \bigcup\{l : 1 .. \#b\ \bullet\ \mathit{find_l}(b(l), r)\}
$$

Bibliography

[Anderson, 1983]   Anderson, J.R., *The Architecture of Cognition*, Harvard University Press, London, 1983.

[Balzer, 1980]   Balzer, R., Erman, L., London, P. and Williams, C., HEARSAY-III: A Domain-independent Framework for Expert Systems, *Proc. First Annual Conference on Artificial Intelligence*, pp. 108-110, 1980.

[Corkhill, 1986]   Corkhill, D.D., Gallagher, K.Q. and Murray, K.E., GBB: A Generic Blackboard Development System, *Proc. Fifth National Conference on Artificial Intelligence (AAAI-86)*, pp. 1008-14, 1986.

[Craig, 1987a]   Craig, I. D., *The BB-SR System*, Research Report no. 94, Department of Computer Science, University of Warwick, Coventry, UK, 1987.

[Craig, 1987b]   Craig, I.D. and Wilson, D.H., *CONFER: A Knowledge System for Bioprocess Control*, Research Report no. 103, Department of Computer Science, University of Warwick, Coventry, UK, 1987.

[Craig, 1988a]   Craig, I.D., *The CASSANDRA Architecture*, Ellis Horwood, Chichester, UK, 1988.

[Craig, 1988b]   Craig, I.D., *Distributed Control in a Blackboard System*, Ph.D. Thesis, Department of Computing, University of Lancaster, 1988.

[Craig, in press]   Craig, I. D., *Blackboard Systems*, Ablex Publishing Corp., Norwood, NJ, *in press.*

[Dijkstra, 1976]   Dijkstra, E.W., *A Discipline of Programming*, Prentice-Hall, Englewood Cliffs, NJ, 1976.

[Feigenbaum, 1982]   Feigenbaum, E.A., Nii, H.P., Anton, J.J. and Rockmore, A.J., Signal-to-signal Transformation: HASP/SIAP Case Study, *Artificial Intelligence Magazine*, Vol. 3, pp. 23-35, 1982.

[Forgy, 1981]   Forgy, C.L., *The OPS5 User Manual*, Technical Report XMU-CS-81-135, Carnegie-Mellon University, 1981.

[Gasser, 1989]   Gasser, L. and Huhns, M.N. (eds.), *Distributed Artificial Intelligence Volume 2*, Pitman, London, 1989.

[Hayes, 1987]   Hayes, I. (ed.), *Specification Case Studies*, Prentice-Hall, London, 1987.

[Hayes-Roth, 1979]   Hayes-Roth, B. and Hayes-Roth, F., A Cognitive Model of Planning, *Cognitive Science*, Vol. 3, pp. 275-310, 1979.

[Hayes-Roth, 1983]   Hayes-Roth, B., *The Blackboard Architecture: A General Framework for Problem Solving?* Report HPP-83-30, Computer Science Department, Stanford University, 1983.

[Hayes-Roth, 1984]   Hayes-Roth, B., *BB1: An Architecture for blackboard systems that control, explain and learn about their own behavior*, Tech. Rep. HPP-84-16, Computer Science Department, Stanford University, 1984.

[Hayes-Roth, 1985]   Hayes-Roth, B., A Blackboard Model for Control, *Artificial Intelligence Journal*, Vol. 26, pp. 251-322, 1985.

[Hayes-Roth, 1986] Hayes-Roth, B., Garvey, A., Johnson, M.V. and Hewett, M., *BB*: A layered environment for reasoning about action*, Technical Report KSL 86-38, Knowledge Systems Laboratory, Stanford University, 1986.

[Hayes-Roth, 1988] Hayes-Roth, B., Buchanan, B., Lichtarge, O., Hewett, M., Altman, R., Brinkley, J., Cornelius, C., Duncan, B., and Jardetzky, O., PROTEAN: Deriving Protein Structure from Constraints, *in* Engelmore, R. and Morgan, T. (eds.), *Blackboard Systems*, Addison-Wesley

Publishing Co., Wokingham, UK, 1988.

[Hoare, 1985] Hoare, C.A.R., *Communicating Sequential Processes*, Prentice-Hall, London, 1985.

[Jones, 1980] Jones, C.B., *Software Development: A Rigorous Approach*, Prentice-Hall, London, 1980.

[Jones, 1986] Jones, C.B., *Systematic Software Development using VDM*, Prentice-Hall, London, 1986.

[Kleene, 1952] Kleene, S.C., *Introduction to Metamathematics*, North-Holland, Amsterdam, 1952.

[Lemmon, 1965] Lemmon, E.J., *Beginning Logic*, Nelson, London, 1965.

[Lesser, 1983] Lesser, V.R. and Corkhill, D.D., The Distributed Vehicle Monitoring Testbed: A Tool for Investigating Distributed Problem Solving Networks, *Artificial Intelligence Magazine*, Vol. 3., no. 3, pp. 15-33, 1983.

[Milner, 1980] Milner, A.J.R.G., *A Calculus of Communicating Systems*, Lecture Notes in Computer Science, Vol. 92, Springer-Verlag, Berlin, 1980.

[Milner, 1989]   Milner, A.J.R.G., *Communication and Concurrency*, Prentice-Hall, London, 1989.

[Morgan, 1990]   Morgan, C., *Programming from Specifications*, Prentice Hall, London, 1990.

[Newell, 1973]   Newell, A., Production Systems: models of control structures, *in* Chase, W.G. (ed.), *Visual Information Processing*, Academic Press, New York, 1973.

[Nii, 1979]   Nii, H.P. and Aiello, N., AGE: A Knowledge-based Program for Building Knowledge-based Programs, *Proc. IJCAI-6*, pp. 645-655, 1979.

[Nii, 1986a]   Nii, H.P., The Blackboard Model of Problem Solving, *Artificial Intelligence Magazine*, Vol. 7, No. 2, pp. 38-53, 1986.

[Nii, 1986b]   Nii, H.P., Blackboard Systems Part Two: Blackboard Application Systems, *Artificial Intelligence Magazine*, Vol. 7, No. 3, pp. 82-102, 1986.

[Nii, 1989]   Nii, H.P., Aiello, N. and Rice, J., Experiments on CAGE and POLIGON: Measuring the Performance of Parallel Blackboard Systems, *in* Gasser, L. (1989).

[Post, 1943]   Post, E., Formal reductions of the general combinatorial decision problem, *American Journal of Mathematics*, Vol. 65, pp. 197-215, 1943.

[Sacerdoti, 1977]   Sacerdoti, E.D., *A Structure for Plans and Behavior*, Elsevier, 1977.

[Searle, 1969]   Searle, J., *Speech Acts*, Cambridge University Press, 1969.

[Shortliffe, 1976]   Shortliffe, E., *Computer-based Medical Consultations: MYCIN*, Elsevier, New York, 1976.

[Simon, 1969]   Simon, H.A., *Sciences of the Artificial*, MIT Press, Cambridge, MA, 1969.

[Spivey, 1988]   Spivey, J.M., *Understanding Z*, Cambridge University Press, 1988.

[Spivey, 1989]   Spivey, J.M., *The Z Notation: A Reference Manual*, Prentice-Hall, London, 1989.

[Stroustrup, 1986]   Stroustrup, B., *The C++ Programming Language*, Addison-Wesley, Reading, MA, 1986.

[Terry, 1983]   Terry, A., *The CRYSALIS Project: Hierarchical Control of Production Systems*, Memo HPP-83-19, Computer Science Department, Stanford University, 1983.

[Waterman, 1978]   Waterman, D.A. and Hayes-Roth, F. (eds.), *Pattern-Directed Inference Systems*, Academic Press, New York, 1978.

[Wilensky, 1983]   Wilensky, R., *Planning and Understanding*, Addison-Wesley, Reading, MA, 1983.

Defined Constructs

This index contains the page numbers of all types, schemata, relations and functions defined in the blackboard and CASSANDRA specification, as well as in the two Appendices. Entries with a "BB" key are defined as part of the blackboard specification. Those with a "CASS" key are defined in the CASSANDRA specification: in some cases, the same name is used for *different* objects. Those entries with an "A" key are defined for the first time in Appendix A, and represent the refined versions of the corresponding entry from the blackboard specification; objects which are repeated in Appendix A and which are defined in the blackboard specification are marked with the key "AR" (the "R" stands for "refinement"). The functions and types defined in Appendix B are marked with the key "AF" (the "F" stands for "Find").

Index

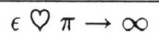